Language Loyalty, Continuity and Change

BILINGUAL EDUCATION AND BILINGUALISM
Series Editors: Professor Nancy H. Hornberger, *University of Pennsylvania, Philadelphia,
USA* and Professor Colin Baker, *University of Wales, Bangor, Wales, Great Britain*

Recent Books in the Series
Continua of Biliteracy: An Ecological Framework for Educational Policy, Research,
and Practice in Multilingual Settings
Nancy H. Hornberger (ed.)
Languages in America: A Pluralist View (2nd edn)
Susan J. Dicker
Trilingualism in Family, School and Community
Charlotte Hoffmann and Jehannes Ytsma (eds)
Multilingual Classroom Ecologies
Angela Creese and Peter Martin (eds)
Negotiation of Identities in Multilingual Contexts
Aneta Pavlenko and Adrian Blackledge (eds)
Beyond the Beginnings: Literacy Interventions for Upper Elementary English
Language Learners
Angela Carrasquillo, Stephen B. Kucer and Ruth Abrams
Bilingualism and Language Pedagogy
Janina Brutt-Griffler and Manka Varghese (eds)
Language Learning and Teacher Education: A Sociocultural Approach
Margaret R. Hawkins (ed.)
The English Vernacular Divide: Postcolonial Language Politics and Practice
Vaidehi Ramanathan
Bilingual Education in South America
Anne-Marie de Mejía (ed.)
Teacher Collaboration and Talk in Multilingual Classrooms
Angela Creese
Words and Worlds: World Languages Review
F. Martí, P. Ortega, I. Idiazabal, A. Barreña, P. Juaristi, C. Junyent, B. Uranga and E. Amorrortu
Language and Aging in Multilingual Contexts
Kees de Bot and Sinfree Makoni
Foundations of Bilingual Education and Bilingualism (4th edn)
Colin Baker
Bilingual Minds: Emotional Experience, Expression, and Representation
Aneta Pavlenko (ed.)
Raising Bilingual-Biliterate Children in Monolingual Cultures
Stephen J. Caldas
Language, Space and Power: A Critical Look at Bilingual Education
Samina Hadi-Tabassum
Developing Minority Language Resources
Guadalupe Valdés, Joshua A. Fishman, Rebecca Chávez and William Pérez
Language Loyalty, Language Planning and Language Revitalization: Recent Writings
and Reflections from Joshua A. Fishman
Nancy H. Hornberger and Martin Pütz (eds)

For more details of these or any other of our publications, please contact:
Multilingual Matters, Frankfurt Lodge, Clevedon Hall,
Victoria Road, Clevedon, BS21 7HH, England
http://www.multilingual-matters.com

BILINGUAL EDUCATION AND BILINGUALISM 60
Series Editors: Nancy H. Hornberger and Colin Baker

Language Loyalty, Continuity and Change
Joshua A. Fishman's Contributions to International Sociolinguistics

Ofelia García, Rakhmiel Peltz
and Harold Schiffman

with Gella Schweid Fishman

MULTILINGUAL MATTERS LTD
Clevedon • Buffalo • Toronto

This volume has been compiled to mark the occasion of Joshua A. Fishman's 80th birthday and is being published in conjunction with a companion volume edited by Nancy H. Hornberger and Martin Pütz, entitled *Language Loyalty, Language Planning, and Language Revitalization: Recent Writings and Reflections from Joshua A. Fishman.* Both books are available from Multilingual Matters Ltd.

Library of Congress Cataloging in Publication Data
A catalog record for this book is available from the Library of Congress.

British Library Cataloguing in Publication Data
A catalogue entry for this book is available from the British Library.

ISBN1-85359-903-4 / EAN 978-1-85359-903-3(hbk)
ISBN 1-85359-902-6 / EAN 978-1-85359-902-6 (pbk)

Multilingual Matters Ltd
UK: Frankfurt Lodge, Clevedon Hall, Victoria Road, Clevedon BS21 7HH.
USA: UTP, 2250 Military Road, Tonawanda, NY 14150, USA.
Canada: UTP, 5201 Dufferin Street, North York, Ontario M3H 5T8, Canada.

Typeset by Wordworks Ltd.
Printed and bound in Great Britain by the Cromwell Press Ltd.

Contents

PART 1: INTEGRATIVE ESSAYS

Fishmanian Sociolinguistics (1949 to the Present)
by Ofelia García and Harold Schiffman
with the assistance of Zeena Zakharia

****

The History of Yiddish Studies: Take Notice!
by Rakhmiel Peltz

****

PART 2: CONCLUDING SENTIMENTS

A Week in the Life of a Man from the Moon
by Joshua A. Fishman

****

PART 3: BIBLIOGRAPHICAL INVENTORY

Joshua A. Fishman's Bibliographical Inventory
compiled by Gella Schweid Fishman

****

To Joshua A. Fishman

Our Teacher, Colleague and Friend

who has taught us
to walk with him by the light of the moon,
to assist marginalized language communities in their search for justice,
to do research that respects the complexity of languages in society,
to enjoy the beauty of ambiguity,
to be irritants in the oyster that is the world,
and above all, to share the pearls of the mind and of the heart with others.

Joshua A. Fishman at the Milbank Chapel of Teachers College, Columbia University, April 6, 2005. © Maria Hodek Hamilton

Foreword

Old age isn't what it used to be. Retirement is a word that has acquired a plural and is now often used with an ordinal number: his first retirement, his second retirement, and so on, a multi-step rite of passage, as it were. How many retirements has Joshua A. Fishman celebrated over the years? This time around, some of his disciples who have seen to it that these occasions were observed in style by editing commemorative volumes and festschrifts – four tomes on the occasion of his 65th birthday – are getting ready to go into retirement themselves. But Joshua Fishman stands tall giving the rest of us the impression that retirement is something that happens once in a while, and when it's over you go back to your desk. Yet he doesn't try to ignore the fleeting time. He would be the first to admit that a busy week and a busy life have to be punctuated by moments of rest, reflection and remembrance, and if and when there is a chance to celebrate it must not be missed. It was only yesterday that he marked the longevity of the *International Journal of the Sociology of Language* by editing a specially enlarged one hundredth issue, but actually more than a decade has passed since.

Again, we are in a celebratory mood and we must be grateful to Joshua A. Fishman for providing the occasion, as well as to those who made sure it did not pass unnoticed. Joshua Fishman's scholarly reputation is firmly established in the academic world (*Gesellschaft*) and does not require another volume to prop it up; but in the community of his students and closer colleagues (*Gemeinschaft*) there is a strong desire to pay tribute to a man who has influenced their lives as much as the scholarly fields in which they have made a name for themselves, be it Bilingual Education, the Sociology of Language, Language Planning or Yiddish Studies. As becomes clear on the pages of this book, Fishman is living testimony to the complex intertwining of both of these 'normal types of human association.' In his work and in his life he has always acknowledged both, which is the secret behind his success in fathoming the depth of language as a social phenomenon and in inspiring others to follow his lead. The subsequent essays by Ofelia García and Harold Schiffman offer an overview of his scholarly achievements that is grounded in the harmonization of the instrumental and the symbolic, embodying the principles of *Gesellschaft* and *Gemeinschaft*. The result of their effort is as useful as a guide to Fishman's work as it is commendable and a fitting homage for the occasion. Rakhmiel Peltz in his essay does as much for Fishman's work on Yiddish, and Gella, his devoted wife, gives us the most complete bibliography of his writings to date. One title is likely to be missing, though, for not to be outdone even on this occasion, Fishman himself contributes an essay about 'a man in the moon' opening the door of his study a gap and allowing us a view at the man behind all the titles.

Florian Coulmas
Tokyo, September 2005

Part 1

Integrative Essays

Fishmanian Sociolinguistics (1949 to the Present)

OFELIA GARCÍA AND HAROLD SCHIFFMAN
with the assistance of Zeena Zakharia

> *They shall yield fruit even in old age;*
> *vigorous and fresh shall they be.*
> Psalm 92, as quoted by J.A. Fishman
> in relation to Yiddish (1991b: 9)

Introduction

Before an intellectual prophet and leader

It has been humbling to reread the scholarly work of Joshua A. Fishman spanning the last 55 years. We both met Fishman after he had been established as the founding father of the Sociology of Language. We knew then that his work had been trailblazing, insightful, inspirational. Being in his presence as a teacher and a colleague was indeed a transforming experience, for he not only taught us well, but also included us in many scholarly enterprises. One of us (García) is frequently heard to exclaim, 'Everything I know, I learned in Fishman 101.' But it took this careful rereading of his work, both his early work as well as his recent work, to understand his prophetic vision, evident as early as 1949 when he published the prizewinning monograph, *Bilingualism in a Yiddish School.*

As Joshua A. Fishman turns 80 years old,[1] we are inspired not only by his gift of intellectual prophesy manifested so early, but also by his extensive scholarly contribution. His fecund scholarship is attested in this volume by the bibliography of well over 1000 items that his wife and partner in the sociolinguistic enterprise, Gella Schweid Fishman, has been able to assemble.[2] We can say about Joshua A. Fishman what the Psalmist in the epigraph of this article attested, for he continues to yield vigorous and fresh fruit even in old age. As we write, Fishman continues to publish – a total of five books, sixteen articles, and two reviews are currently in press. As we will see, Fishman's intellectual contributions are important, not only because they anticipate many future understandings, thus rendering his prophesy important, but also because they are broad-ranging, making him a true intellectual giant.

Fishman's work dedicates much attention to leaders who develop and mobilize positive ethnolinguistic consciousness. For example, *Bilingualism in the Barrio* studies the language consciousness and language loyalty of Puerto Rican intellectuals. And both in his first major research study, 'Language Loyalty in the United States' (1960–1965), as in its update, 'Language Resources in the United States' (1981–1985), the views of ethnic activists received special attention (see, for example, 'Ethnic Activists View the Ethnic Revival and its Language Consequences: An Interview Study of Three American Ethnolinguistic Minorities').[3] Fishman has also intensively studied the leadership role that Nathan Birnbaum held at the Tschernovits Language Conference on Yiddish (see, for example, Fishman, 1987).

This essay gives attention to the role of Joshua A. Fishman as a leader who has mobilized and energized younger scholars throughout the world to study language and behavior, especially as it relates to ethnolinguistic consciousness. Beyond anticipation and the size of his intellectual endeavor,[4] Fishman has been, and continues to be, a leader in an intellectual field – one who has mobilized hundreds, if not thousands, of scholars, educators, language planners and government bureaucrats to study multilingualism and to act on its behalf, and especially on behalf of language minorities. At times Fishman has openly expressed his interest in having a leadership role. Writing about bilingual education, he states, '[I]t is my fond and fundamental hope to *lead* bilingual educators in the USA and elsewhere to consider themselves to be a *single* community of interest, each learning from the other and correcting each other's experimental and attitudinal limitations' [emphasis ours] (Fishman, 1976: viii).[5] Fishman's scholarship is not only ideologically mobilized, but it is energizing for the rest of us who read him and study him.

Joshua A. Fishman's clear leadership role in the founding and development of the sociology of language is unquestionable and has been well established by various scholars. Fernando Peñalosa (1981: 4), for example, calls Fishman 'the leading figure in the development and characterization of the sociology of language as an identifiable discipline.' According to Glyn Williams (1992: 97), Fishman, 'more than anyone, has been responsible for the development of the sociology of language.' Wright (2004: 11) calls Fishman, 'a key figure in LPLP (Language Policy Language Planning) studies.' In a recent text on sociolinguistics, Florian Coulmas (2005: 158) describes Fishman as the scholar 'who more than anyone else laid the groundwork for the scientific investigation of language shift.' And Spolsky (2004: 188) has lately said: 'The study of the efforts of linguistic minorities to preserve their languages is another field initiated by the creative scholarship of Joshua Fishman. Just as his work pioneered research into language maintenance and the spread of English, so he too inaugurated the field that he calls reversing language shift.' In Dell Hymes' foreword to Fishman's first text on the sociology of language, Hymes (1972: v) writes: 'In several major areas of the field [sociology of language] – language loyalty, language development, bilingualism – Professor Fishman has been a leader in research; at the same time, he has worked to build the field as a whole.'

But which field is it that Fishman has built? It is clear that the work of Joshua A. Fishman goes beyond the two disciplines that the term 'sociology of language' evokes. His intellectual enterprise is grounded in language in society, but also encompasses psychology, political science, anthropology, history, education, geography, religion and literature. The danger of continuing to refer to the field that Fishman has so richly developed as 'sociology of language' is that it reduces it only to sociological inquiry about language. We propose here, based on Fishman's own reclaiming of the term 'sociolinguistics' (see 'Growing pains' section below), that we speak of *Fishmanian sociolinguistics,* as a way to build a space for the rich interdisciplinary field that he has developed and in which language in society remains at the core.

This essay

Though we are unable to fully do justice to Joshua A. Fishman's intellectual genius, we nonetheless have found permission to do so in Fishman's own words, which we quote below. Speaking about the way in which research should and could be done and the way it is done in the real world, Fishman asks:

> Why is there such a difference? Because researchers are limited in time, funds, ideas and ability; nevertheless, they must do the best they can with what they have. They cannot wait until the best of all possible worlds comes to pass (for it never will), so they try to *conduct their studies as best they can.* (Fishman, 1996a: 7)

We have tried to write this integrative essay 'as best we can,' knowing full well that it cannot represent or fully grasp Joshua A. Fishman's profound scholarship.

Because this volume includes Peltz's integrative essay about Joshua A. Fishman's work about Yiddish and in Yiddish, we omit the Yiddish category from our analysis. But we acknowledge from the outset the important role that Yiddish has had in Fishman's work. Fishman has always acknowledged the importance of what he calls 'listening to Yiddish with the third ear' in his work (1990: 114).

This integrative essay identifies some of the conceptual threads in Joshua A. Fishman's work over the last 50 years and attempts to analyze, in Fishman's (1971: 607) own words, 'How the worm has turned!' The essay is organized along conceptual threads that appear interwoven, and even entangled, in Fishman's own work, often in relationship to each other.

Although artificially separated here, we have chosen to disentangle them for the reader so that we might provide some guideposts as to how Fishman's thinking has remained the same, and yet has evolved. *Sociology of Language*, the interdisciplinary enterprise established and developed by Joshua A. Fishman himself, has evolved into what we might call today, because of its integrative and yet distinctive character – *Fishmanian Sociolinguistics*. Fishmanian Sociolinguistics subsumes the following categories of study:

- language and behavior;
- multilingualism;
- language maintenance/language shift/reversing language shift;
- language spread;
- language attitudes and language and ethnicity/nationalism/identity/religion/power;
- language planning and language policy;
- bilingual education and minority language group education.

In drawing out the threads in this volume, we quote Joshua A. Fishman extensively. We do so because much of his early work has not been reprinted, and it remains out of reach for younger scholars. His words here provide the light to the guideposts that bring his ideas alive.

Language and Behavior and Fishmanian Sociolinguistics

The pioneering efforts

Trained as a social psychologist[6] Joshua A. Fishman was strongly influenced during his high school years by the work of Max Weinreich and his son Uriel Weinreich on Yiddish Linguistics. Fishman's interest in language in different sociocultural settings was evident when, as a young professor of social psychology at The City College of New York, he used Joseph Bram's Language and Society as a required text. After a brief stay as Director of Research for the College Entrance Examination Board, Fishman returned to his native Philadelphia as Associate Professor of Human Relations and Psychology and Director of Research at the Albert M. Greenfield Center for Human Relations at the University of Pennsylvania, where he taught the first course in Sociology of Language during the 1958/59 academic year. In 1960, after receiving his first major grant for sociolinguistic research for his 'Language Resources Project,' Fishman returned to New York City as Professor of Psychology and Sociology at Yeshiva University, where he also served as Dean of the Ferkauf Graduate School of Humanities and Social Sciences. From 1966 to 1972 his Doctoral Program in Language and Behavior became the first interdisciplinary program at Ferkauf, later succeeded by the PhD Program in Bilingual Educational Developmental Psychology (1981 to 89).[7]

Sociolinguistics has been said to have taken shape during the 1964 summer seminar at Indiana University's Bloomington campus, sponsored by the Social Science Research Council and the National Science Foundation. This seminar, which took place within the general framework of the annual summer Linguistic Institute, brought together the major actors of what would be the sociolinguistic enterprise – Gumperz, Haugen, Labov, Bright, Ervin, Rubin and Grimshaw, among others. Although this marks the official beginnings of sociolinguistics for some, Fishman makes clear that by 1964, he had been teaching the sociology of language for five years; he had submitted his 'Language Loyalty in the United States' report to the United States Office of Education; and he was putting finishing touches on his first edited volume about the topic, *Readings in the Sociology of Language*, which was published four years later in 1968.[8]

Definitions

A 1965 article entitled 'Who Speaks What Language to Whom and When?' established in a nutshell the question that sociology of language was to pursue for the next 40 years. In the first major publication to name the field, *Readings in the Sociology of Language* (1968), Fishman describes why the sociology of language is needed:

> Since languages normally function in a social matrix and since societies depend heavily on language as a medium (if not as a symbol) of interaction, it is certainly appropriate to expect that their observable manifestations, language behavior and social behavior, will be appreciably related in many lawful ways. (Fishman, 1968: 6)

Fishman defines the sociology of language as an enterprise that:

> [E]xamines the interaction between these two aspects of human behavior: the use of language and the social organization of behavior. Briefly put, the sociology of language focuses upon the entire gamut of topics related to the social organization of language behavior, including not only language usage per se, but also language attitudes and overt behaviors toward language and toward language users. (Fishman, 1972a: 1)

But the sociology of language is concerned with more than just language behavior. Sociology of language, Fishman (1991b: 2) says, 'is centrally concerned not only with societally patterned behavior through language but with societally patterned behavior *toward* language, whether positive or negative' [emphasis ours]. It is this belief in *social action* on behalf of language that spurs the shaping of the subfields of Language Maintenance, Reversing Language Shift, and Language Planning, which we treat later in the chapter.

From the beginning, Fishman talks about sociology of language as an interdisciplinary and future-oriented field. Sociology of language, Fishman (1968: 6) says, needs 'work and workers with sensitivity and sympathy' and as such, is an inclusive, rather than an exclusive field. The sociology of language is (Fishman, 1968: 5) *'one of several recent approaches* to the study of the patterned co-variation of language and society' [emphasis ours].

Growing pains: Sociolinguistics vs. sociology of language. '*And never the twain shall meet*?' (1972a: 278)

The term sociolinguistics was broadly used by Joshua A. Fishman during the early developmental phase of Fishmanian sociolinguistics. Publishing the very first textbook under the title *Sociolinguistics: A Brief Introduction* in 1970, Fishman used the term 'sociolinguistics' to include both behavior toward language (attitudes, movements, planning) and language concomitants of social processes, large and small (societal formation, societal interaction, societal change and dislocation). But Fishman constantly argued for balance and interpenetration between linguistics and sociology, and he pushed linguistics to truly include sociolinguistics:

> If economics answers all questions with supply and demand, and psychology with it all depends, then the first contribution of sociolinguistics to linguistics is doubtlessly to make us aware of the fact that the relations and interpenetrations between language and society are 'a little more complicated than that,' whatever that may be. (Fishman, 1972a: 311)

This call for the expansion of linguistics to be more inclusive of social concerns is one that Fishman has continued to make throughout his career:

> Certainly, linguistics as a science and linguists as scientists cannot and should not try to escape from the values and loyalties, dreams and intuitions, visions and sensitivities that move them and that touch them. (Fishman, 1982, as cited in 1989: 575–6)

Just a few years after the legendary Bloomington seminar of 1964, Fishman started differentiating what he then called 'modern sociolinguistics' from what he defined as the sociology of language. In 1967, at an International Seminar held in Moncton, Canada, Fishman proposed a critique of 'modern sociolinguistics.' This paper, published as 'The Description of Societal Bilingualism' both in the proceedings of the conference edited by L.G. Kelly in 1967, and also included in the 'Theoretical Addendum' to his 1971 *Bilingualism in the Barrio*, criticizes the focus of sociolinguistics on micro processes. Fishman (1971: 610) warns that 'We need studies of societal bilingualism that do not get so lost in the minutiae of description (in terms of any current equilibrium model) that they are unable to demonstrate changes in the bilingual pattern as a result of social change.'

By 1972, Fishman was beginning to have doubts about the use of the term 'sociolinguistics.' In *Language in Sociocultural Change*, Fishman (1972a: 268) argued against the use of the term 'sociolinguistics' saying, 'It smacked to me of linguistic priority, if not of linguistic imperialism.' He adds,

> The term [sociology of language] now stands in my mind for the reborn field, the revitalized field, whereas 'sociolinguistics' has increasingly come to stand for a 'kind of linguistics' and, therefore, for a possibly important preoccupation, but for one with which I do not and cannot fully identify. ... [T]he sociology of language must be much more vigorously in touch with social and comparative history, with social geography and with political science than with linguistics. (Fishman, 1972a: 270, 272)

As such, his 1972 introductory text was titled, *The Sociology of Language: An Interdisciplinary Social Science Approach to Language in Society.*

Joshua A. Fishman's use of the two terms – sociolinguistics and sociology of language – in his work reflects his changing relationships with the field. From 1968 to 1972, he preferred the term 'sociolinguistics,' and this appeared in the title of his articles ten times, whereas 'sociology of language' was not used in any title during that period. 'Sociolinguistics' was used in Fishman's work from 1968 to 1972 to refer to the language of developing programs, national development, bilingualism, neighborhoods and censuses. In 1972, however, both 'sociology of language' and 'sociolinguistics' start to appear in titles, with sociology of language receiving more attention. That year, Fishman used the term 'sociology of language ' in six of his titles, and reserved 'sociolinguistics' for only two. Throughout the mid-1970s and 1980s, Fishman referred to his contribution and the field he was shaping as Sociology of Language, and used the term 'sociology of language' to refer to his work, although he used the term 'sociolinguistics' in a 1973 title in connection to nationalism, and again in 1979 ('The Sociolinguistic "Normalization" of the Jewish People'), and 1982 ('Sociolinguistic Foundations of Bilingual Education').

Despite the growth of the field, by 1990 Fishman signaled that the sociology of language had entered a mid-life crisis. He complained that instead of 'progressing firmly on two legs, sociolinguistics was trying to move ahead primarily on the linguistic front while merely 'shuffling on the social.' His was a call to put 'socio more into prominence' (1991a: 128). When at the end of the 20th century it became clear to Fishman that sociolinguistics had taken off as a branch of linguistics, leaving sociology behind, he insisted on placing his work within 'the sociolinguistics enterprise,' which he envisioned in his edited volume, *Handbook of Language and Ethnic Identity*, as an 'embrace of both sociology of language and sociolinguistics' (Fishman, 1999: 152). Throughout the years, Fishman has clamored for inclusion and balance between the linguistic and the social, and he has not ceased to lose hope that the field will work hard to do both: 'The field will only really fulfill its potential when we have the critical mass of case study knowledge that will allow us to aggregate the particular to get a clear view of the general' (Fishman, 2002: x).

With prophetic vision, Fishman had argued in 1972 that the term socio-linguistics would not disappear because 'it is too catchy.' But he opposed the division of sociology of language into two separate parts – one of socio-linguistics of language, and the other of sociolinguistics of society (as Fasold, 1984, did years later) – arguing instead for the *interpenetration* of language in society and society in language that makes the division impossible. Fishman claimed that language and societal behavior are 'equal partners rather than one or the other of them being "boss" and "giving orders" to the other' (1972a: 301). 'Micro- and macro-sociolinguistics are both conceptually and methodologically complementary,' Fishman (1971: 598) reminds us. Arguing for inclusiveness and expansion in the sociolinguistic enterprise, he says:

> I am neither a prophet nor the son of a prophet but I do know what my 'druthers' are and which are so fanciful as to be best kept to myself. I hope that the links between micro and macro will become ever stronger, to the point that they will be viewed much like the links between organic and inorganic chemistry: important and self evident rather than dubious or controversial... Without bridges, the gap between micro and macro will grow... The middle ground is repre-sented by the vision that calls for the relationship between small events or processes and large scale aggregates or structures, for the natural and the formalized, for the empirical as well as for theoretical parsi-mony.' (Fishman, 1972a: 280)

It is the middle ground that Fishman develops throughout his work, and that is the core of Fishmanian sociolinguistics.

Growth and hopes

Precisely to develop the 'middle ground,' the interpenetration, Joshua A. Fishman founded both a book series and a journal. Since 1972 he has been the editor of Walter de Gruyter/Mouton's *Contributions to the Sociology of Language* (for a complete list of the volumes published, see Appendix 1). Starting with Fishman's own *Advances in the Sociology of Language*, the series has published 80 titles of senior and junior scholars from around the world, many of which have become classics. Although published in English, the series was quick to include scholars from developing countries. Early atten-tion was also paid to the developing world. For example, in the 1970s, the titles included language cases in Indonesia and Malaysia, Albania and New Guinea. The most recent books address such diverse language-in-society situations as Mexico's indigenous languages, Australia's many languages and Englishes, multilingualism in China, and languages in New York City.

Since 1974, Joshua A. Fishman has also been the General Editor of *The International Journal of the Sociology of Language* (IJSL), the most important academic publication in the field of international macro-sociolinguistics. Reflecting on the characteristics of the journal, Fishman describes them as:

> (a) interdisciplinary, reaching far beyond the field of linguistics (particularly, beyond narrowly linguistics-focused sociolinguistics), (b) truly international in content, and (c) macro-level oriented with a special concern for the status of indigenous and immigrant minority language communities. (Fishman 1997c: 237)

The growth of the field itself is reflected in the fact that in the early years, only three issues appeared each year, but by 1976 four issues were being published annually. After 1981, six issues appeared every year (see Appendix 2, for a list of the *IJSL* titles). Again, from the beginning, attention was paid to different areas of the world – issues in the 1970s were dedicated to languages in Israel, Southeast Asia, Sweden and Finland, Belgium, the American southwest, and to languages as varied as Romani and Yiddish. Since the 1990s, *IJSL* has, in Fishman's words (1997c: 238), 'provided sociolinguistic endeavor with difficult-to-achieve entrée' into China, Korea, the Maghreb, Poland, the Czech Republic, Hungary, South Africa, Sub-Saharan Africa, Morocco, Aboriginal Australia and Latin America.

Multilingualism

Multilingualism in Fishmanian sociolinguistic perspective

Joshua A. Fishman's early interest in Yiddish distinguished him from other early sociolinguists who were interested in language variation within the same language. From the very beginning, Fishman had a special interest in bilingual situations precisely because of the more marked sociolinguistic variations that this afforded and the possibility of studying this variation with clearer parameters. Recently Fishman (1999) commented on his interest in multilingualism:

> Bilingual or multilingual settings are very commonly studied in order to gauge sociolinguistic variation (and to relate such variation to the identity and purpose of speakers on different occasions and in different contexts), because the variation between languages *is easier to monitor (particularly by sociologists)* than is the variation within one and the same language. [emphasis ours] (Fishman, 1999: 153)

Fishman has always been interested in multilingualism as *an intra-group* phenomenon that is *widespread and stable*, rather than as an inter-group process. His early work focused on developing and mobilizing conscious-ness of minority languages and ethnicities in the United States, a country with a skewed vision of bilingualism as a 'vanishing phenomenon, as a temporary dislocation from a presumably more normal state of affairs' (Fishman, 1971: 584) – see, for example, his books *Bilingualism in a Yiddish School, Language Loyalty in the United States, Yiddish in America,* and *Bilingualism in the Barrio.* But very early on (1968), Fishman broadened his atten-tion to include inter-group bilingualism also, as his *Language Problems of Developing Nations* book demonstrates. His work, however, never aban-doned the interest in, and focus on, widespread and stable intra-group bilingualism. In the present era of globalization, when multilingualism is increasingly an intra-group phenomenon within inter-group interactions, Fishman´s conception of multilingualism is more valid than ever before.

Fishman's work defines 'multilingualism' as the interaction between bilingualism (preferred by psychologists) and diglossia (preferred by soci-ologists). (For more on this, see the 'Diglossia' section below.) As such, multilingualism in Fishmanian sociolinguistics focuses on the intra-group widespread and stable use of two or more languages.

Viewing multilingualism differently

The importance of Fishmanian sociolinguistics for the study of multi-lingualism is precisely that it goes beyond the term 'bilingual' as under-stood in the 1960s by psychologists, linguists and sociologists. Much of Fishman's early work is devoted to debunking the ideas proposed by psychologists on how to study and understand bilingualism, especially the concepts of *balanced bilingualism* and *dominance* that were so prevalent in the psychological literature concerning bilingualism in the 1960s.

Speaking against the concept of *dominance* as tested by psychologists with translation speed tests, Fishman argues that where bilingualism is socially constructed, and not merely an occupation or hobby, very little translation occurs. Speaking against translation speed tests, he wrote: 'such usage makes it exceedingly cumbersome to deal with those bilinguals whose dominant (i.e. most used) language is not their most proficient language...' (Fishman, 1971: 557). Years later, Tove Skutnabb-Kangas (1988) would expand upon this difference between function and competence as she developed a definition of mother tongue based on the plural criteria of function, competence, origin and identification.

The debunking of *balanced bilingualism* and the advancement of Fishman's concept of domains of language behavior (see the next section) reminds us of the notion of 'plurilingualism' that has become so important in the Euro-pean Union today. European plurilingualism today is defined as 'profi-ciency, of varying degrees, in several languages and experience of several cultures' (*Common European Framework of Reference for Languages,* 2002: 168).

For Coste (2001: 15), plurilingualism involves practices and values that are not equivalent or even homologous in different languages, but that are *integrated, variable, flexible and changing*. This is an expansion of Fishman's early notion that balanced bilingualism is an impossibility.

Linguists have sometimes been the culprits in contributing to the misunderstandings surrounding bilingualism. Following Weinreich's (1953) *Languages in Contact*, linguists have looked at the two languages separately as reflecting two groups, and not one group. In typical Fishman mocking style, Fishman says in 1971 (p. 561): 'The linguist has traditionally seen his task, in relation to the study of bilingualism, as being similar to that of a housewife looking for smears of wet paint.' In ways that remind us of the hybridity proposed by Bakhtin (1981) and that is so prevalent in the postmodernist work of scholars like Bhahba (1994), Anzaldúa (1997) and Gutiérrez *et al.* (1999), and sociolinguists like Canagarajah (2005), Fishman blames linguists for having a model of pure monolithic *langue* that leads them to find interference only as something harmful. He argues for studying the bilingual varieties as varieties in their own right. Fishman (1971: 562) claims: 'Like other people bilinguals constitute speech communities characterized by certain general social patterns of rights, obligations daily round and interactions.' The ways in which languages are used are not random, but are governed by norms of bilingual usage understood by the members of the bilingual community itself.

Fishman (1971: 3) has also pointed out that second language acquisition, a favorite topic of study for many psycholinguists who study bilingualism, is not of interest to the sociology of language since 'bilingualism is acquired by exposure to, and interaction with, a community that lives in accord with the norms of usage and that is involved in the normal process of change to which most communities and most norms are exposed.' Fishman warns:

> Any speech community is characterized by definite norms of language and behavior, which not only encompass the speech varieties (or languages) that exist within the speech community for its own internal communicative needs but also relate them to the types of other-than-speech behaviors – the interactions, the mutual rights and obligations, the roles and statuses, the purposes and identifications – in which various networks within the community are engaged. It follows that the description and measurement of an individual's bilingualism (as of an individual's repertoire range with respect to the language varieties that exist even within monolingual communities of any complexity) should reflect and disclose the sociolinguistic norms of the speech networks and the speech community of which he is a part, precisely because these sociolinguistic norms underlie the individual's bilingualism. (Fishman, 1971: 3)

Referring to the spread of English 33 years later, Brutt-Griffler (2004: 138) expands upon this concept to propose 'macroacquisition' as the 'acquisition of a second language by a speech community. It is a process of social second language acquisition, the embodiment of the process of language spread and change, or language change through its spread.'

Fishman's criticism of how bilingualism has been studied also extends to sociologists who have not conducted their own self-reports but who have depended on governmental censuses. Fishman questions the traditional social categories that sociologists use and cries out for lower-order validation of such categories with different populations, in diverse situations. Fishman's early contributions include the development of instruments that could be used to assess language use and behavior (see, for example, *Bilingualism in the Barrio*).

Joshua A. Fishman's ways of looking at multilingualism have given psychologists, linguists and sociologists new understandings about how languages function in stable, widespread, intra-group bilingualism. As Fishman (1971: 605) himself said, 'Instead of witch-hunting for bilingual interference, modern sociolinguistics recognizes the linguistic repertoires of bilingual speech communities as an instance of the repertoires that characterize all functionally diversified speech communities.'

A Fishmanian sociolinguistic model for the study of multilingualism: Methodological propositions

Joshua A. Fishman's early work provided a sociolinguistic model for studying multilingualism and at the same time it advanced theories about how multilingualism functioned in society. Both the theoretical and the methodological propositions were founded on the sociocultural contextualization of the data, as well as the interrelationships of the parameters.

An important methodological contribution made by Fishman's early work was his proposal that researchers have to identify with the speech community they are studying. This is a position that Fishman has maintained throughout his scholarly life. In 1991, he said: 'The sociology of language, like all of social science, is inevitably perspectival and a good bit of any observers' values and beliefs therefore rub off on his or her observations' (1991b: 8). And in his recent article on 'sociolinguistics' in the *Handbook of Language and Ethnicity* (1999: 160) he added: 'Without adequately taking into consideration the 'insider' views, convictions and interpretations, no full or richly nuanced understanding of the behaviors being researched is possible.'

In *Bilingual Education: An International Perspective* (1976), Fishman talks about his focus not only on empirical data, but also on communicating feelings and values. The preface starts out by saying:

This is a partisan volume. Not only is it unabashedly in favor of bilingual education, but it is strongly in favor of a certain context for bilingual education: a context that values it as enrichment for one and all. ... I have written this book because I want to bring this view, and the data and reasoning on which it is based, to teachers, teacher-trainees, educational administrators, a wide variety of other educational specialists, and educationally concerned laymen. ... I hope I will be pardoned for feeling deeply and for communicating feelings and values in addition to information and conclusions. I believe it is my duty as an empirical researcher to do the former as well as the latter because bilingual education urgently requires not only attention and understanding but also sympathy, assistance and dedication. (Fishman, 1976: viii)

Fishman has defended this 'voice from within,' even when the political tide supports research that is contrary to this position and has left him with little funding for research. In his book titled, *In Praise of the Beloved Language* (1996a), he explains:

The chief debit of the 'voice from within' is that it is self-interest biased, but at least it is admittedly so. However, the voices from without are also necessarily biased – in perspective and in expected audience and reward (and therefore, also in self-interest) – no matter how much they dress themselves up in the garb of science, objectivity, theory and fashionable philosophy or ideology. Like insider views, outsider views too are often reductionist and simplistic (and therefore, neither fully informed nor informing), a charge that outside viewers have long hurled at insider viewers. (Fishman, 1996a: 119)

But to this insider's view, Fishman, the researcher, has always added an analytical perspective. In his book *Language and Nationalism* (1972b), he speaks about how the three nationalist movements that are at the center of his life – Yiddish secularism, Hebrew Zionism and the African American movement – have shaped his interest in language and nationalism. But he describes how he obtained scholarly distance:

I have decided to do so [understand them better] by engaging in a once removed, twice removed, thrice removed mode of analysis, in the hope that the wider canvas would illumine the narrower, while the narrower passion would drive me on to examine one hidden corner after another in the broader picture. (Fishman, 1972b: xiii)

As a way to study multilingualism, the Fishmanian sociolinguistic model (1971) relies first on ethnographic observations through which behavioral or attitudinal clusters associated with different speech varieties are hypothesized. These clusters are then used for further observations, interviews, questionnaires, or attitude scales.

Fishman's methodological contributions to large-scale social investigations consist of the early development of self-report instruments, censuses, questionnaires, interview guides and word association tests, that were then subjected to factor analysis, analyses of variances and multiple regression analyses. But methodology to him is subservient to the topic at hand. In what was to be his second large scale sociolinguistic study, *Bilingualism in the Barrio*, Fishman (1971: xiii) says: 'It is one of the hallmarks of scientific social inquiry that methods are selected as a result of problem specifications rather than independently of them.' This is an area to which Fishman has always paid attention. As Research Director of the College Board in the late 1950s, he used correlations, regressions and identification of predictors that attempt to approximate criteria, but he demanded that selection and admissions to college must be anchored in a philosophy of education (Fishman & Passanella, 1960).

Throughout his work, Fishman has been concerned with the tension between group data and individual data, but he has not been moved to give one up for the other. He sustains:

> The need to summarize and group language usage data necessarily leads to some loss of refinement when proceeding from specific instances of actual speech in face to face interaction to grouped or categorized data. However, such summarization or simplification is an inevitable aspect of the scientific process of discovering meaning in continuous multivariate data by attending to differential relationships, central tendencies, relative variabilities and other similar characterization. (Fishman, 1972a: 91)

Because the same process may result in differences in varied cases, Fishman proposes that a comparative method be used to find cross-cultural and diachronic regularities. As early as 1968, he suggested four scenarios for comparative work with language groups being the same or different, and similar or dissimilar with regards to primary sociocultural processes and contact types. The four resulting scenarios are (Fishman, 1972a: 103):

(1) *same* language group in two separate interaction contexts: *similar;*
(2) *same* language group in two separate interaction contexts: *dissimilar;*
(3) *different* language groups in two separate interaction contexts: *similar;*
(4) *different* language groups in two separate interaction contexts: *dissimilar.*

As Fishman's conceptual universe grew, his methodology continued to reflect his positive attitude toward the minority speech community or the problem that he was studying. He also developed ways of continuing to compare and contrast his thinking on particular sociolinguistic situations with others, and his own thinking with those of others in what he says may 'not be the best of all possible worlds.' This is evident, for example, in the book that he dedicates to positive ethnolinguistic consciousness, *In Praise of the Beloved Language* (1996a). Drawing from examples of the many languages that make up the compendium of languages in the book, Fishman (1996a: 4) proceeds to compare the answers that these texts reveal about the following questions:

- What are the positive views about their vernaculars that have been expressed by peoples the world over?
- Are there any regularities to these views, across time and across space?
- Are there more common and less common themes and, if so, which are which?
- Are some themes more distinctly European and others less so, or have some themes now become rather uncommon in Europe while they have become more common elsewhere?

With considerable detail, Fishman tells us how he went about creating the categories for the content analysis.

Fishman is mostly interested in social factors, dimensions and parameters, rather than individuals:

> The individual, any individual, is merely error variance from the perspective of social research. Each individual's behavior is over-determined in terms of his or her personal dynamics. Social research, on the other hand, is concerned with factors, dimensions and parameters that are demonstrable over and above the varying tendencies, dispositions and idiosyncrasies of unique individuals. All of our much vaunted statistical tests are built upon this very principle: to contrast between-group variance with within-group variance. Only when the former is sufficiently greater than the latter do we call our findings 'statistically significant'. (Fishman, 1987: 2)

Yet Fishman often also pays attention to individuals. He devotes an entire book to the man who had captured his imagination as the organizer of the First Yiddish Language Conference in Austro-Hungarian Tshernovits in 1908 – Nathan Birnbaum.

Fishman's 2001, *Can Threatened Languages be Saved*? is a collection of case studies that puts to the test his theoretical conceptualizations about Reversing Language Shift (see below). In many contributions, Fishman tests his own conceptualizations, and in so doing, draws other scholars to reflect and expand upon his own theories and cases. In the preface to *Can Threatened Languages be Saved?* Fishman (2001) writes:

Just as any single-authored volume inevitably overestimates the degree of coherence and confirmation vis-à-vis the author's views, any multi-authored volume is likely to reveal a reverse imbalance, over-representing differences and disconfirmations relative to the views of that same particular author's approach. (Fishman, 2001: xiii)

One of us (García) always remembers Fishman, the teacher, saying that 'increasing the variance' was important in all research. It is a lesson that Fishman the scholar has always acted upon, demanding that the voices of 'little people' and 'little languages' also be included.

Recently, Fishman has chided the ethnographic revolution of the post-modern world for paying little attention to ethnicity and not considering poetic and romantic imagery and folk analogies. As he puts it,

We have often championed late modernizers and 'native peoples,' but we have even more commonly refocused our intellectualizations from modernization to post-modernization without letting these peoples speak their own words or disclose their own hearts and minds. (Fishman: 1996a: 120)

Fishman has never closed the door to ways of looking deeply in various ways. About his work, he has said:

I feel strongly that there is more 'out there' (even more to the sociology of language) than science can grasp, and I have a personal need for poets, artists, mystics and philosophers too for a deeper understanding of all that puzzles me. (Fishman, 1990: 123)

A Fishmanian sociolinguistic model for the study of multilingualism: Theoretical propositions

Domains

One of the main early concepts proposed by Fishman to study multi-lingualism was that of *domain*. The concept of domain, Fishman explains, was first elaborated among *Auslandsdeutsche*[9] students in pre-World War II multilingual settings. Domains 'are defined, regardless of their number, in terms of institutional contexts and their congruent behavioral co-occur-rences. They attempt to summate the major clusters of interaction that occur in clusters of multilingual settings and involving clusters of interloc-utors' (Fishman, 1971: 586). Domains allow scholars to make connections between clusters of interaction and interlocutors and more concrete social situations.

The interest in defining 'domains' grew out of Fishman's methodological concern that analytic parameters be in touch with reality and be abstracted from domain – appropriate persons, places and times. Domains structure the data of social behavior. Fishman tells us that domain variance is the most *parsimonious* and fruitful designation of the societally or institutionally clusterable occasions in which one language (variant, dialect, style, etc.) is habitually employed rather than (or in addition to) another. (Fishman, 1972a: 80)

Throughout his work, Fishman has reserved a special place for the family domain, saying that: 'Multilingualism often begins in the family and depends upon it for encouragement if not for protection' (Fishman, 1972a: 82). And much later, when he proposes his model for Reversing Language Shift (RLS, see below), Fishman (1991b: 113) declares: 'Without intergenerational mother tongue transmission, no language maintenance is possible. That which is not transmitted cannot be maintained.' This is why in the *Graded Intergenerational Disruption Scale* proposed in his RLS model, Stage 6 – the stage in which language X (the minority or non-dominant language) is the normal language of informal, spoken interaction between and within the family – is crucial to language maintenance and RLS. Commenting on globalization and the multimodal discourses that have been made possible by recent technology, Fishman insists on the power of the family over the power of the Internet, stating that:

> Nothing can substitute for face-to-face interaction with real family imbedded in real community. Ultimately, nothing is as crucial for basic RLS success as intergenerational mother tongue transmission. *Gemeinschaft* (the intimate community whose members are related to one another via bonds of kinship, affection and communality of interest and purpose) is the real secret weapon of RLS. (Fishman, 2001: 458)

Diglossia

Another of the major contributions of Joshua A. Fishman to the study of societal multilingualism has been his extension and expansion of the concept of *diglossia* as proposed by Ferguson (1959). Ferguson used diglossia to describe a society that used a H(igh) variety of a language in religion, education and other domains, and a L(ow) variety in the home and lower work sphere. Fishman (1964) traces the maintenance and disruption of diglossia to the national or societal level and extends it to include cases of societal bilngualism. He warns that 'socially patterned bilingualism can exist as a stabilized phenomenon only if there is functional differentiation between two languages' (Fishman, 1971: 560) and says:

> If the roles were not kept separate (compartmentalized) by the power of their association with quite separate though complementary values, domains of activity and everyday situations, one language or variety would displace the other as role and value distinctions became blurred or merged. (Fishman, 1972a: 140)

Fishman renders the compartmentalization between the H(igh) and L(ow) language in the form of a diagram:

$$\frac{H}{L}$$

with the line between the two indicating functional separation, a boundary. Fishman explains that without diglossia, stable balanced bilingualism cannot be obtained, and continues:

> From the point of view of sociolinguistics, any society that produces functionally balanced bilinguals (i.e. bilinguals who use both their languages equally and equally well in all contexts) must soon cease to be bilingual because no society needs two languages for one and the same set of functions. (Fishman, 1972a: 140)

Diglossia provides the impetus for language maintenance or shift, which we will discuss later. Fishman declares:

> Without separate though complementary norms and values to establish and maintain functional separation of the speech varieties, that language or variety which is fortunate enough to be associated with the predominant drift of social forces tends to displace the others. (Fishman, 1972a: 149)

In 1987, in the book that he dedicates to Nathan Birnbaum, the organizer of the First Yiddish Conference in Tschernovits in 1908, Fishman reiterates:

> A culture that can no longer control its own boundaries is doomed to a cultural version of the 'acquired immune deficiency syndrome.'...There must be a boundary that cannot be overstepped. (Fishman, 1987: 138)

Diglossia, as the stable maintenance of two complementary value systems and thus two languages, is expressed in two complementary sets of domains. Fishman distinguishes bilingualism from diglossia as follows:

> [B]ilingualism is essentially a characterization of individual linguistic versatility while diglossia is a characterization of the societal allocation of functions to different languages or varieties. (Fishman, 1972a: 145)

In 1967, Fishman published his now famous and much cited 'Bilingualism With and Without Diglossia; Diglossia With and Without Bilingualism.' In this article, he outlined four possible situational cells:

(1)   diglossia with bilingualism;
(2)   diglossia without bilingualism;
(3)   bilingualism without diglossia;
(4)   neither diglossia nor bilingualism.

Fishman devotes most attention to the fruitful bilingualism of the first of these (diglossia with bilingualism) which he illustrates with examples such as Paraguay where Guaraní is used at home and Spanish is used in education, religion, government and work. Social groups in this cell are usually fairly large speech communities that offer a range of compartmentalized roles, as well as access to those roles to its members (Fishman, 1971).

The second cell (diglossia without bilingualism) is exemplified by polities that are for the most part 'economically underdeveloped and unmobilized.' In these polities, the elites speak one language and the masses another, but they have never really formed a single speech community – 'their linguistic repertoires were discontinuous and their inter-communications were by means of translators or interpreters' (Fishman, 1972a: 143).

Bilingualism without diglossia exists in social groups with great social unrest or rapid social change, such as is the case of immigrants and refugees. Finally, there are very few societies where neither diglossia nor bilingualism occur.

But as the world has become more interdependent, Fishman's concept of diglossia has acquired some fluidity. In 1985 he warns that diglossia requires control, but not the 'freezing' of intercultural boundaries.' Speaking about the relationship between English and Dutch in the Netherlands, Fishman explains:

> The result of such boundary maintenance is that English never becomes a requirement for membership in the Dutch ethnoculture, although it does become a widespread skill advantageously associated with such membership. ... It [English] is definitely not intended to be, nor will it become, an inside language of Dutch society at large. (Fishman, 1985, as cited in 1989: 227)

Despite the insistence that there must be some functional allocation between two languages in order for stable intra-group bilingualism to be maintained, Fishman posits that he espouses cultural pluralism, rather than cultural separatism. For North American ethnolinguistic minorities, he supports 'language maintenance within the framework of *mutual interaction* with American core society' (Fishman, 1972a: 22). Fishman increasingly acknowledges the interdependency of a globalized world:

> In a world that is continually more and more interactive and interdependent, modernization can be delayed and 'locally colored,' but rarely can it be interminably delayed or fully controlled. (Fishman, 1996a: 93)

When Fishman conceptualizes the field of Reversing Language Shift (RLS), he concedes overlapping and interactive functions. But he insists on the protection and stability of what he calls the X-ish functions, in the face of Y-ish functions, with X representing co-territorial threatened languages, and *Y* denoting unthreatened or less threatened languages. Fishman (1991b: 85) explains that 'Bilingualism is protective of *X*-ishness and *interactive* with *Y*-ishness' [emphasis ours].

Fishman (2001) acknowledges that threatened languages (*Th* below) usually aspire to discharge the powerful functions of employment, higher education, mass media, government, etc. That is, threatened languages aim to fulfill those functions that diglossia had previously noted as High, as well as the informal and less powerful functions to which it had been previously relegated (previously noted as Low).

But Fishman describes a more realistic and initial goal for threatened languages in which some of the social functions that had previously been relegated to the more powerful (or High) language; for example, secondary education or local employment; would be shared with the non-threatened language (*n-Th* below). Fishman represents this diglossic relationship, with powerful functions above the line, as:

$$\frac{n\text{-}Th/Th}{Th}$$

That is, although the Th(reatened) language, previously noted as L(ow), may share some of the functions of the n(on)-Th(reatened) language, previously noted as H(igh) in the more formal and powerful domains, the informal domains of intimacy and informality, and especially home, must be reserved solely for the Th(reatened) language. In other words, there must not be any fluidity over the horizontal line, and the Th(reatened) language carefully guards its functions in the home domain.

Fishman warns that RLS's goal is not just to elevate the threatened language so that it is in a position to assume powerful functions. It must also *guard the invasion of the non-threatened powerful language into the less powerful domains, especially the family*, where it can destroy the possibility of intergenerational transmission by destroying the creation of any mother tongue speakers within one generation. It is especially *X*, the threatened language, that has to be functionally separated. Fishman explains:

> When intragroup bilingualism is stabilized so that *X*-ish has its functions and *Y*-ish has its functions and these two sets of functions overlap minimally, then *X*-ish will have its own space, functions in which it and it alone is normatively expected. (Fishman, 1991b: 85)

Facing the threats of globalization in the 21st century, Fishman acknowledges the importance of the 'Big Brother language.' He concedes that: '[A]n internal societal re-allocation of languages to functions is pursued that will also be partially acceptive of the culturally stronger Big Brother language' (Fishman, 2001: 7). Speaking of what he calls late- and later-modernizer languages, he states that they:

may find that multilingualism and multiliteracy are actually their best options for more quickly attaining both symbolic vernacular recognition on the one hand and the greater material advantages that are associated with languages of wider communication on the other. (Fishman, 1999: 161)

Language Maintenance/Language Shift/Reversing Language Shift

Language maintenance/language shift

Language maintenance and language shift have been important fields of inquiry in the sociology of language from the very beginning ('Language Maintenance and Language Shift as a Field of Inquiry,' 1964). They were originally defined thus:

> The study of language maintenance and language shift is concerned with the relationship between change or stability in habitual language use, on the one hand, and ongoing psychological, social or cultural processes of change and stability, on the other hand. (as cited in Fishman, 1971: 603, note 3)

In 1968, Fishman revisits this definition and extends it by saying:

> The study of language maintenance and language shift is concerned with the relationship between change (or stability) in language usage patterns, on the one hand, and ongoing psychological, social or cultural processes, on the other hand, in populations that utilize more than one speech variety *for intra-group or for inter-group purposes.*' [emphasis ours] (Fishman, 1968: 76)

Fishman's initial interest in intra-group multilingualism was quickly extended to encompass inter-group processes, as he faced the developing world and his interest in language planning (see below). It is this extension that he highlights in his revised definition.

The three main topics of language maintenance and language shift are identified as (Fishman, 1964, 1968):

(1) habitual language use and the measurement of degree and location of bilingualism along sociologically relevant dimensions;
(2) psychological, social and cultural processes and their relationship to stability or change in habitual language use;
(3) behavior toward language, including attitudinal behavior, cognitive behavior or overt behavior.

In a style that is typical of Fishman throughout his career, he articulates his theoretical conceptualization of language maintenance and language shift by presenting a series of counter-arguments to his thinking, which he then critiques (Fishman, 1972a):

(1)   language maintenance is a function of intactness of group member-ship or group loyalty, particularly nationalism;
(2)   urban dwellers are more inclined to shift. Rural dwellers who are more conservative and isolated are less inclined;
(3)   the most prestigious language displaces the less prestigious language.

To the first argument, Fishman provides counter-evidence from such varied ethnolinguistic groups as the Guayquyeries of Venezuela, the lower caste groups in India, the Raetoromans in Switzerland and the *Auslandsdeutsche* in the midst of Polish and Ukrainian majorities. He concludes:

> Language maintenance may depend most on nationalist ideologies in populations whose lives have otherwise been greatly dislocated and it may also depend least on such ideologies in those populations that have best preserved their total social context against the winds of change. (Fishman, 1972a: 97)

Fishman then makes the point that language loyalty and language revival movements are mostly urban phenomena, and gives example of some low prestige languages that have historically displaced more presti-gious ones. By so doing, Fishman proposes that the same process may have different outcomes in different societies and at different times. He says, for example:

> Urbanization may result in language shift away from hitherto tradi-tional language in some cases, in language shift back to traditional languages in other cases, while revealing significantly unaltered main-tenance of the status quo in still others. (Fishman, 1972a: 100)

The significance of this quote is that it contains the germinating seeds for Fishman's later work on reversing language shift (RLS) – see next section.

With a vision that well anticipates Richard Ruiz's (1984) division of language ideology as viewing language as a problem, as a resource, or as a right, Fishman says about language in the United States:

> The recommendations advanced here are derived from the point of view that language maintenance in the United States is desirable, in that the non-English language *resources* of American minority groups have already helped meet our urgent national need for speakers of various non-English languages, and that these resources can be rein-forced and developed so as to do so to a very much greater extent in the future. [emphasis ours] (Fishman, 1972a: 18)

The seeds for RLS are also in Fishman's 1966 article titled 'Planned Reinforcement of Language Maintenance in the United States. Suggestions for the Conservation of a Neglected National Resource.' This article already puts Fishman in the position of recommending and planning social action on behalf of threatened languages. He explains:

> [M]ost social scientists feel more comfortable with diagnosis (study design, instrument construction, data collection, data analysis, data interpretation) than with therapy (recommendations for action, planning action, involvement with action-oriented branches of government or segments of the community).... Although it is frequently admitted that applied settings can provide powerful stimulation for theoretical developments, the leap from the role of scholar to that of *consultant or activist* is still rarely attempted among behavioral scientists. [emphasis ours] (Fishman, 1972a: 16, 17)

Fishman, however, dares to make the leap to activist, and also has the courage to admit his values and biases – his social philosophy. He tells us: 'Recommendations leading to language reinforcement imply a willingness to espouse certain values, and *to assist* certain groups in an informed pursuit of "the art of the possible"' [emphasis ours] (Fishman, 1972a: 19). Clearly the seeds for RLS were sown in the 1960s and early 1970s.

Reversing language shift (RLS)

While many scholars complain about threatened and endangered languages in the world today, Fishman has turned his conceptualization of language maintenance and language shift into a program of social action. Threatened languages, Fishman (1991b) reminds us, are not replacing themselves demographically and are unrelated to higher social status. But something can be done to assist them; resources such as intelligence, funds, time and effort can be mobilized. Fishman first establishes that RLS is both necessary and desirable. Posing the question, 'Can anything be done?' he answers in the affirmative, and suggests that one has to decide 'which functions to tackle first ... and which specific steps to take in order to (re)gain those functions among specific target populations' (Fishman, 1991b: 12). Fishman proposes his *Graded Intergenerational Disruption Scale (GIDS)* where, the higher the score, the lower the language maintenance prospects of a group.

The GIDS provides a way by which groups can assess the threatened state of their languages (*X*) and can mobilize resources on their behalf:

Stage 8: *X* spoken by socially isolated old folks;

Stage 7: *X* spoken by people who are socially integrated and ethnolinguistically active, but beyond child-bearing age;

Stage 6:   *X* is normal language of informal spoken interaction between and within all three generations of family, with *Y* reserved for greater formality and technicality than those common of daily family life;

Stage 5:   *X* is also used for literacy in home, school and community, but such literacy is not reinforced extra-communally;

Stage 4:   *X* is used in lower education that meets requirements of compulsory education laws;

Stage 3:   *X* is used in lower work sphere, outside of the community, and involving interaction between both speech communities;

Stage 2:   *X* is used in lower governmental services and mass media, but not higher levels;

Stage 1:   *X* is used in higher level educational, occupational, governmental and media efforts.

The crucial stage beyond which there is no intergenerational mother tongue transmission, and therefore, no possibility of language maintenance is Stage 6. As we noted before, 'Face-to-face interaction with real family imbedded in real community,' Fishman (2001: 458) reminds us, 'is the real secret weapon of RLS.' Reacting to the importance that scholars of multimodal discourse give to the web community (Jewett & Kress, 2003; Kress, 2003), Fishman (2001: 455) says that 'community and 'virtual community' are not the same thing at all as far as intergenerational mother tongue transmission are concerned.'

Groups that fall between stages 5 and 8 are attempting to work out some kind of diglossia, what Fishman sees as the program minimum of RLS. Groups that fall between stages 1 and 4 have transcended diglossic status, and are in search of increased power sharing.

RLS is especially important in the 21st century as a way to balance globalization. Fishman says:

> RLSers aim at nothing more than to achieve greater self-regulation over the processes of sociocultural change which globalisation fosters. They want to be able to tame globalisation somewhat, to counterbalance it with more of their own language-and-culture institutions, processes and outcomes. (Fishman, 2001: 6)

Thus, RLS theoretical contributions make room for both – globalization and particularism. Fishman (2001) points to the important multilingual and multi-ethnic interactions that will be necessary in the world of the future:

> The languages of the world will either all help one another survive or they will succumb separately to the global dangers that must assuredly await us all (English included) in the century ahead. (Fishman, 2001: 481)

Language Spread

As we have seen, Fishman's sociology of language was first concerned with the measurement of habitual language use and the sociocultural processes leading to or inhibiting language maintenance and language shift in immigrant settings. But from the beginning, Fishman also turned to the study of the opposite side of this coin, namely the diffusion process of a language of wider communication. In 1967, he published the first article that was to deal with this topic: 'The Breadth and Depth of English in the United States.' The spread of English offered a new perspective for the study of language maintenance and language shift. On the one hand, English was widely present in very different societal contexts. On the other hand, it was present in many educational systems, and was often more read than spoken. Furthermore, sociocultural processes, and especially the role of power, were more visible in the study of English language spread than in the study of language maintenance and shift of immigrant communities. Fishman says:

> Bilingualism is repeatedly skewed in favor of the more powerful, with the language of greater power being acquired and used much more frequently than that of lesser power. (Fishman, 1976, as cited in 1989: 241)

About English, Fishman adds:

> On the whole, English as an additional language is more learned than used and more used than liked. The three (learning, using and liking) are little related to each other. (Fishman, 1976, as cited in 1989: 254)

The fact that English is not particularly liked worldwide is linked to its power. Fishman asserts:

> Small languages and weak polities in the modern world quickly realize that they require strong partners to protect and complement them. Large languages and strong polities lack this realization and, therefore, run a particular risk of parochialism, provincialism, and philistinism – a risk that is all the more terrifying because miscalculations derived therefrom can have truly calamitous results. (Fishman *et al.*, 1977: 334)

It is a lesson for the United States and the powerful English-speaking world that Fishman delivers again and again.

But from the beginning, Fishman also explains that the spread of English does not have to result in the loss of local languages. This early position reminds us of Louis-Jean Calvet's (1999) 'gravitational model' of diglossia, a model that proposes that today's spread of global powerful languages like English can coexist and not threaten local languages. In fact, Fishman,

Cooper and Conrad (1977) prophesy that the use of local languages might increase as a result of English language spread:

> English is clearly the major link-language in the world today and that alone shows signs of continuing as such, at least in the short run, while the use of local languages for official literacy/education-related purposes is also likely to increase. (Cooper & Conrad, 1977: 56)

In 1980, in an article titled 'Language Maintenance and Ethnicity,' Fishman had already identified the two contradictory trends that according to Maurais and Morris (2004) characterize languages in the globalized world of the 21st century:

(1) the spread of a single lingua franca (English) 'for supra-local, econo-technical, political, diplomatic, educational and touristic purposes';
(2) the recognition of more languages than ever before 'for governmental and governmentally protected functions.' (as cited in Fishman, 1989: 220)

And yet, Fishman, Cooper and Conrad call for the English-speaking world to assist the rest of the world in preserving their local vernaculars. Fishman says:

> International sociolinguistic balance rests on the spread of English, the control of English, and the fostering of local/regional/national vernaculars. ... Of these three, the one that is currently most dynamic is that relating to the vernaculars, many of which are straining for further recognition. Thus it becomes all the more crucial not only whether native speakers of English can hold on to their technological superiority but also whether they can really meet the 'others' halfway in the crucial sociopsychological arena of *mutual acceptance*. [emphasis ours] (Fishman *et al.*, 1977: 335)

Fishman pursues this topic of the role of English in former British and American colonies in the book he edits with Andrew Conrad and Alma Rubal-López, *Post-Imperial English: Status Change in Former British and American Colonies 1940–1990*. In a series of case studies authored by different scholars, Fishman studies the presence of English along seven dimensions – elementary education, tertiary education, print media, non-print media, technology/commerce/industry, governmental services and operations and indigenous informal usage. Although most cases confirm the presence of English especially in the econotechnical realms at the supra-local level, Fishman concludes that there is no evidence of alienation from the local culture, and certainly no evidence of linguicide. Despite the threats to endangered languages, which Fishman acknowledges and has spent his academic life trying to protect and save, it is the need for assistance to local indigenous vernaculars that Fishman's work emphasizes. In other words, he wastes no intellectual energy trying to stop the spread of English. He acknowledges that:

> The socioeconomic factors that are behind the spread of English are now indigenous in most countries of the world and part and parcel of indigenous daily life and social stratification. (Fishman, 1996b: 637)

So it is the role of the vernacular, and its weaker (or at least weakening) status in indigenous daily life that is important for Joshua A. Fishman, with language attitudes and ideologies playing an important role in the shaping of that role.

Language Attitudes and Language and Ethnicity/ Nationalism/Identity/Religion/Power

Language attitudes

Fishmanian sociolinguistics has always included research aimed at discovering 'the nature, determinants, effects and measurement of attitudes' (Cooper & Fishman, 1974: 6). That is, affective behaviors always have had a place in sociology of language studies, alongside overt behaviors and cognitive behaviors. But Fishman has also signaled the contradictions between affective and overt behaviors. In an article on 'Language Policy in the USA,' Fishman (1989: 408) comments that 'it is possible for language attitudes to improve in compensatory fashion as both use and knowledge decrease.'

In 1996, Fishman dedicated an entire book to language attitudes. His *In Praise of the Beloved Language. A Comparative View of Positive Ethnolinguistic Consciousness* is an attempt to understand language attitudes towards the vernacular. Fishman makes clear that although nationalist movements have used these attitudes in mobilizing populations, positive ethnolinguistic consciousness is not in itself nationalism. Fishman also acknowledges that positive ethnolinguistic consciousness is not the only type of language consciousness. Language consciousness can also be inter-ethnic, and even supra-ethnic in the case of shared lingua francas.

The concept of positive ethnolinguistic consciousness ties the understandings of language attitudes with those of language identity and language and nationalism which we will discuss below. Fishman explains that:

> The phenomenology of most ongoing positive ethnolinguistic consciousness recognizes a ... reality in which the ethnic language, the ethnic identity and the ethnic culture (behaviors, beliefs, artifacts) are all completely intertwined. It is this very intertwining that constitutes the 'heart of the matter.' (Fishman, 1996a: 61)

Despite this intertwining, we address each of these components individually below.

Language and ethnicity

In a 1997 essay entitled 'Language and Ethnicity: The View from Within,' Joshua Fishman explains that the term ethnicity is derived from the Greek *'ethnos'* and shares its negative semantic load of 'unrefined.' The earliest Greek translation of the Hebrew Bible used the term *'ethnos'* as the counterpart to the Hebrew *'goy'* which meant 'god-obeying.' When the terms race, national origin and culture became inapplicable because they were no longer useful, the term ethnicity was brought to the fore.

In an early article that Fishman published in 1965 entitled 'Varieties of Ethnicity and Varieties of Language Consciousness,' Fishman says:

> Ethnicity refers most basically to a primordial holistic guide to human behavior ... An all-embracing constellation, limited in its contacts with the outside world, limited in its consciousness of self, limited in the internal differentiation or specialization that it recognizes or permits; a 'given' that is viewed as no more subject to change than one's kin and one's birthplace; a 'given' that operates quite literally with these two differentiations (kinship and birthplace) uppermost in mind; a 'given' in which kinship and birthplace completely regulate friendship, worship and workmanship. (as cited in Fishman, 1972a: 180)

More than 15 years later, in an article entitled 'Language Maintenance and Ethnicity,' Fishman (1989: 180) defines ethnicity as 'peopleness, i.e. belonging or pertaining to a phenomenologically complete, separate, historically deep cultural collectivity, a collectivity polarized on perceived authenticity.' Ethnicity, Fishman says much later, is about macro-group 'belongingness' or the identification dimensions of culture. He distinguishes it from culture by saying that ethnicity is both narrower than culture and more perspectival than culture, that is, 'the attribution of ethnicity is fundamentally subjective, variable and very possibly non-consensual' (Fishman, 1997b: 329). But Fishman (1972a: 180) warns that 'primordial ethnicity is a web that comes apart and becomes segmentized, bit by bit during periods of sociocultural change.'

Of language, Fishman (1996a: 61) says: 'Language is an intimately experienced and highly valued verity, a palpable object of esteem, affection, reverence and dedication.' According to Fishman (1989: 673), language 'is both part of, indexical of, and symbolic of ethnocultural behavior.' The 'beloved language,' he tells us is 'flesh of our flesh and bone of our bone' (Fishman, 1996a: 91).

The fact that language is the link to ethnicity is a constant thread throughout all of Fishman's work.

> [L]anguage is the recorder of paternity, the expresser of patrimony and
> the carrier of phenomenology. Any vehicle carrying such precious
> freight must come to be viewed as equally precious, as part of the
> freight, indeed, as precious in and of itself. The link between language
> and ethnicity is thus one of sanctity-by-association. (Fishman, 1989: 32)

In the book that he devotes to positive ethnolinguistic consciousness, *In Praise of the Beloved Language*, Fishman (1996a) explains that language is a symbol system of the human species. Every vernacular can become symbolic of the speech community, utilized intergenerationally and for cultural boundary-maintenance. Some languages have a sanctity dimension, that is, they are expressed as the spirit or the soul of the ethnonational collectivity. Some are outright Holy languages in which the word of God and the disciples and prophets was spread – Biblical Hebrew, Koranic Arabic, Sanskrit, Pali, Classical Mandarin, Javanese, Syriac, Latin, Greek, Coptic, Armenian, Ethiopic, Old Church Slavonic and several scriptural languages of the Eastern Orthodox Churches. The majority of the world's ethnocultures, Fishman (1997b) reminds us, are predominantly linked to traditionally associated religions. Most of the time the language and ethnicity link is clear, denoting kinship, heritage, hearth and home.

In ways that remind us of the work on linguistic ideologies of anthropologists today (Irvine & Gal, 2000; Pavlenko & Blackledge, 2004; Woolard, 1998), Fishman (1991b: 388) explains that language 'not only implies and reflects core boundaries but it constantly creates and legitimizes them as well.' Fishman (1997b) further points out that the link between language and ethnicity is variable; that is, sometimes language is a prime indicator of ethnicity, and at other times it is marginal and optional. Ethnicity itself 'waxes and wanes and changes in response to more powerful and encompassing developments' (Fishman, 1983, as cited in 1989: 686).

Fishman also introduces the concept of language as a resource, and as a worldwide societal asset. He dedicates much of his work to understanding Benjamin Lee Whorf's contributions and especially what he calls 'Whorfianism of the third kind' (Fishman, 1982). Whorf, a student of Edward Sapir, had extended Sapir's argument that each language represents a worldview, and posited that particular languages carve up experience according to their structures and categories. But beyond the *linguistic relativity* and the *linguistic determinism* hypotheses that Whorf posed, and that have been discarded as untenable, Fishman (1989: 568) values Whorf as a 'neo-Herderian champion of a multilingual, multicultural world in which "little peoples" and "little languages" would not only be respected, but valued.' The work of Johann Gottfried Herder (1744–1803) is cited frequently by Fishman, who supports Herder's views that the mother tongue expresses a nationality's soul and that:

[L]anguage was also the surest way for individuals to safeguard (or recover) the authenticity they had inherited from their ancestors as well as to hand it on to generations yet unborn, and finally, that world-wide diversity in language and in culture was a good and beautiful thing in and of itself, whereas imitation led to corruption and stagnation. (Fishman, 1972b: 46)

The link between language and ethnicity can be 'energized by collective grievances,' Fishman (1996a: 161) explains. He suggests that the relationship between language and ethnicity is not uni-directional:

Just as ethnic identity is fostered by intergroup grievances, so the language use corresponding to such identity is fostered. Thus when use of one's ethnically associated language is restricted or denigrated, the users who identify with it are more likely to use it among themselves ... than if no such grievance existed. (Fishman, 1996a: 154)

Taking sides, as always, with those who grieve, Fishman warns:

When the late-modernizing or late-autonomy-gaining worm finally turns, it will necessarily disturb the peace and quiet of those who have attained recognition earlier and at the latecomers' expense. But in their own eyes the latecomers 'turning' will not only seem justified but long-overdue and, indeed, merely following an example well established in the surrounding world of nations and peoples. ... In the pursuit of ethnolinguistic dreams, what's sauce for the goose is oft-times considered sauce for the goslings as well, whether or not this is realistic or desired by the now older, wiser and fatter geese. (Fishman, 1996a: 91)

Fishman (1996a: 93) warns us that ethnolinguistic consciousness of what he calls 'late' or 'peripheral' languages will 'continue to alarm self-satisfied neighbors' and 'disturb the peace of those who are already contextually comfortable.' The only way to work out this dilemma is 'greater reciprocal bilingualism, with each side evincing a willingness to compromise "its position maximum"' (Fishman, 1996a: 93).

Responding to scholars and critics who view the process of globalization as making ethnicity and language differences unnecessary, Fishman notes:

Some of the very processes of globalization and post-modernism that were supposed to be most deleterious to purportedly 'parochial' identities have actually contributed most to their re-emergence as 'part-identities.' The increasing ubiquity of the civil state, of civil nationalism and, therefore, of a shared supra-ethnic civil nationalism as part of the identity constellation of all citizens, has resulted in more rather than less recognition of multiculturalism at the institutional level and a more widespread implementation of local ethnicity as a counterbalance to civil nationalism at the level of organized part-identity. (Fishman, 2001: 460)

As globalization has advanced, the link between language and ethnicity has become more salient in consciousness. And it is precisely globalization that is responsible for the social action language programs proposed by RLS, as well as the transformation of many threatened languages and their speakers. Fishman proposes that:

> With increased intensities and frequencies of intergroup contacts and competition, on the one hand, and with the resulting weakening of traditional life in the face of cultural influences that are experienced as 'supra-ethnically' modern (rather than as specifically 'other-ethnic'), on the other hand, a protective and differentiating counteraction is often cultivated. Under these circumstances, the language and ethnicity link can not only become the basis of social action but it can also be transformative for those among whom it is salient. (Fishman, 1997b: 330)

According to Fishman (2001), it is precisely globalization that makes 'localization' important:

> [T]he coming of globalization in certain aspects of human functioning makes 'localization' even more important in modern part-identity, equally so for state-nation, nation-state and sub-state populations. (Fishman, 2001: 455)

Language and nationalism

Joshua A. Fishman devotes an entire book to the topic of *Language and Nationalism* (1972b). In the two long essays that make up that book, Fishman distinguishes between the concepts of ethnic group, nationality and nation on the one hand, and state, polity or country on the other. Ethnic group, Fishman says 'is simpler, smaller, more particularistic, more localistic' than nationality. Nationalities are 'sociocultural units that have developed beyond primarily local self-concepts, concerns and integrative bonds' that do not necessarily have their own autonomous territory (Fishman, 1972b: 3). Nation, however, is 'any political-territorial unit which is largely or increasingly under the control of a particular nationality' (Fishman, 1972b: 5). A state, polity or country may not be independent of external control, and unlike a nation, does not always have a single predominant nationality.

Fishman also distinguishes between nationalism and nationism. He defines nationalism as 'The more inclusive organization and the elaborated beliefs, values and behaviors which nationalities develop on behalf of their avowed ethnocultural self-interest...' (Fishman, 1972b: 4). Nationism, however, is the 'cluster of behaviors-beliefs-values pertaining specifically to the acquisition, maintenance and development of politically independent territoriality' (Fishman, 1972b: 4). Fishman (1972b: 194) explains further that 'Nationism – as distinguished from nationalism – is primarily concerned not with ethnic authenticity but with operational efficiency.'

Nationalism often uses language as the link with a glorious past and as a link with authenticity, either directly by claiming that the mother tongue is a part of the soul, or indirectly by widespread oral and written imagery. According to Fishman (1972b), nationalism is 'transformed primordial ethnicity' that leads to functioning on a larger scale. *Language Loyalty*, the title of Fishman's first major study of languages in the United States, is a component of nationalism.

Fishman has always distinguished between positive ethnolinguistic consciousness and nationalism. He defends his interest in positive ethno-linguistic consciousness by declaring, 'I draw a line ... between contributing to an understanding of positive ethnolinguistic consciousness and fostering an acceptance of nationalistic horrors' (Fishman, 1996a: 5). And to the question of whether positive ethnolinguistic consciousness, and for that matter, nationalism, can also be put to negative use, Fishman (1996a: 6) replies: '[I]t certainly can, but so can word processors, education, motherhood, cherry pies and early spring.'

Language and identity

In *Language and Nationalism*, Fishman (1972b) refers to the continued need for identity in the latter part of the 20th century:

> The need for identity, for community, to make modernity sufferable, is greater than it was and will become greater yet, and woe to the elites in universities, governments and industries – who do not recognize this, or even worse, who consider it to be only a vestigial remnant of nine-teenth-century thinking. (Fishman, 1972b: 83)

And facing the globalization of the 21st century, Fishman speaks against the social disorganization of post-modern and supra-ethnic societal func-tioning:

> [R]ationality has not fully satisfied the Pandora's box of human long-ings, i.e., it has neither created nor corresponded to an inner reality that responds or corresponds to various other 'wave lengths' in human social motivation as well. (Fishman, 1996a: 58)

Fishman concedes that today 'ethnic identity is contextually constructed' and that 'group membership may be multiple':

> The global and the specific are now more commonly found together, as

partial (rather than as exclusive) identities, because they each contribute to different social, emotional and cognitive needs that are co-present in the same individuals and societies and that are felt to require and to benefit from different languages in order to give them appropriate expression (Fishman, 1999: 450).

This conviction that multiple-group membership is possible is an early constant for Joshua A. Fishman. For example, in *Bilingual Education: An International Sociological Perspective* (1976), he points out that the human cultural experience is different from plant or animal evolution precisely because of its capacity for multiple memberships. He says: 'It [human cultural experience] not only exhibits but can be aware of and can value multiple-group membership' (Fishman, 1976: 8).

But Fishman objects to the concept introduced by Anderson (1983) of 'imagined communities.' Communities, according to Fishman, may be imagined, but they are not *imaginary*. He agrees with Richard Jenkins' (1997) position, on which he draws extensively:

> Although ethnicity is imagined [in the sense that most members will never interact with each other face to face and that, therefore, the group is an abstraction which they must conceive of an identify with], it is not imaginary ... Somewhere between irresistible emotion and utter cynicism, neither blindly primordial nor completely manipulable, ethnicity and its allotropes are principles of collective identification and social organization in terms of culture and history, similarity and difference, that show little sign of withering away ... It is hard to imagine the social world in their absence. (Fishman, 1996a: 447)

Because ethnic identity is a sociopsychological variable, minorities are more conscious than majorities of their own ethnic identity, Fishman (1996a) tells us. But this doesn't mean that ethnic identity doesn't exist for all humanity.

Language and power

Fishman's work in defending minority and immigrant languages is centered on his conviction that languages have to be safeguarded to ensure a democratic climate of expression. In 1966, in an article entitled 'Planned Reinforcement of Language Maintenance in the United States,' Fishman writes:

> Our political and cultural foundations are weakened when large population groupings do not feel encouraged to express, to safeguard, and to develop behavior patterns that are traditionally meaningful to them. Our national creativity and personal purposefulness are rendered more shallow when constructive channels of self-expression are blocked and when alienation from ethnic-cultural roots becomes the

necessary price of self-respect and social advancement, regardless of the merits of the cultural components of these roots. (1966, as cited in 1972a: 23).

Using languages in ways that describe the positioning of power differently, but that attest to unequal relations of power nonetheless, Fishman (1990: 113) describes his work as 'centralizing the periphery' and working on the 'cultivation of marginality' (Fishman, 1990: 115). Reflecting on his attraction for the periphery, he says:

> The periphery magnifies and clarifies. Above all, it refuses to take matters for granted. It refuses to confuse peripherality with unimportance, or weakness in numbers or in power, with weakness vis-à-vis equity, justice, law and morality (Fishman, 1990: 113).

Since the 1990s, some sociolinguists have focused on the relationship between inequality and power and language and society (Fairclough, 1989; Pennycook, 1989; Tollefson, 1991, 1995). Pierre Bourdieu (1991) has posited that linguistic practices are symbolic capital that is distributed unequally in the linguistic community. Fishman's work is indeed cognizant and aware of the economic and social rewards that some languages hold. In fact, one of his most recent co-edited books (with Martin Pütz) is titled, '*Along the Routes to Power': Explorations of Empowerment through Language*. But Fishman is even more concerned with the *non-material* values that are so important in the whole sociolinguistic enterprise. Fishman warns that by focusing so much on power, a 'reductionist school of thought' is 'missing the real elephant' (Fishman, 1991b: 19). In introducing the field of Reversing Language Shift, Fishman critiques this reductionism:

> The entire intellectually fashionable attempt to reduce all ethnocultural movements to problems of 'who attains power' and 'who gets money' is exactly that: reductionist. It reduces human values, emotions, loyalties and philosophies to little more than hard cash and brute force. These misguided attempts, regardless of the great names associated with them and the pseudo-intellectual fashionableness that they occasionally enjoy because of their purported 'realism,' inevitably impoverish rather than enrich our understanding of the complexity of human nature and of sociocultural reality. They cannot help us grasp the intensity of ideals and idealism of commitments and altruism, that are at the very heart of much social behavior in general and of RLS behavior in particular.
>
> And it is not the flea but the elephant that is being overlooked by such reductionist schools of thought. (Fishman, 1991b: 19)

Fishman cautions that it is not language alone that is standing in opposition to the power potential of people who speak *X* languages (threatened) in interaction with those who only speak *Y* (non-threatened):

> *X*ians are invariably bilingual ... and, therefore, in no way cut off from the economic rewards that are presumably inherent in *Y*ish. ... If only knowledge of *Y*ish stood between *X*ish workers and *Y*ish-controlled rewards, the economic well-being of the former would be much better off than it usually is. Furthermore, the economic reward dimension is not the only one that defines *X*ish individual and social identity ... Societally weaker languages always need more than mere economic rationales. It is not labour-market access but economic power which is disproportionately in *Y*ish hands and that is a problem that will rarely be overcome on linguistic grounds alone. As a result, even *X*ian bilingualism usually does not lead to any redistribution of economic power and, that being the case, the maintenance of *X*ish identity and cultural intactness becomes all the more important for community problem solving, health, education and cultural creativity. Vulgar materialism ... does not begin to do justice to the nuanced and completely interrelated human values, behaviours and identities that are essentially non-materialist or even anti-materialist in nature. ... Isn't it the mark of higher cultures to have other than material values, the latter being merely the most elementary expression of individual and group needs? (Fishman, 2001: 453)

Language and religion

Joshua A. Fishman's interest in language and religion is not new. 'The Maintenance and Perpetuation of Non-English Mother Tongues by American Ethnic and *Religious Groups*' (italics ours) was the subtitle of *Language Loyalty in the United States* (1966). Many of the chapters of that book pay attention to language use and religion. In the Preface, Fishman names language and religion as two of the important factors spurring his interest in language loyalty in the United States. He asks:

> How many of us, even among professional historians or students of religion in America, know that a Polish national Catholic Church grew up on our shores, rather than in Poland proper, because so many Polish-Americans were distressed by the policy of American Catholic leaders toward language and culture maintenance? Or that a similar state of affairs almost came into being among Franco-Americans in New England? How many of us know about the language problems that convulsed several German and Norwegian Lutheran denominations for well over half a century, or of the language issues that have

influenced Jewish ethnic, religious and intellectual life in America? (Fishman, 1966: 10)

In particular, the chapter in *Language Loyalty in the United States* by John E. Hofman on 'Mother Tongue Retentiveness in Ethnic Parishes,' included a study of language use in the sermons and instruction in Roman Catholic, Greek Catholic and Eastern Orthodox ethnic parishes.

But it was only recently that Joshua A. Fishman devoted an entire volume to the topic of language and religion. Co-edited with Tope Omoniyi, *Explorations in the Sociology of Language and Religion* (2006) includes contributions from Brazil, USA, Nigeria, Singapore, Australia, Israel, England, Germany, Georgia, Scotland and South Africa. And the Sociolinguistics Symposium 16 in Limerick, Ireland will include a panel on the Sociology of Language and Religion in honor of Joshua A. Fishman's 80th birthday during the summer of 2006.

Language Planning and Language Policy

The language problems of developing nations were an early scholarly interest of Joshua A. Fishman, one pursued with his lifelong friend and colleague, Charles A. Ferguson. In 1968, Fishman, Ferguson and Das Gupta edited *Language Problems of Developing Nations*, one of the first texts in the field that became Language Planning and Policy.

Language policy

Fishman differentiates between language planning and language policies, a distinction that other scholars tend to ignore, or minimize (see, for example, Spolsky, 2004). Language planning, Fishman maintains, is the processes that come *after* language-policy decisions have been reached (1972b). Fishman identifies *three types of language policies* for three corresponding types of societies:

(1) *Type A: Amodal.* There is consensus in these societies that there is neither an overarching sociocultural or political past and no indigenous Great Tradition (a Great Tradition being a 'widely accepted and visibly implemented belief and behavior system of indigenously validated greatness' (Fishman1972c: 194)). Usually a Language of Wider Communication (LWC) is selected as a national or official language.

(2) *Type B: Unimodal.* There are long-established sociocultural unities with rather well-established political boundaries. There is a single Great Tradition available. Usually a single indigenous or indigenized language is selected as the national language.

(3) *Type C: Multimodal.* There are conflicting or competing multiplicities of Great Traditions. The nation must stand for a supra-nationalistic goal,

since nationalism is associated with traditional regional (sub-national) identities. Usually regional official languages are selected, and a LWC is selected as co-official. Bilingualism is expected.

Language planning

Fishman (1973: 24–25) defines language planning as a 'set of deliberate activities systematically designed to organize and develop the language resources of the community in an ordered schedule of time.' But like all planning, language planning also requires a justification for the movement in the specified direction. Fishman's model of language planning is based on Haugen's original conceptualization of the field (Haugen, 1966) which included four categories: (1) norm selection, (2) codification, (3) elaboration and (4) implementation. Fishman likewise speaks of code selection, codification and elaboration. He posits, however, that language planning can foster unity and authenticity via differentiation of two sources: (1) undesirable external linguistic influences and (2) internal linguistic alternatives.

Fishman studies language planning from two vantage points: (1) status planning and (2) corpus planning. He cautions that status planning is usually embroiled in conflictual inter-ethnic struggles, since it is the area of material statuses and rewards (Fishman, 1997b). Corpus planning, on the other hand, consists of tending to the 'outer vestments (nomenclature, standardized spellings, grammars and stylistic conventions) that modern pursuits and modern institutions require' (Fishman, 1997b: 337). Although Fishman posits that language policy precedes language planning, his study of First Congresses (1993) made him aware of an embryonic stage of language planning in which no authoritative policy decisions have yet been reached.

Fishman (1994) has responded to the neo-Marxist and post-structuralist critiques toward language planning (Luke & Baldauf, 1990; Tollefson, 1991), while recognizing the difficulties with the field: (1) that it is conducted by elites, (2) that it reproduces sociocultural and econotechnical inequalities, (3) that it inhibits or counteracts multiculturalism and (4) that it espouses world-wide Westernization and modernization. According to Fishman:

> Authorities will continue to be motivated by self-interest. New structural inequalities will inevitably arise to replace the old ones. More powerful segments of society will be less inclined to want to change themselves than to change others. Westernisation and modernisation will continue to foster both problems and satisfactions for the bulk of humanity. Ultimately language planning will be utilised by both those who favor and those who oppose whatever the socio-political climate may be. (Fishman, 1994: 98)

Fishman's latest work is focused on the status agenda in corpus planning and the interpenetration of both – the pair of Siamese-twins, he calls them. He explains:

> It is a gossamer web that they weave. It cannot be woven out of praises alone, for were there nothing but praises to be uttered for the beloved language as it is, then corpus planning itself would be unnecessary if not impossible. On the other hand, it cannot be fostered by emphasizing the current debits of the beloved language, for were that to be done it would play into the hands of its detractors and opponents. (Fishman, 1996a: 114)

Although Fishman understands that people in general do not like the prospects of social intervention in languages and their uses, he argues that it is inevitable if all languages are to be seated 'at the table':

> If one seeks a place at the table of the respected and the self-respecting, if one seeks a share in the good things of the world, not least among them being respect, comfort and security, then one's beloved language too must be elevated. The language symbolizes the people, it represents them, it speaks volumes for them, and if they are to be heard and heard-out, then it must speak from a position of honor and security as well. However, the circular interconnectedness between language and people is also fully matched by a circular interconnectedness between status planning and corpus planning. One cannot make a silk purse out of a sow's ear and an effective elevation in status can rarely be attained or maintained without considerable change in the nature of the language itself. And so it inevitably comes about that the beloved language, whose loveliness was initially given in nature, and, indeed, is seen as part of its own ineffable nature, comes to require intervention so that it can more rapidly become visibly and audibly suitable for the new and higher functions that are pursued on its behalf. (Fishman, 1996a: 92)

Developing this concept further, Fishman (2000) has suggested that all language planning, whether corpus planning or status planning, is related to a super factor of independence/interdependence. Fishman proposes four different categories that are organized around the different poles of independence and interdependence:

(1) *Ausbau/Einbau. Ausbau planning*[10] is a building away process motivated by a desire to distance a language from its structurally similar big brother. This is the case of Urdu/Hindi, of Macedonian/Bulgarian, or of Landsmäl/Ryksmäl. Linguistic distancing is an indicator of a wish for independence and distancing – social, cultural and political.

Einbau planning, on the other hand, refers to drawing two languages closer together, emphasizing similarities and interdependence. This is the case of the current Romanian treatment of Moldavian, or of former Soviet treatment of Ukrainian and Belarusian

(2) *Uniqueness/Internationalization.* Planning for *Uniqueness and Authenticity* requires ensuring that language is independent of others. This is why, for example, St Stephen of Perm developed a writing system for Komi based on a similarity to the traditional Komi decorative designs. Planning for *internationalization,* on the other hand, wishes for interdependence with the modern scientific and technological ways of naming. This was the case, for example, of Atatürk who Westernized Turkish based on French influences that he thought would make Turkish capable of modern use.

(3) *Purification/Regionalization.* Planning for *Purification* is related to Ausbau and Uniqueness, but it differs from Ausbau in that the fears are not directed against the 'Big Brother' alone. And it differs from Uniqueness in that a single source of contamination is rejected. Purification has been a factor in planning for the independence of the revival of Hebrew, for example, from the contamination of Yiddish. Planning for *Regionalization,* on the other hand, has to do with *Sprachbund,* an entire cluster of sister languages that are acceptable sources for borrowings and influences. For example, Turkic languages are the resources for Central Asian languages; Malay and Indonesian are resources for each other; and Nordic languages are resources for one another, with the exclusion of Danish.

(4) *Classicization/Vernacularization.* There are many examples of planning for *classicization:* Hindi (from Sanskrit), Tamil (from Old Tamil), Arabic (from Quranic Arabic). Planning for *vernacular* use, however, favors popular usage.

In the end, Fishman (2000: 114) tells us, 'all corpus planning that is oriented toward modernization and interaction with [the] community of modern peoples and nations must also settle for [an] inevitable degree of interdependence as well.' Language planning, he explains,

> when engaged in under auspices of modernization and with modernization as the goal, generally results in making languages even more capable of translating American life, even when suffusing the translations with the aura and the pretense of greater or lesser degrees of indigenization.' (Fishman, 2000: 50)

Bilingual Education and Minority-Language Group Education

Scholarly interest

Bilingual education was Joshua A. Fishman's earliest area of study ('Bilingualism in a Yiddish School: Some Correlates and Non-correlates,' 1949). Almost 60 years ago, this study already contained the motivations for the development of the sociology of language. García (1991) has pointed out that the 'Bilinguality Relationship Scale' used in the study contains questions that foreshadow Fishman's now famous 'Who Speaks What Language to Whom and When.' And the independent variables of the study – play preferences, school adjustment, family adjustment, number of friends, self-identity with nationality and attitude toward Yiddish – are the same variables that Fishman later explores in studies of language, ethnicity and schooling. Fishman's familiarity with the Yiddish Workmen's Circle Schools in Philadelphia prepared him for his work on bilingual education.

Fishman's first major research project and publication, *Language Loyalty in the United States* (1966), dedicates a chapter to 'the ethnic group school and mother tongue maintenance in the United States,' a topic that he has pursued throughout his lifetime. Once the Bilingual Education Act was passed in 1968, many publications on bilingual education followed. Fishman devoted three more books to the topic of bilingual education: *Bilingual Education: An International Sociological Perspective* (1976); *Bilingual Education: Current Perspectives. Social Science* (1977); and *Bilingual Education for Hispanic Students in the United States* (1982). And in 1979 he released his final report for the National Institute of Education on 'The Ethnic Mother Tongue School in America.' Between 1970 and 1985, Joshua A. Fishman published 15 articles on the topic; these were reprinted again and again.[11]

Fishman devotes a great deal of effort to documenting the existence of Ethnic Mother Tongue Schools (EMT schools) because:

> These schools must be included in our educational, social and intellectual bookkeeping, more for the sake of our national well-being than for their sake, since even the United States cannot afford to overlook some 6000 schools attended by as many as 600,000 children. (Fishman, 1980: 236)

Furthermore, he explains: 'Rather than reflections of foreignness, ethnic community mother tongue schools are actually reflections of dealing with both indigenousness and mainstream exposure' (Fishman, 1980: 243).

It is important to point out that Fishman was never 'led astray' by the frenzy that surrounded The Bilingual Education Act, that is, Title VII of the Elementary and Secondary Education Act. His work, both that of *Language Loyalty in the United States,* and also the research that later became *Bilingualism in the Barrio,* was frequently quoted in the deliberations that led to the passage of the Bilingual Education Act in 1968. And some of his terminology, especially the word 'transitional' to substitute for 'compensatory,' has been adopted by governmental, scholarly and popular circles. His support for the education of language minorities, especially Spanish-speaking minorities, has been unquestionable. The 1982 volume edited with Gary Keller and dedicated to Hispanic students is precisely a reflection of this support. In addition, his concern about public bilingual education for poor Latino and Native American students has been approached through the prism of the importance of ethnic-mother-tongue schools, organized and supported by the ethnolinguistic group itself.

Education

Joshua A. Fishman has defined education broadly. As Dean at Yeshiva University, he proposed the merging of Education, Liberal Arts and Behavioral and Social Sciences saying that '[Education] is first and foremost an intellectual endeavor striving to increase knowledge about man and the process whereby he learns, grows, changes and influences others' (Congressional Record A, 3594, July 11, 1966).

Fishman has also claimed that schools cannot 'go at it alone.' In an article entitled 'Minority Mother Tongues in Education' he says:

> [E]ducation is a socializing institution and must never be examined without concentrating on the social processes that it serves and the social pressures to which it responds. (as cited in Fishman, 1989: 467)

Fishman (1989: 467) goes on to say that '[S]chools alone cannot guarantee the continuity of cultures, if for no other reason than that schools are generally no more than intervening (serving) rather than independent (causal) variables with respect to such continuity.'

That schools are just intervening variables is an important idea in Fishman's early defense of public bilingual education. He cautions that:

> [B]ecause there are so many other pervasive reasons why such children [poor minority children] achieve poorly, the goals of majority-oriented and -dominated schools (and societies), removing this extra burden above – and leaving all else as it was – does not usually do the trick, particularly when the teachers, curricula and materials for bilingual education are as nonoptimal as they currently usually are. (Fishman, 1976: 28)

For bilingual education to succeed, general support is needed. Fishman (1976: 111) contends that: 'not only is community consensus needed if bilingual education is to succeed, but ... help of the unmarked language community is needed every bit as much as, if not more than, that of the marked language community.' His interest in bilingual education was concerned with increasing knowledge about speech communities – both language minority and language majority ones – as they interacted with each other and were transformed.

Early typologies and warnings

In 1970, Joshua A. Fishman and John Lovas published the now well-known 'Bilingual Education in Sociolinguistic Perspective'.[12] Two years after the implementation of the United States' Bilingual Education Act, Fishman and Lovas identified the features still lacking: (1) lack of funds, (2) lack of personnel, (3) lack of evaluated programs. This contribution provided insights into societal bilingualism that educators, psychologists and linguists involved with bilingual education programs had been missing.

Fishman pointed to three different language situations in communities that planners of bilingual education should be aware of:

(1) a community in the process of language shift;
(2) a community determined to maintain its own language in many or all social domains;
(3) a community with one or more nonstandard varieties in one or more languages and their differential use from one societal domain to another and from one speech network to another.

And he warned that bilingual education (BE) programs must ascertain the sociolinguistic situation of the community before one program or the other is chosen.

Fishman (1972d: 89) proposes a typology of bilingual education based on different kinds of communities and school objectives:

(1) *Type I. Transitional BE*, where the mother tongue is used in early grades until the dominant language is developed. This program corresponds to an objective of language shift.
(2) *Type II. Monoliterate BE*, where both languages are used for aural-oral skills, but literacy skills in the mother tongue are not pursued.
(3) *Type III. Biliterate BE–Partial Bilingualism*, where fluency and literacy in both languages are pursued, but literacy in the mother tongue is restricted to certain subject matter, usually that which relates to the ethnic group. Ethnic-mother-tongue day schools are generally of this type.
(4) *Type IV. Biliterate BE–Full Bilingualism*, where both languages are used as media of instruction for all subjects, and students develop all skills in both languages in all domains.

Fishman warns that although full biliterate-bilingualism programs seem to be desirable, there are dangers in pursuing them, saying:

A fully-balanced bilingual speech community seems to be a theoretical impossibility because balanced competence implies languages that are functionally equivalent and no society can be motivated to maintain two languages if they are really functionally redundant. Thus, this type of program does not seem to have a clearly articulated goal with respect to societal reality. (Fishman, 1976: 89)

Continuing to develop the link between types of education and types of speech communities, Fishman published 'Bilingual and Bidialectal Education' (1972) where he attempted to apply to bilingual education the model he had developed for language planning in 'National Languages and Languages of Wider Communication in the Developing Nations' (1969). Fishman (1972a: 332–337) proposes three different types of *language education policies*, advancing by a quarter-century the field that was later known by that name:

(1) *Type A policies:* None of the mother tongue varieties are considered school-worthy because they're not tied to any great tradition and are not believed to have integrative potential. The educational authorities select for educational use a language which is not a mother tongue, and often is the standard variety of the language of wider communication (LWC). Examples of these policies are countries in West Africa such as Gambia and Sierra Leone.

(2) *Type B policies:* There is an internally integrative great tradition, but additional traditions must also be recognized. Usually the standard is reserved for written language and education is bidialectal. Teachers and students are of the same speech community. Examples of these policies are most parts of Switzerland and Germany.

(3) *Type C policies:* Several competing great traditions exist usually regionally. Each locality must teach a link language for communication with other localities. Students will be educated in their own mother tongue, and also in another tongue. Examples: Belgium, Switzerland or India.

Fishman not only proposes alternatives, but discusses their consequences and points out to infelicities in each of the types of policies. In Type A policies where the LWC is chosen for education, Fishman indicates that teachers must nevertheless begin by using the mother tongue of the pupils. Another consideration for this type of language education policy is whether to adopt the curriculum and standards set where the LWC is spoken or whether to develop these indigenously. An even greater problem occurs when polities have a high rate of illiteracy. It is well known that this type of policy, where the LWC used in education is not the mother tongue, presents great difficulties for adult literacy.

But the biggest concern with this type of language education policy is precisely that it is artificial and may not result in educational success.

Fishman points, however, to the reality that many indigenous groups insist on this type of education, regardless of limitations. That is, it is not simple imposition of the most powerful that results in such language education policies. Representing the powerful standard or dialect with a capital D (before Gee (1996) had suggested the D for his use of Discourse), Fishman writes:

> The insistence on D and D only (for all students for all subjects) is potentially nonfunctional even though it may be a widely shared view rather than one imposed from without in many ways. It artificializes education to the extent that it identifies it with a variety that is not functional in the life of the community. (Fishman, 1972: 334)

Type B policies, in which the D is used for some subjects and a more indigenous variety is used for other subjects, also presents additional questions. For example, polities would have to decide what should be taught, in which language, and for how long.

International perspectives and advantages

In 1976, Fishman published *Bilingual Education: An International Sociological Perspective*, a book that he had been working on since 1972 when he was Visiting Professor of Sociology of Language at the Hebrew University in Jerusalem. The book includes the results of an empirical study that focuses on three specific criteria across 100 of the 1000 secondary bilingual education programs:

(1) What are the averaged grades awarded across all subjects and all years of study?
(2) How do bilingual secondary schools compare to monolingual secondary schools in their immediate areas serving comparable populations insofar as averaged grades are concerned?
(3) How pleased are students with respect to their bilingual secondary schooling in terms of its impact on their academic, personal and social development? (Fishman, 1976: 94–95)

The resulting published work was a significant contribution to the field of bilingual education. It communicated Fishman's (1976: ix) support for the field ('bilingual education is "good for everybody"'). Part 1 of the book proposes and then defends the four principles in which Fishman bases his support of bilingual education:

(1) bilingual education is good for the majority group;
(2) bilingual education is good for the minority group;
(3) bilingual education is good for education;
(4) bilingual education is good for language teachers.

The arguments for bilingual education that Fishman presents in this book are eerily relevant today. For example, Fishman supports bilingual education because it responds to multiple-group membership, a concept prevalent in post-modern scholarship. He writes: 'Only bilingual and bicultural education provides for multiple memberships and for multiple loyalties in an integrative fashion... ' (1976: 9). He also supports the social equality aspects of bilingual education, saying:

> If bilingual education does nothing else, it at least equalizes the children of marked- and unmarked-language backgrounds by providing each of them some instruction via their own mother tongue as well as some via the 'other' group's mother tongue. (Fishman, 1976: 119)

Fishman points out that yet another advantage of bilingual education is the economic possibilities that it affords bilinguals. He notes that others might see this as selfish, and clarifies:

> Economic self-interest is presumably acceptable if pursued by the oil lobby, by the teachers' unions, and by our most reputable universities, but is considered meanly divisive if pursued by Hispanics, Native Americans, or other ethnics. (Fishman, 1989: 408)

Fishman's intention in writing a book on international bilingual education is clearly to provide a cross-cultural dimension that would guide and lead bilingual educators everywhere, allowing them to consider themselves a 'single community of interest, each learning from the other and correcting each other's experimental and attitudinal limitations' (Fishman, 1976: viii). He prophesied that bilingual education would continue to be important and become even more important as English spreads, saying:

> We seem to be living in a period of world history in which a larger number of local languages are being given educational recognition at the very same time that a relatively few world languages (primarily English) are also gaining wider currency. Both of these trends, disparate though they may appear to be on the surface, are contributing to the overall growth of bilingual education. (Fishman, 1977: 31)

A significant contribution of this book is the chapter that argues that bilingual education is good for language teachers, a foreshadowing of what Krashen (1996, for example) advanced decades later as the advantage of bilingual education over TESOL. Fishman makes two important theoretical contributions in this regard: (1) that the increased contextualization provided by bilingual education is important for language learning, and (2) that second language teaching must target specific communicative functions.

Fishman (1976: 36) values bilingual education for 'its maximization of language learning for the communication of messages that are highly significant for senders and receivers alike.' This position is related to

Krashen's (1979) comprehensible input hypothesis and his idea of *i+1* for second language learning – representing input (*i*) plus a bit more (+1) than the student already knows). But Fishman's ideas are also related to Vygotzky's concept of scaffolding, and to what second language educators today have translated as more contextualization, relevancy and immediacy (Gibbons, 2002; Walqui, 2002).

Fishman (1976: 38–39) also points out that second language learners need languages for restricted ranges of functions, and that teachers 'ought to specify the contexts in which the student plans to use the target language.' Furthermore:

> No one knows how to speak a language appropriately in all contexts in which it is used, because no one has access to all the societal roles in which the language is used and which constrain language usage. (Fishman, 1976: 39)

In the 21st century, as we saw above, the European Union has advanced the concept of plurilingualism for all its citizens. The CLIL/EMILE pedagogy that is being developed (Baetens Beardsmore, 1999) clearly specifies language functions and targets, with second languages being used to teach only certain subjects and for certain functions.

Critic of the Bilingual Education Act

Although a supporter of bilingual education, Fishman makes his antipathy towards the Bilingual Education Act clear, and he denounces its monolingual goals:

> The Act was primarily an act for the Anglification of non-English speakers and not an act for Bilingualism. 'Bilingualism' has become a newspeak euphemism for non-English mother tongue. 'Bilinguals' are thus non-English mother tongue speakers; bilingual teachers are those who teach them/ bilingual programs are those that Anglify them.... The act is basically not an act for bilingualism, but rather, an act *against* bilingualism. [emphasis ours] (Fishman, 1989: 405)

The bilingual education programs supported by Title VII (presently Title III of No Child Left Behind) rarely have interest either in the minority language or in the minority child. Instead in many schools the only interest is the rapid acquisition of English.

About the US government's lack of interest in developing and teaching the minority languages, Fishman (1989: 469) proposes, 'There is no or little constructive interest among the central authorities in how well they are taught in their own language, since these learnings are not considered by national authorities to be really in the national interest.' And about the lack of interest in the minority child, he explains:

[I]f there are still doubts as to the psycho-educational advantage of initial instruction via the minority child's mother tongue, it is only because of the overwhelming concern for that acquisition of the societally dominant language rather than for his or her more pervasive intellectual, emotional and self-definitional development or for the future of his or her minority community. (Fishman, 1989: 468)

Fishman is interested in the protection and development of the minority language precisely because of its advantages for the minority child and the minority community. He reveals that many of the public bilingual education programs do not have the child's best interest at heart.

Transitional vs. enrichment bilingual education

From the very beginning, Joshua A. Fishman stood against the trans-ethnifying aspects of transitional bilingual education. Much of the volume *Bilingual Education: International Perspectives* is devoted to speaking against transitional/compensatory models, as well as in favor of enrichment bilingual education. In Fishman's ironic style, he conceptualizes *transitional bilingual education* as a disease and explains how it is that using the mother tongue can lead to language shift:

If a non-English mother tongue is conceptualized as a disease of the poor, then in true vaccine style this disease is to be attacked by the disease bacillus itself. A little bit of deadened mother tongue, introduced in slow stages in the classroom environment, will ultimately enable the patient to throw off the mother tongue entirely and to embrace all-American vim, vigor and stability. (Fishman, 1976: 34)

Fishman cautions that transitional bilingual education is simply bad for the minority language:

As for the 'common garden variety' of American transitional bilingual education, there is a growing suspicion that for the marked group child, it is doing more harm to native language mastery and to native community participation than whatever good it may be doing in terms of academic achievement, English mastery or participation in un-marked role. (Fishman, 1972a: 46)

He refuses to give scholarly attention to transitional bilingual education because it is only a small part of the education of a child. Years later, he explains that mother tongue education,

should not be trivialized by evaluating merely the degree to which initial instruction via the disadvantaged language maximizes acquisition and mastery of the advantaged one. To do so is not only tantamount to adding insult to injury; it is also to lose sight of the true relationship between language, society and culture. (Fishman, 1989: 479)

Fishman (1972a: 48) also warns that '[t]ransitional-compensatory bilingual education is scheduled to "self-destruct" in the not too distant future.' He explains this self-destruction in the following way:

> If it does not succeed in improving the English mastery of those assigned to it, it would necessarily be called to task, and discontinued since such improvement is its major avowed purpose. However, should it succeed in this restricted task, then it would be discontinued purportedly as being no longer necessary. The result may well be a species of the *'double bind'* so well known in the etiology of schizophrenia, with compensatory bilingual education characterized by not having enough leverage or opportunity with respect to the dominant (Anglo) society in order to successfully negotiate progress toward economic-social-political status roles for its clientele, on the one hand, and then, in addition, not having enough of an economic-social-political base within its own ethnic environments to foster real respect, mastery and attachment to the ethnic mother tongues either. [emphasis ours] (Fishman, 1977: 23)

Fishman refers to this 'double bind' ('damned if you do; damned if you don't') of the Bilingual Education Act throughout all his writings on the subject (see, for example, Fishman, 1978). And in the 21st century, the success of the anti-bilingual education referenda in California, Arizona and Massachusetts seem to be a reflection of Fishman's early vision regarding the difficulties that public bilingual education was to face in the future.

At the same time that Fishman (1976: viii) attacks transitional bilingual education, he advances his passion for *'enrichment for one and all*, rather than merely as compensation for down-and-out minorities or as a group-maintenance opportunity for reawakening ones' [emphasis ours]. In fact, he states (1976: 9): 'It is the poor little rich kids who most desperately need bilingual and bicultural education.' Advancing again by decades the coming of 'English Plus,' Fishman says: 'In the long run it means just as much mastery of *English plus* more vibrant cultural pluralism, both for the minorities and for the majority as well' (Fishman, 1976: 121).

Two-way dual language bilingual education

Joshua A. Fishman establishes that it is important for ethnolinguistic minorities to first become heard and socially equal before they can stress interdependence with majorities. Speaking of the case of the United States, Fishman proposes:

> America's non-English speaking minorities may very well have to

place greater stress upon good bilingual education and other, even more effective forms of social protest and social equalization before they can afford the equanimity of stressing good intergroup relations as a goal to aim at from a position of strength. (Fishman, 1977: 42)

Nevertheless, Fishman has a vision that these goals of social equalization may be possible in a better future. He says:

There is a vision of American magnanimity involved, but more than that, a vision of American possibilities, opportunities, appreciations, sensitivities, that we all should savour. 'Brotherhood' does not mean uniformity. A shared diversity can be the true meaning of the American promise: 'to crown thy good with brotherhood from sea to shining sea.' (Fishman, 1989: 415)

But he again warns that school cannot go at it alone to impart this vision.

Fishman advances the vision of joint schooling for students with different linguistic profiles – what we today call two-way dual language education – but he warns that this goal cannot be restricted to the schools alone:

If both types of children can ultimately wind up in the same classroom, one motivated by transitional and maintenance considerations and the other by enrichment considerations, an optimal *modus vivendi* will have been attained.... However, if enrichment language policy is limited or restricted to the schools alone, it will fail as surely as either transitional or maintenance policy when similarly restricted. What is needed is an enrichment policy that views the multilingualization of American urban life as a contribution to the very quality of life itself. (Fishman, 1989: 414)

Indeed, Fishman foresees the problems that two-way dual language bilingual programs are encountering in the United States today, as their enrichment philosophy does not correspond to the view of bilingualism that most US citizens hold (García, 2006).

With regard to the participation of English-speaking students in such programs, Fishman (1989: 405) warns that the '[r]ealities of urban demography being what they are, such magnanimity does not go much beyond the co-presence of Blacks and Hispanics.' Indeed today it is mostly Latinos with different linguistic profiles who make up the student-body of two-way dual language programs. And it is students of color, African-Americans and others of African descent, but also Indians, Pakistanis and many others, who make up the English-speaking part of most two-way dual language programs.

Conclusion

Summing up the scholarly achievements of a seminal thinker like Joshua A. Fishman is a daunting task. We who have followed in his footsteps often find that it is like following a giant – we have to make a huge effort to understand what he has done, even as we recommend to our students that they read carefully, and also read between the lines. And as we compare our own meager work to his, we often find ourselves thinking that no matter what the topic is, Fishman has already taken care of it. He has already written about it, presaging later developments, laying out the groundwork. We find ourselves stumbling to make our own contributions fit, and make sense. It is this 'Olympian overview' that Fishman provides that makes everything else seem inconsequential – we can only provide examples from other contexts that corroborate what he has written, or at best add a detail here and there that extends his ideas into an area that was previously ignored or forgotten.

But there is another aspect of his work that makes it different from work in other disciplines or fields, and that is his tremendous humanity, his caring about languages and peoples, and the careful, avuncular mentoring he has extended to all who work in this paradigm. The atmosphere is one that encourages and fosters exploration and innovation, rather than the kind of adversarial infighting one finds in other fields and disciplines. We are grateful that we work in an area that is exemplified by this magnanimous spirit, and can encourage students to continue to read his work and learn from it.

Notes

1. In 1991, on the occasion of Joshua A. Fishman's 65th birthday, four volumes were published in his honor. John Benjamins published three *Focusschrift in Honor of Joshua A. Fishman* on three different sociolinguistic topics: *Bilingual Education* (Ofelia García, ed.), *Language and Ethnicity* (J.R. Dow, ed.) and *Language Planning* (David F. Marshall, ed.). In addition, Mouton de Gruyter published *The Influence of Language on Culture and Thought: Essays in Honor of Joshua A. Fishman's Sixty-Fifth Birthday* (Robert L. Cooper and Bernard Spolsky, eds).
2. The bibliographic inventory compiled by Gella Schweid Fishman and included in Cooper and Spolsky (1991) contained a total of 718 items. Today, the bibliographic inventory contains a listing of more than 1200 entries.
3. This article, co-authored with Esther Lowy, Michael Gertner, Itzek Gottesman and William Milán originally appeared in 1983 in the *Journal of Multilingual and Multicultural Development*, 4: 237–54. It was reprinted in Fishman 1989, pages 530–549.
4. Fishman's work is widely cited in the literature. A search of Google Scholar, in summer 2005, yielded 181 references. Appendix 3 lists the titles and numbers of those references attested by Google Scholar where there were two or more citations.
5. Because this volume includes (in Part 3) an exhaustive bibliography of Joshua A.

Fishman's work, in the references section at the end of this chapter we include only the works from which we quote directly.

6. Joshua A. Fishman received his PhD in Social Psychology from Columbia University in 1953.

7. García (1991) includes a more extensive biography of Joshua A. Fishman that readers might find helpful. Readers are also referred to Fishman, 1990.

8 For more on the role of this seminar, see Fishman (1997a) in Paulston and Tucker (eds).

9 The researchers on *Auslandsdeutsche* were primarily German scholars concerned with what had happened to the German language during emigration, i.e. *im Ausland*. The most important pioneer in this field was Heinz Kloss (Kloss, 1940).

10 It should be noted that this usage differs from Kloss (1929), who first proposed it, as well as later versions of it (e.g. Kloss, 1967). The term *Einbau*, however, is Fishman's own.

11 Fishman's articles on bilingual education include: Bilingual education in sociolinguistic perspective (1970); Bilingual and bidialectal education: An attempt at a joint model for policy description (1972); Bilingual education in sociological perspective (1972); Bilingual education: What and why? (1973, reprinted 1976, 1978, 1979); The sociology of bilingual education (1974, reprinted 1976, 1977, 1989); Bilingual education and the future of language teaching and language learning (1975; reprinted 1976); Bilingual education: Hope for Europe's migrants (1976); The international sociology of bilingual secondary education (1976); Bilingual education: A perspective (1977); Standard vs. dialect in bilingual education (1977, reprinted 1979); The Bilingual Education Act: High time for a change (1977); Bilingual education: Ethnic perspectives (1977); A model for bilingual and bidialectal education (1977); Bilingual education and the future of language teaching and language learning (1978); Philosophies of bilingual education in societal perspective (1979, reprinted 1989); The significance of the ethnic community mother tongue school (1979, reprinted 1985); Ethnic community mother tongue schools in the USA (1980, reprinted 1981, 1989); Minority language maintenance and the ethnic mother tongue school (1980); Bilingual education, language planning and English (1980); Bilingual education in the United States under ethnic community auspices (1980); Bilingual education (1982); Mother tongues as media of instruction in the United States (1982); The Americanness of the ethnic community school (1983); The use of minority mother tongues in the education of children (1983, reprinted 1989); Non-English language ethnic community schools in the USA (1985, reprinted 1989).

12 This article was reprinted in 1972 in Bernard Spolsky´s *The Language Education of Minority Children*.

Appendix 1: Joshua A. Fishman's Contributions to the *Sociology of Language* (CSL) Book Series

The following is a list of works edited by Joshua A. Fishman for the *Sociology of Language* (CSL) series. Titles are listed under year of publication and in alphabetical order by author/editor. This list was compiled with the assistance of Rebecca Walters, Mouton de Gruyter and Zeena Zakharia, Teachers College, Columbia University.

1972 Fishman, J.A. (ed.) *Advances in the Sociology of Language: Selected Studies and Applications* (Vol. 2).

Lewis, E.G. *Multilingualism in the Soviet Union: Aspects of Language Policy and its Implementation.*

1973 Fellman, J. *The Revival of Classical Tongue: EliezerBen Yehuda and the Modern Hebrew Language.*

1975 Dillard, J.L. (ed.) *Perspectives on Black English.*

1976 Alisjahbana, S.T. *Language Planning for Modernization: The Case of Indonesian and Malaysian.*

Byron, J. *Selection among Alternates in Language Standardization: The Case of Albanian.*

Dillard, J.L. *Black Names.*

1977 de Francis, J. *Colonialism and Language Policy in Viet Nam.*

Grayshon, M.C. *Towards a Social Grammar of Language.*

Greenbaum, S. *Acceptability in Language.*

Luelsdorff, P.A. (ed.) *Soviet Contributions to the Sociology of Language.*

Rubin, J., Jernudd, B.H., DasGupta, J., Fishman, J.A. and Ferguson, C.A. (eds) *Language Planning Processes.*

Uribe-Villegas, O. *Issues in Sociolinguistics.*

1978 Gordon, D.C. *The French Language and National Identity (1930–1975).*

Jessel, L. *The Ethnic Process: An Evolutionary Concept of Languages and Peoples.*

1979 Billigmeier, R.H. *A Crisis in Swiss Pluralism. The Romansh and Their Relations with the German- and Italian-Swiss in the Perspective of a Millennium.*

Saulson, S.B. *Institutionalized Planning: Documents and Analysis of Revival of Hebrew.*

Wurm, S.A. (ed.) *New Guinea and Neighboring Areas: A Sociolinguistic Laboratory.*

1980 Dillard, J.L. (ed.) *Perspectives on American English.*

Khleif, B.B. *Language, Ethnicity, and Education in Wales.*

1981 Fishman, J.A. (ed.) *Never Say Die! A Thousand Years of Yiddish in Jewish Life and Letters.*

Key, M.R. *The Relationship of Verbal and Nonverbal Communication.* Second printing.

1982 Cobarrubias, J. and Fishman, J.A. (eds) *Progress in Language Planning. International Perspectives.*

Forster, P.G. *The Esperanto Movement.*

1983 Veltman, C. *Language Shift in the United States.*

1985 Dillard, J.L. *Toward a Social History of American English.*

Fishman, J.A., Gertner, M.H., Lowy, E.G. and Milán, W.G. *The Rise and Fall of the Ethnic Revival: Perspectives on Language and Ethnicity.*
Kreindler, I.T. (ed.) *Sociolinguistic Perspectives on Soviet National Languages: Their Past, Present and Future.*
Mehrotra, R.R. *Sociolinguistics in Hindi Contexts.*
Parkinson, D.B. *Constructing the Social Context of Communication: Terms of Address in Egyptian Arabic.*
Wolfson, N. and Manes, J. *Language of Inequality.*

1986 Evans, A.D. and Falk, W.W. *Learning to be Deaf.*
Fishman, J.A. (ed.) *The Fergusonian Impact. In Honor of Charles A. Ferguson on the Occasion of his 65th Birthday (Vol. 1: From Phonology to Society; Vol. 2: Sociolinguistics and the Sociology of Language).*
Haarmann, H. *Language in Ethnicity: A View of Basic Ecological Relations.*
Preisler, B. *Linguistic Sex Roles in Conversation: Social Variation in the Expression of Tentativeness in English.*

1987 Haugen, E. *Blessings of Babel: Bilingualism and Language Planning. Problems and Pleasures.*

1988 Braun, F. *Terms of Address: Problems of Patterns and Usage in Various Languages and Cultures.*
Flaitz, J. *The Ideology of English: French Perceptions of English as a World Language.*
Harman, L.D. *The Modern Stranger. On Language and Membership.*
Heller, M. (ed.) *Codeswitching: Anthropological and Sociolinguistic Perspectives.*

1989 Coleman, H. (ed.) *Working with Language: A Multidisciplinary Consideration of Language Use in Work Contexts.*
García, O. and Otheguy, R. (eds) *English Across Cultures. Cultures Across English. A Reader in Cross-Cultural Communication.*
Haarmann, H. *Symbolic Values of Foreign Language Use. From the Japanese Case to a General Sociolinguistic Perspective.*
Jernudd, B.H. and Shapiro, M.J. (eds) *The Politics of Language Purism.*
Key, M.R. and Hoenigswald, H.M. (eds) *General and Amerindian Ethno-linguistics. In Remembrance of Stanley Newman.*

1990 Adams, K.L. and Brink, D.T. *Perspectives on Official English. The Campaign for English as the Official Language of the USA.*
Janicki, K. *Toward Non-Essentialist Sociolinguistics.*

1991 Clyne, M. (ed.) *Pluricentric Languages. Differing Norms in Different Nations.*
Coulmas, F. (ed.) *A Language Policy for the European Community. Prospects and Quandaries.*
Fierman, W. *Language Planning and National Development: The Uzbek Experience.*
Haarmann, H. *Basic Aspects of Language in Human Relations. Toward a General Theoretical Framework.*
McGroarty, M.E. and Faltis, C.J. (eds) *Languages in School and Society: Policy and Pedagogy.*
Watts, R.J. *Power in Family Discourse.*

1992 Brenzinger, M. (ed.) (1992) *Language Death: Factual and Theoretical Explorations with Special Reference to East Africa.*

1993 Fishman, J.A. (ed.) *The Earliest Stage of Language Planning. 'The First Congress'* *Phenomenon.*

1995 Harlig, J. and Pléh, C. (ed.) *When East Met West: Sociolinguistics in the Former* *Socialist Bloc.*
Pütz, M. (ed.) *Discrimination Through Language in Africa? Perspectives on the* *Namibian Experience.*

1996 Fishman, J.A., Conrad, A.W. and Rubal-Lopez, A. (eds) *Post-Imperial English.* *Status Change in Former British and American Colonies, 1940–1990.*
Hellinger, M. and Ammon, U. *Contrastive Sociolinguistics.*
Dalls, K.K. *Language Loss and the Crisis of Cognition. Between Socio- and* *Psycholinguistics.*
Robinson, C.D. *Language Use in Rural Development: An African Perspective.*

1997 Clyne, M. (ed.) *Undoing and Redoing Corpus Planning.*
Fishman, J.A. *In Praise of the Beloved Language: A Comparative View of Positive* *Ethnolinguistic Consciousness.*
García, O. and Fishman, J.A. (eds) *The Multilingual Apple: Languages in New* *York City.*
Goldstein, T. *Two Languages at Work: Bilingual Life on the Production Floor.*
Hornberger, N.H. *Indigenous Literacies in the Americas: Language Planning from* *the Bottom up.*

1998 PuruShotam, N.S. *Negotiating Language, Constructing Race: Disciplining Differ-* *ence in Singapore.*
Smith, M.G. *Language and Power in the Creation of the USSR, 1917–1953.*

1999 Clyne, M. and Kipp, S. *Pluricentric Languages in an Immigrant Context: Spanish,* *Arabic and Chinese.*
Kunihiro, T., Inoue, F. and Long, D. (eds) *Sociolinguistics in Japanese Contexts/* *Takesi Sibata.*

2000 Owens, J. *Arabic as a Minority Language.*

2001 Ammon, U. (ed.) *The Dominance of English as a Language of Science. Effects on* *Other Languages and Language Communities.*
Wolf, H.G. *English in Cameroon.*

2002 García, O. and Fishman, J.A. (eds) *The Multilingual Apple: Languages in New* *York City* (2nd edn).
Jones, M.C. and Esch, E. (eds) *Language Change: The Interplay of Internal,* *External and Extra-Linguistic Factors.*
Wei, L., Dewaele, J.M. and Housen, A. (eds) *Opportunities and Challenges of* *Bilingualism.*

2003 Tuten, D.N. *Koineization in Medieval Spanish.*
Zhou, M. *Multilingualism in China: The Politics of Writing Reforms for Minority* *Languages 1949–2002.*

2004 Leitner, G. *Australia's Many Voices: Australian English: The National Language* (Vol. 1).
Leitner, G. *Australia's Many Voices. Ethnic Englishes, Indigenous and Migrant* *Languages. Policy and Education* (Vol. 2).

2005 Hidalgo, M. (ed.) *Mexican Indigenous Languages at the Dawn of the Twenty-First* *Century.*

Pütz, M., Fishman, J.A. and Neff-van Aertselaer, J. (eds) *'Along the Routes to Power': Explorations of Empowerment Through Language.*

Appendix 2: Joshua A. Fishman's Contributions to the *International Journal of the Sociology of Language* (*IJSL*)

The following is a list of works published in the *International Journal of the Sociology of Language (IJSL)* series, for which Joshua A. Fishman served as General Editor. Titles are listed under year of publication and by issue number. This list was compiled with the assistance of Rebecca Walters, Mouton de Gruyter and Zeena Zakharia, Teachers College, Columbia University.

1974 1   Fishman, J.A. (ed.) *The Sociology of Language in Israel.*
      2   Spolsky, B. and Bills, G.D. (eds) *The American Southwest.*
      3   Cooper, R.L. (ed.) *Language Attitudes I.*

1975 4   Fishman, J.A. (ed.) *'Singles' Issue.*
      5   Rubin, J. (ed.) *Sociolinguistics in Southeast Asia.*
      6   Cooper, R.L. (ed.) *Language Attitudes II.*

1976 7   Dillard, J.L. (ed.) *Socio-Historical Factors in the Formation of the Creoles.*
      8   Berry, J. (ed.) *Language and Education in the Third World.*
      9   Rona, J.P. and Wölck, W. (eds) *The Social Dimension of Dialectology.*
      10   Nordberg, B. (ed.) *Sociolinguistic Research in Sweden and Finland.*
      11   Rubin, J. (ed.) *Language Planning in the United States.*

1977 12   Dressler W. and Wodak-Leodolter, R. (eds) *Language Death.*
      13   Fishman, J.A. (ed.) *'Singles' Issue.*
      14   Lewis, E.G. (ed.) *Bilingual Education.*

1978 15   Verdoodt, A. (ed.) *Belgium.*
      18   Fishman, J.A. (ed.) *'Singles' Issue.*

1979 19   Hancock, I.F. (ed.) *Romani Sociolinguistics.*
      20   Lamy, P. (ed.) *Language Planning and Identity Planning.*
      21   Ammon, U. (ed.) *Dialect and Standard in Highly Industrialized Societies.*
      22   Fishman, J.A. (ed.) *'Singles' Issue.*

1980 23   Sager, J.C. (ed.) *Standardization of Nomenclature.*
      24   Fishman, J.A (ed.) *Sociology of Yiddish.*
      25   Williamson, R.C. and van Eerde, J.A. (eds) *Language Maintenance and Language Shift.*
      26   Fishman, J.A. (ed.) *Variance and Invariance in Language Form and Context.*

1981 27   Walters, J. (ed.) *The Sociolinguistics of Deference and Politeness.*
      28   Clyne, M.G. (ed.) *Foreigner Talk.*
      29   Tabouret-Keller, A. (ed.) *Regional Languages in France.*
      30   Fishman, J.A. (ed.) *The Sociology of Jewish Languages.*
      31   Currie, H.C. (ed.) *Sociolinguistic Theory.*
      32   Fishman, J.A. (ed.) *Unguarded and Monitored Language Behavior.*

1982 33   Kreindler, I. (ed.) *The Changing Status of Russian in the Soviet Union.*
      34   Polomé, E.C. (ed.) *Rural and Urban Multilingualism.*
      35   Ellis, J. and Ure, J. (eds) *Register Range and Change.*

36 McKay, G.R. (ed.) *Australian Aborigines: Sociolinguistic Studies.*
37 Harris, T.K. (ed.) *Sociology of Judezmo: The Language of the Eastern Sephardim.*
38 Fishman, J.A. (ed.) *From Conceptualization and Performance to Planning and Maintenance.*

1983 40 Leitner, G. (ed.) *Language and Mass Media.*
41 Cooper, R.L. (ed.) *Sociolinguistic Perspective on Israeli Hebrew.*
43 Fishman, J.A. (ed.) *Face-to-Face Interaction.*

1984 45 Fishman, J.A. (ed.) *The Decade Past, the Decade to Come* (10th anniversary issue).
46 Giles, H. (ed.) *The Dynamics of Speech Accommodation.*
47 Ros i Garcia, M. and Strubell i Trueta, M. (eds) *Catalan Sociolinguistics.*
49 Coleman, H. (ed.) *Language and Work 1: Law, Industry, Education.*
50 Fishman, J.A. (ed.) *International Sociolinguistic Perspectives.*

1985 52 Magner, T.F. (ed.) *Yugoslavia in Sociolinguistic Perspective.*
53 Aguirre, Jr, A. (ed.) *Language in the Chicano Speech Community.*
54 Tabouret-Keller, A. (ed.) *Sociolinguistics in France: Current Research in Urban Settings.*
55 Mehrotra, R.R. (ed.) *Sociolinguistics Surveys in South, East and Southeast Asia.*
56 Cooper, R.L. (ed.) *Sociolinguistic Perspective on Theoretical and Applied Issues.*

1986 57 Preston, D.R. (ed.) *Sociolinguistic Taxonomics.*
59 Jernudd, B.H. *Chinese Language Planning: Perspectives from China and Abroad.*
61 Jernudd, B.H. and Ibrahim, M.H. (eds) *Aspects of Arabic Sociolinguistics.*

1987 63 Cooper, R.L. (ed.) *Language in Home, Community, Region and Nation.*
64 Gorter, D. (ed.) *The Sociology of Frisian.*
65 Apte, M.L. (ed.) *Language and Humor.*
66 Williams, G. (ed.) *The Sociology of Welsh.*
67 Fishman, J.A. (ed.) *The Sociology of Jewish Languages.*
68 Dow, J.R. (ed.) *New Perspectives on Language Maintenance and Language Shift I.*

1988 69 Dow, J.R. (ed.) *New Perspectives on Language Maintenance and Language Shift II.*
70 ó Riagáin, P. (ed.) *Language Planning in Ireland.*
71 Rickford, J.R. (ed.) *Sociolinguistics and Pidgin-Creole Studies.*
72 Pauwels, A. (ed.) *The Future of Ethnic Languages in Australia.*
73 Stalpers, J. and Coulmas, F. (eds) *The Sociolinguistics of Dutch.*
74 Coulmas, F. (ed.) *Language Planning and Attitudes.*

1989 75 Mehrotra, R.R. (ed.) *Sociolinguistics in India.*
76 Zuanelli Sonino, E. (ed.) *Italian Sociolinguistics: Trends and Issues.*
77 Hornberger, N.H. (ed.) *Bilingual Education and Language Planning in Indigenous Latin America.*
78 Janicki, K. (ed.) *Sociolinguistics in Poland.*
79 Wherritt, I. and García, O. (eds) *US Spanish: The Language of Latinos.*
80 Coulmas, F. (ed.) *Current Issues in Language Planning and Language Education.*

1990 81 Yuan, C. and Marshall, D.F. (eds) *Sociolinguistics in the People's Republic of China.*
82 Haarmann, H. and Hwang, J.R. (eds) *Aspects of Korean Sociolinguistics.*
83 Coulmas, F. (ed.) *Zur Soziolinguistik des Deutschen / Varieties of German.*
84 Coulmas, F. (ed.) *Spanish in the USA: New Quandaries and Prospects.*
85 Pollard, V. (ed.) *Caribbean Languages: Lesser-known Varieties.*
86 Coulmas, F. (ed.) *Perspectives on Language Contact and Language Policy.*

1991 87 Ennaji, M. (ed.) *Sociolinguistics of the Maghreb.*
88 Sibayan, B.P. and Gonzalez, A.B. (eds) *Sociolinguistic Studies in the Philippines.*
89 Gomes de Matos, F. and Bortoni, S.M. (eds) *Sociolinguistics in Brazil.*
90 de Bot, K. and Fase, W. (eds) *Migrant Languages in Western Europe.*
91 Fishman, J.A. (ed.) *Yiddish: The Fifteenth Slavic Language.*
92 Coulmas, F. (ed.) *New Perspectives on Linguistic Etiquette.*

1992 93 Taylor, A.R. (ed.) *Language Obsolescence, Shift and Death in Several Native American Communities.*
94 Bull, T. and Swan, T. (eds) *Language, Sex and Society.*
95 Ammon, U. and Kleineidam, H. (eds) *Language-Spread Policy I: Languages of Former Colonial Powers.*
96 Lastra, Y. (ed.) with the assistance of de la Mora, A. *Sociolinguistics in Mexico.*
97 Hongkai, S. and Coulmas, F. (eds) *News from China: Minority Languages in Perspective.*
98 Coulmas, F. (ed.) *Attitudes and Accommodation in Multilingual Societies.*

1993 99 Siegel, J. (ed.) *Koines and Koineization.*
100/1 Fishman, J.A. (ed.) *Anniversary Issue: Preparing for the 21st Century.*
102 Schnepel, E.M. and Prudent, L.F. (eds) *Creole Movements in the Francophone Orbit.*
103 Eastman, C.M. (ed.) (1993) *Language in Power.*
104 Verdoodt, A.F. and Sonntag, S.K. (eds) (1993) *Sociology of Language in Belgium (Revisited).*

1994 105/6 Bourhis, R.Y. (ed.) *French-English Language Issues in Canada.*
107 Ammon, U. (ed.) *Language Spread Policy II: Languages of Former Colonial Powers and Former Colonies.*
108 Landry, R. and Allard, R. (eds) *Ethnolinguistic Vitality.*
109 Varro, G. (ed.) *Language, the Subject, the Social Link: Essays offered to Andrée Tabouret-Keller by the members of LADIDIS.*
110 Fishman, J.A. (ed.) *Ethnolinguistic Pluralism and Its Discontents: A Canadian Study, and Some General Observations.*

1995 111 Kontra, M. and Pléh, C. (eds) *Hungarian Sociolinguistics.*
112 Ennaji, M. (ed.) *Sociolinguistics in Morocco.*
113 Devlin, B., Harris, S., Black, P. and Guruluwini Enemburus, I. (eds) *Australian Aborigines and Torres Strait Islanders: Sociolinguistic and Educational Perspectives.*
114 Hidalgo, M. (ed.) *Sociolinguistic Trends on the US–Mexican Border.*
115 Jahr, E.H. (ed.) *Sociolinguistics in Norway.*
116 Coulmas, F. (ed.) *'Singles' Issue: Language Politics and Accommodation.*

1996 117 Elizaincín, A. (ed.) *Sociolinguistics in Argentina, Paraguay and Uruguay.*

118 Dua, H.R. (ed.) *Language Planning and Political Theory.*
119 Verhoeven, L. (ed.) *Vernacular Literacy in Non-Mainstream Communities.*
120 Gustavsson, S. and Starý, Z. (eds) *Minority Languages in Central Europe.*
121 Grin, F. (ed.) *Economic Approaches to Language and Language Planning.*
122 Coulmas, F. (ed.) *'Singles' Issue: Concepts of Language in Asia and Other Non-Western Societies.*

1997 123 Ennaji, M. (ed.) *Berber Sociolinguistics.*
124 Greenberg, M.L. (ed.) *The Sociolinguistics of Slovene.*
125 Abdulaziz, M.H. (ed.) *Sociolinguistic Issues in Sub-Saharan Africa.*
126 Alatis, J.E., Straehle, C.A. and Ronkin, M. (eds) *Aspects of Sociolinguistics in Greece.*
127 Hamel, R.E. (ed.) *Linguistic Human Rights in a Sociolinguistic Perspective.*
128 Coulmas, F. (ed.) *Issues in Language Contact and Social Power Relations.*

1998 129 Ide, S. and Hill, B. (eds) *Women's Languages in Various Parts of the World.*
130 Omar, A.H. (ed.) *Linguistic Issues in Southeast Asia.*
131 Topolinjska, A. (ed.) *The Sociolingistic Situation of the Macedonian Language.*
132 McCarty, T.L. and Zepeda, O. (eds) *Indigenous Language Use and Change in the Americas.*
133 Varro, G. and Boyd, S. (eds) *Americans in Europe: A Sociolinguistic Perspective. Probes in Northern and Western Europe.*
134 Coulmas, F. (ed.) *Language Choice Issues.*

1999 135 Videnov, M. and Angelov, A. (eds) *Sociolinguistics in Bulgaria.*
136 McCormick, K. and Mesthrie, R. (eds) *Post-Apartheid South Africa.*
137 Landau, J.M. (ed.) *Language and Politics: Theory and Cases.*
138 Isaacs, M. and Glinert, L. (eds) *Pious Voices: Languages Among Ultra-Orthodox Jews.*
139 Hennoste, T. (ed.) *Estonian Sociolinguistics.*
140 Coulmas, F. (ed.) *Linguistic Symbolism, Political and Individual.*

2000 141 Bamgbose, A. (ed.) *Sociolinguistics in West Africa.*
142 Ramírez González, C.M. and Torres, R. (eds) *Language Spread Policy III: Languages of Former Colonial Powers and Former Colonies: The Case of Puerto Rico.*
143 Omoniyi, T. (ed.) *Islands and Identity in Sociolinguistics: Hong Kong, Singapore and Taiwan.*
144 Kamwangamalu, N.M. (ed.) *Language and Ethnicity in the New South Africa.*
145 Kallen, J.L., Hinskens, F. and Taeldeman, J. (eds) *Dialect Convergence and Divergence Across European Borders.*
146 Coulmas, F. (ed.) *Problems of Multilingualism and Social Change in Asian and African Contexts.*

2001 147 Filipovic, R. and Kalogjera, D. (eds) *Sociolinguistics in Croatia.*
148 Modarresi, Y. (ed.) *Aspects of Sociolinguistics in Iran.*
149 Hidalgo, M. (ed.) *Between Koineization and Standardization: New World Spanish Revisited.*
150 Grivelet, S. (ed.) *Diagraphia: Writing Systems and Society.*
151 Radovanovic, M. and Major, R.A. (eds) *Serbian Sociolinguistics.*
152 Coulmas, F. (ed.) *Language Contact Issues.*

2002 153 de Bot, K. and Stoessel, S. (eds) *Language Change and Social Networks.*

154 Ricento, T. and Wiley, T.G. (eds) *Revisiting the Mother-Tongue Question in Language Policy, Planning and Politics.*

155/6 Garcia, E.E. (ed.) *Bilingualism and Schooling in the United States.*

157 Fishman, J.A. (ed.) *Focus on Diglossia.*

158 Coulmas, F. (ed.) *Linguistic Choices by Individuals, Organizations, and Speech Communities.*

2003 159 Kirstiansen, T. and Jørgensen, J.N. (eds) *The Sociolinguistics of Danish.*

160 Tabouret-Keller, A. (ed.) *Sociolinguistics in France: Theoretical Trends at the Turn of the Century.*

161 David, M.K. (ed.) *Language Maintenance or Language Shift: Focus on Malaysia.*

162 Nekvapil, J. and Cmejrková, S. (eds) *Language and Language Communities in the Czech Republic.*

163 Belnap, R.K. (ed.) *Arabic Sociolinguistics as Viewed by Western Arabists.*

164 Coulmas, F. (ed.) *Language Expansion and Linguistic World.*

2004 165 König, G. (ed.) *Sociolinguistics in Turkey.*

166 Bargiela-Chiappini, F. (ed.) *Organizational Discourse.*

167 King, K.A. and Hornberger, N.H. (eds) *Quechua Sociolinguistics.*

168 Goutsos, D. (ed.) *The Sociolinguistics of Cyprus I (Studies from the Greek Sphere).*

169 Blanchet, P. and Schiffman, H. (eds) *Revisiting the Sociolinguistics of Occitan: A Presentation.*

170 Coulmas, F. (ed.) *Focus on Africa: Sociolinguistic Changes in a Changing World.*

2005 171 Cenoz, J. and Gorter, D. (eds) *Trilingual Education in Europe.*

172 Lotherington, H. and Benton, R. (eds) *Pacific Sociolinguistics.*

173 Bradley, D. (ed.) *Language Policy and Language Endangerment in China.*

174 Azurmendi, M.J. and Martínez de Luna, I. (eds) *Presenting the Basque Case.*

175/6 Coulmas, F. and Heinrich, P. (eds) *Changing Language Regimes in Globalizing Environments: Japan and Europe.*

Appendix 3:
Google Scholar Citations of Joshua A. Fishman's Work

This table is correct as of August 2005. Only citations of more than one are included. Books are rendered in italics, chapters and articles appear in regular font. Where two entries appear to be the same, the first is usually the title of an article or chapter, the second the title of a book (often the one in which the article or chapter appears).

Number of citations	Publication date	Title of publication
123	1991	Reversing language shift
96	1991	*Reversing Language Shift: Theoretical and Empirical Foundations of Assistance to Threatened Languages*
75	1989	*Language & Ethnicity in Minority Sociolinguistic Perspective*
44	2001	*Can Threated Languages be Saved? Reversing Language Shift, Revisited: A 21st Century Perspective*
46	1967	Bilingualism with and without diglossia: Diglossia with and without bilingualism
37	1972	The sociology of language
34	1978	*Language Loyalty in the United States*
24	1977	*Language and Ethnicity*
23	1973	*Language and Nationalism: Two Integrative Essays*
22	1964	Language maintenance and language shift as fields of inquiry
22	1970	*Sociolinguistics: A Brief Introduction*
21	1996	*Post-Imperial English: Status change in former British and American colonies* (with A.W Conrad and A. Rubal-Lopez)
19	1972	*The Sociology of Language: An Interdisciplinary Social Science Approach to Language in Society*
19	1971	*Bilingualism in the Barrio*
19	1991	*Bilingual Education: Focusschrift in Honor of Joshua A. Fishman* (edited by O. García)
17	1990	What is reversing langauge shift (RLS) and how can it succeed
17	1980	Bilingualism and biculturalism as individual and societal phenomena
17	1999	*Handbook of Language and Ethnic Identity*
17	1972	Language and nationalism
16	1976	*Bilingual Education: An International Sociological Perspective*
17	1965	Who speaks what language to whom and when
15	1968	*Readings in the Sociology of Language*
13	1968	Nationality-nationalism and nation-nationism
12	1968	Language problems of developing nations
12	1970	Language attitude studies: A brief survey of methodological approaches

11	1964	Language loyalty in the United States: The maintenance and perpetuation of non-English mother tongues
11	1985	*The Rise and Fall of the Ethnic Revival: Perspectives on Language and Ethnicity* (with M.H. Gertner, E.G. Lowy, W.G. Milan)
10	1985	The rise and fall of the ethnic revival
9	1972	*Language in Sociocultural Change*
9	1974	The study of language attitudes
9	1976	Advances in the sociology of language
9	1998	The new linguistic order
9	1996	What do you lose when you lose your language
8	1972	Domains and the relationship between micro-and macro-sociolinguistcis
8	1999	Sociolinguistics
8	1982	Whorfianism of the third kind: Ethnolinguistic diversity as a worldwide societal asset
8	1997	Maintaining languages, what works, what doesn't
7	1976	Advances in language planning
7	1977	*The Spread of English: The Sociology of English as an Additional Language*
7	1977	The spread of English
7	1997	*The Multilingual Apple: Languages in New York City* (with O. García)
7	1970	Bilingual Education in sociolinguistic perspective
7	1994	On the limits of ethnolinguistic democracy
7	1983	Sociology of English as an additional language
6	1971	National languages and languages of wider communication in the developing nations
6	1968	Sociolinguistics and the language problems of the developing countries
6	1956	An examination of the process and function of social stereotyping
6	1997	*In Praise of the Beloved Language: A Comparative View of Positive Ethnolinguistic Consciousness*
5	1985	Language maintenance and ethnicity
5	1996	Introduction: Some empirical and theoretical issues
5	1997	Linguistic human rights from a sociolinguistic perspective (with R.E. Hamel)
5	1973	Language modernization and planning in comparison with other types of national modernization
5	1977	Bilingual education: Current perspectives. The social science perspective
5	1994	Critiques of language planning: A minority languages perspective
5	1994	English only
5	1978	*Advances in the Study of Societal Multilingualism*

Number of citations	Publication date	Title of publication
4	1983	*Progress in Language Planning: International perspectives*
4	1968	Some contrasts between linguistically homogeneous and linguistically heterogeneous polities
4	1968	A sociology of bilingual education
4	1996	Summary and interpretation: Post-imperial English 1940–1990
4	1974	Language planning and language planning research: The state of the art
4	1979	Bilingual education, language planning and English
4	1981	Societal bilingualism: Stable and transitional
4	1980	Minority language maintenance and the ethnic mother tongue school
4	2001	300-plus years of heritage language education in the United States
3	1974	Yiddish in Israel: A case-study of efforts to revise a monocentric language policy (with D.E. Fishman)
3	2001	From theory to practice (and vice versa): Review, reconsideration and reiteration
3	1968	Sociolinguistic perspectives on the study of bilingualism
3	1987	Language spread and language policy for endangered languages
3	1997	In praise of the beloved language
3	1993	*The Earliest Stage of Language Planning: The 'First Congress' Phenomenon*
3	1991	*Yiddish: Turning to Life*
3	1993	Ethnolinguistic democracy: Varieties, degrees and limits
3	1988	Ethnocultural issues in the creation, substitution and revision of writing systems
2	1985	Language, ethnicity and racism
2	2001	Digraphia maintenance and loss among Eastern European Jews: Intertextual and interlingual print
2	1989	Bilingual education and language planning in indigenous Latin America
2	1985	*Readings in the Sociology of Jewish Languages*
2	1971	Sociolinguistique
2	1980	Social Theory and ethnography: Language and ethnicity in Eastern Europe
2	1977	*Advances in the Creation and Revision of Writing Systems*
2	1985	*Ethnicity in Action: The Community Resources of Ethnic Languages in the United States*
2	1982	Sociolinguistic Foundations of Bilingual Education
2	1991	*Language and Ethnicity: Focusschrift in Honor of Joshua A. Fishman on the Occasion of his 65th Birthday* (edited by J.R. Dow)

References:
Joshua A. Fishman works cited

We include here (in date order) only those works – often a collection of work – from which we quote verbatim. For a more complete list of Fishman's works referred to in this chapter, please consult the bibliographical inventory compiled by Gella Schweid Fishman, which forms Part 3 of this volume.

Fishman, J.A. and Passanella, A. (1960) College admission-selection studies. *Review of Educational Research* 30, 298–310.

Fishman, J.A. (1964) Language maintenance and language shift as a field of inquiry. *Linguistics* 9, 32–70.

Fishman, J.A. (1965) Who speaks what language to whom and when? *La Linguistique* 2, 67–88.

Fishman, J.A. (1966) *Language Loyalty in the United States. The Maintenance and Perpetuation of Non-English Mother Tongues by American Ethnic and Religious Groups*. The Hague: Mouton.

Fishman, J.A. (1967) The description of societal bilingualism. In L.G. Kelly (ed.) *The Description and Measurement of Bilingualism* (pp. 275–284). Toronto: Toronto University Press.

Fishman, J.A. (ed.) (1968) *Readings in the Sociology of Language*. The Hague: Mouton.

Fishman, J.A., Cooper, R.L., Ma, R. *et al.* (1971) *Bilingualism in the Barrio: Language Science Monographs* 7. Bloomington, IN: Indiana University Press.

Fishman, J.A. (1972a) *Language in Sociocultural Change. Essays by Joshua A. Fishman*. Stanford: Stanford University Press.

Fishman, J.A. (1972b) *Language and Nationalism. Two Integrative Essays*. Rowley, MA: Newbury House.

Fishman, J.A. (ed.) (1972c) *Advances in the Sociology of Language* II. The Hague: Mouton.

Fishman, J.A. and Lovas, J. (1972d) Bilingual education in sociolinguistic perspective. In B. Spolsky (ed.) *The Language Education of Minority Children* (pp. 83–93). Rowley, MA: Newbury House.

Fishman, J.A. (1973) Language modernization and planning in comparison with other types of national modernization and planning. *Language in Society* 2, 23–44.

Cooper, R.L. and Fishman, J.A. 1974. The study of language attitudes. *International Journal of the Sociology of Language* 3: 5–20.

Fishman, J.A. (1976) *Bilingual Education: An International Sociological Perspective*. Rowley, MA: Newbury House.

Fishman, J.A. (1977) *Bilingual Education: Current Perspectives. Social Science*. Arlington, VA: Center for Applied Linguistics.

Fishman, J.A., Cooper, R.L. and Conrad, A. (1977) *The Spread of English: The Sociology of Language as an Additional Language*. Rowley, MA: Newbury House.

Fishman, J.A. (1978) A gathering of vultures, the 'legion of decency' and bilingual education in the USA. *NABE Journal* 21, 13–16.

Fishman, J.A. (1980) Ethnic community mother tongue schools in the USA: Dynamics and distributions. *International Migration Review* 14, 235–247.

Fishman, J.A. (1982) Whorfianism of the third kind: Ethnolinguistic diversity as a worldwide asset. *Language in Society* 11: 1–14.

Fishman, J.A. (1983) The rise and fall of the 'ethnic revival' in the USA. *Journal of Intercultural Studies* 4 (3), 5–46.

Fishman, J.A., Gertner, M.H., Lowy, E.G. and Milan, W.G. (1985a) *The Rise and Fall of the Ethnic Revival: Perspectives on Language and Ethnicity*. Berlin: Mouton de Gruyter.

Fishman, J.A. (1985) The societal basis of the intergenerational continuity of additional languages. In K.R. Jankowsky (ed.) *Scientific and Humanistic Dimensions of Language. Festchrift for Robert Lado* (pp. 551–558). Amsterdam: John Benjamins.

Fishman, J.A. (1987) *Ideology, Society and Language: The Odyssey of Nathan Birnbaum*. Ann Arbor, MI: Karoma.

Fishman, J.A. (1989) *Language and Ethnicity in Minority Sociolinguistic Perspective*. Clevedon: Multilingual Matters.

Fishman, J.A. (1990) My life through my work: My work through my life (autobiography). In K. Koerner (ed.) *First Person Singular* (Vol. 2; pp. 105–124). Amsterdam: John Benjamins.

Fishman, J.A. (1991a) Putting the 'socio' back into the sociolinguistic enterprise. *The International Journal of the Sociology of Language* 92, 127–138.

Fishman, J.A. (1991b) *Reversing Language Shift: Theory and Practice of Assistance to Threatened Languages*. Clevedon: Multilingual Matters.

Fishman, J.A. (1991c) *Yiddish: Turning to Life: Sociolinguistic Studies and Interpretations*. Amsterdam: John Benjamins.

Fishman, J.A. (1994) Critiques of language planning: A minority languages perspective. *Journal of Multilingual and Multicultural Development* 15 (2 and 3), 91–99.

Fishman, J.A. (1996a) *In Praise of the Beloved Language: A Comparative View of Positive Ethnolinguistic Consciousness*. Berlin: Mouton de Gruyter.

Fishman, J.A., Conrad, A.W. and Rubal-López, A. (eds) (1996b) *Post-Imperial English. Status Change in Former British and American Colonies, 1940–1990*. Berlin: Mouton de Gruyter.

Fishman, J.A. (1997a) Bloomington, summer of 1964: The birth of American sociolinguistics. In C.B. Paulston and G.R. Tucker (eds) *The Early Days of Sociolinguistics: Memories and Reflections* (pp. 87–95). Dallas, TX: Summer Institute of Linguistics Publications.

Fishman, J.A. (1997b) Language and ethnicity: The view from within. In F. Coulmas (ed.) *The Handbook of Sociolinguistics* (pp. 327–343). Oxford: Blackwell Publishers.

Fishman, J.A. (1997c) Reflections about (or prompted by) *International Journal of the Sociology of Language (IJSL)*. In C.B. Paulston and G.R. Tucker (eds) *The Early Days of Sociolinguistics: Memories and Reflections* (pp. 237–241). Dallas, TX: Summer Institute of Linguistics Publications.

Fishman, J.A. (ed.) (1999) *Handbook of Language and Ethnic Identity*. New York: Oxford University Press.

Fishman, J.A. (2000) The status agenda in corpus planning. In R.D. Lambert and E. Shohamy (eds) *Language Policy and Pedagogy: Essays in Honor of A. Ronald Walton* (pp. 43–51). Amsterdam: John Benjamins.

Fishman, J.A. (ed.) (2001) *Can Threatened Languages Be Saved?* Clevedon: Multilingual Matters.

Fishman, J.A. (2002) Introduction. *MOST Journal on Multicultural Societies* 4 (2), i–x.

Other works cited

Anderson, B. (1983) *Imagined Communities*. London: Verso.

Anzaldúa, G. (1997) *Borderlands/La frontera: The New Mestiza*. San Francisco: Aunt Lute Books.

Baetens-Beardsmore, H. (1999) La consolidation des expériences en éducation plurilingue. In D. Marsh and B. Marland (eds) *CLIL Initiatives for the Millenium.* Jyväskylä: University of Jyväskylä.

Bakhtin, M.M. (1981) *The Dialogic Imagination: Four Essays.* (M. Holquist, ed., M. Holquist and C. Emerson, trans.). Austin, TX: University of Texas Press.

Bhabha, H.K. (1994) *The Location of Culture.* London: Routledge.

Bourdieu, P. (1991). *Language and Symbolic Power.* Cambridge: Harvard University Press.

Brutt-Griffler, J. (2004) *World English: A Study of its Development.* Clevedon: Multilingual Matters.

Calvet, L.J. (1999) *Pour une écologie des langues du monde.* Paris: Plon.

Canagarajah, S. (ed.) (2005) *Reclaiming the Local in Language Policy and Practice.* Mahwah, NJ: Lawrence Erlbaum.

Common European Framework of Reference for Languages (2002) Online document: http://www.coe.int/T/E/Cultural_Co-operation/education/Languages/Language_Policy/Common_Framework_of_Reference/

Coste, D. (2001) La notion de compétence plurilingue. In *Actes du Séminaire: l'Enseignement des Langues Vivantes, Perspectives.* Paris: Ministère de la Jeunesse de l'Education et de la Recherche, DES. On WWW at http://www.eduscol.education.fr

Coulmas, F. (2005) *Sociolinguistics: The Study of Speakers' Choices.* Cambridge: Cambridge University Press.

Fairclough, N. (1989) *Language and Power.* London: Longman.

Fasold, R. (1984) *The Sociolinguistics of Society.* Oxford: Basil Blackwell.

Ferguson, C.A. (1959) Diglossia. *Word* 15 (2), 325–340.

García, O. (ed.) (1991) *Bilingual Education. Focusschrift in Honor of Joshua A. Fishman on the Occasion of His 65th Birthday* (Vol. 1). Amsterdam/Philadelphia: John Benjamins Publishing Company.

García, O. (2006) Lost in transculturation: The case of bilingual education in New York City. In M. Pütz, J.A. Fishman and J. Neff-van Aertselaer (eds) *'Along the Routes to Power': Explorations of the Empowerment through Language.* Berlin/New York: Mouton de Gruyter.

Gee, J.P. (1996) *Social Linguistics and Literacies. Ideology in Discourses.* London: Taylor and Francis.

Gibbons, P. (2002) *Scaffolding Language: Scaffolding Learning. Teaching Second Language Learners in the Mainstream Classroom.* Portsmouth, NH: Heinemann.

Gutiérrez, K., Baquedano-López, P. and Tejada, C. (1999) Rethinking diversity: Hybridity and hybrid language practices in the third space. *Mind, Culture and Activity* 6 (4), 286–303.

Haugen, E. 1996. *Language Planning and Language Conflict. The Case of Modern Norwegian.* Cambridge, MA: Harvard University Press.

Hymes, D. (1972) Foreword. In J.A. Fishman, *The Sociology of Language. An Interdisciplinary Social Science Approach to Language in Society* (pp. v–viii). Rowley, MA: Newbury House.

Irvine, J. and Gal, S. (2000) Language ideology and linguistic differentiation. In P. Kroskrity (ed.) *Regimes of Language: Ideologies, Polities and Identities* (pp. 35–84). Santa Fe, NM: School of American Research Press.

Jenkins, R. (1997) *Rethinking Ethnicity.* London: Sage.

Jewett, C. and Kress, G. (2003) *Multimodal Literacy.* New York: Peter Lang.

Kloss, H. (1929). *Nebensprachen: Eine sprachpolitische Studie über die Bezienhungen eng Verwandter Sprachgemeinschaften*. Wien: Wilhelm Braumüller, Universitäts-Verlagsbuchhandlung.

Kloss, H. (1940) *Das Volksgruppenrecht in den Vereinigten Staaten von Amerika* (Vol. 1). Essener Verlagsanstalt: Essen.

Kloss, H. (1967) *Abstand* languages and *Ausbau* languages. *Anthropological Linguistics* 9 (7), 29–41.

Krashen, S.D. (1979) Language acquisition and language learning in the late-entry bilingual education program. *Language Development in a Bilingual Setting* (pp. 100–112). Pomona, CA: National Multilingual Multicultural Materials Development Center.

Krashen, S.D. (1996) *Under Attack: The Case Against Bilingual Education*. Culver City, CA: Language Education Associates.

Kress, G. (2003) *Literacy in the New Media Age*. New York: Routledge.

Luke, A. and Baldauf, Jr, R.B. (1990) Language planning and education: A critical rereading. In R.B. Baldauf, Jr and A. Luke (eds) *Language Planning and Education in Australasia and the South Pacific* (pp. 349–356). Clevedon: Multilingual Matters.

Maurais, J. and Morris, M. (eds) (2004) *Languages in a Globalising World*. Cambridge: Cambridge University Press.

Pavlenko, A. and Blackledge, A. (eds) (2004) *Negotiation of Identities in Multilingual Contexts*. Clevedon: Multilingual Matters.

Peñalosa, F. (1981) *Introduction to the Sociology of Language*. Rowley: Newbury House.

Pennycook, A. (1989) The concept of method, interested knowledge and the politics of language teaching. *TESOL Quarterly* 23 (4), 589–618.

Ruiz, R. (1984) Orientations in language planning. *NABE Journal* 8 (2), 15–34.

Skutnabb-Kangas, T. (1988) Multilingualism and the education of minority children. In T. Skutnabb-Kangas and J. Cummins (eds) *Minority Education: From Shame to Struggle* (pp. 9–44). Clevedon: Multilingual Matters.

Spolsky, B. (2004) *Language Policy*. Cambridge: Cambridge University Press.

Tollefson, J. (1991) *Planning Language, Planning Inequality: Language Policy in the Community*. London: Longman.

Tollefson, J. (ed.) (1995) *Power and Inequality in Language Education*. Cambridge: Cambridge University Press.

Walqui, A. (2002) Conceptual framework. Scaffolding instruction for English learners. Unpublished manuscript. WestEd, San Francisco.

Weinreich, Uriel. 1953. *Languages in Contact: Findings and Problems*. The Hague: Mouton.

Williams, G. (1992) *Sociolinguistics. A Sociological Critique*. London and New York: Routledge.

Woolard, K. (1998) Introduction: Language ideology as a field of inquiry. In B. Schieffelin, K. Wollard and P. Kroskrity (eds) *Language Ideologies: Practice and Theory* (pp. 3–47). New York and Oxford: Oxford University Press.

Wright, S. (2004) *Language Policy and Language Planning: From Nationalism to Globalisation*. Hampshire: Palgrave Macmillan.

The History of Yiddish Studies: Take Notice!

RAKHMIEL PELTZ

Minority Languages and Cultures Have Their Own Research Agendas

In the history of ethnic minorities, the development of societal self-consciousness of the significance and necessity of documenting the group's history and *modus vivendi* through organized scholarship always occurs late in the group's history. Although historical narratives are at the fore-front of the oral transmission of family and group history, the development of disciplined efforts to analyze and document experience and behavior takes place much later in history for minorities than for dominant groups and cultures. Accordingly, although cultural and religious groups that are not in control of major political and social institutions evolve successful methods of remembering their histories and transmitting their rituals, very often they lack the formal, advanced research efforts and organizations that ensure the spread of information through books and other media, as well as through school systems and institutions that train teachers and scholars. Or at best, these latter efforts emerge much later than the analogous initiatives of the dominant cultures and religions. Furthermore, for the minorities, such institutions are likely underfunded, unstable and short-lived.

In 19th century Europe, after the Enlightenment and Emancipation, scholarly research academies were well established for majority cultures. By the end of that century, 'the peoples without history,' had started to clamor for this high level of societal, institutional, cultural construction. Although Jews, and particularly European Jews, had for centuries been vigorously involved in *yeshivos* (their own institutions for advanced study of sacred texts written in Hebrew and Aramaic, specifically the *Torah and Talmud*), the more secularized study of the history of the people and its folkways and literature did not arise until the 19th century in Germany. By the 18th century the center of gravity of European Jewry had moved to Eastern Europe, and by the beginning of the 20th century several Jewish intellectuals argued and planned for academies that would collect, analyze and teach the culture of most of Europe's Jewry throughout its experience during the preceding millennium – a culture created and transmitted in its vernacular, Yiddish. In the confines of this essay, it will not be possible to discuss in detail the indications that demonstrate that many of the documenters perceived the language and culture as being at risk and that their efforts would serve to preserve it. It is my intention a century later to delineate the contours of research on Yiddish language and culture and the lacunae that have remained in the record, especially with regards to the analysis and documentation of the complex position of Yiddish language in its social contexts. *En passant* I must note that, even 60 years after the decimation of the heartland of Yiddish in Eastern Europe by the Nazis and their collaborators, Yiddish is still the lingua franca of many traditional Jewish communities in different parts of the globe that transmit it from generation to generation.

Scholarly research on Yiddish has a long history that spans some 500 years. Although there is no universally accepted criterion for what constitutes an act of scholarship, the historians of Yiddish research (i.e. starting with Borokhov, 1913a; Weinreich, 1923), most likely under the influence of the Viennese Yiddish philologist Alfred Landau, included rudimentary efforts at systematization, manifestations of a self-conscious analytical process and citations to the literature, all of which speak to the formation of an intellectual tradition. The beginnings hark back to 1514, to the school of Humanists who worked in Latin and whose interest in the Hebrew Bible led them to Yiddish glosses, spelling, phonology, pronunciation and lexical analyses. The motley crew of early researchers included serious Jewish and Christian scholars and authors, along with Christian missionaries intent on converting the Jews, as well as criminologists searching for entry into thieves' cant. With time, much of the research was devoted to documenting early examples of Yiddish literature that, by dint of the evidence of its existence, would demonstrate beyond any doubt that Yiddish was a bona fide language and culture.

Eventually even the research efforts on behalf of the 'little' languages and traditions would accept the methods of the humanities worked out for the classic and by then modern major proponents. However, the more controversial and variable components of the research enterprise would also become part of the purview of the field. If, indeed, the language and culture of minority vernaculars are the carriers of the heart and soul, actually the identity of the nationality and ethnic group, as Herder had persuaded, then the provenance of research into the vernacular could include all issues that are vital to the group. The Yiddishist school of research that reigned during the first half of the 20th century was started in clearest terms by Borokhov (1913b), who viewed Yiddish as a broad field of inquiry in and of itself, and championed the publication of all research studies in Yiddish. The uniqueness of the Yiddishist researchers is that their highest goal was to serve nationalist Jewish goals by meeting the Yiddish language needs of Jewish social institutions and by recording the long history of Yiddish culture, practically unknown up to that time. In describing these broader romantic aims of Yiddish philology, Borokhov (1917/1966: 217) got carried away and included the fields of grammar, language history, word construction, dialects, literature, literary history, folklore, archaeology, folk traditions, customs, moral and art history. He based his classifications on the curricula of academic programs in philology and of published studies of German philologists. Borokhov's own charge, as evidenced in the statement of his goals, was broader and grandiose: '*Mayn tsvek iz nit di shprakh, oykh nit di literature, nit di sotsyale antviklung – nor di kultur, velkhe nemt in zikh altsding*' ('My goal is not the language, nor the literature, not societal development – but the culture, and that includes everything'). The philologist is not merely an academic researcher, but rather a nationalistic leader who has faith in the future of the language: '*Far a filolog iz nor miglekh ... az zayn obyekt lebt un vet lebn*' ('For a philologist it is only possible ... that his research object lives and will continue to live'). This is a far cry from the way we define philology today, namely the analysis of old texts.

Borokhov had written of the need for a scholarly academy based on Yiddish culture. In the mid-1920s, three such research centers were founded in Eastern Europe. The sectional divisions of these academies were very similar: (1) in Vilna: philology, pedagogy, history and social economics; (2) in Minsk: language, literature, history and economics-demography; (3) in Kiev: philology, history, literature and later pedagogy.

We should recognize that Yiddish, the previousy ignored and denigrated mother tongue that represented the L (low) functions of the diglossia relationships vis-à-vis the H (high) functions of Hebrew and Aramaic was now flexing its muscles. For a short period, until World War II in Eastern Europe, and, for another three or four decades to a more limited extent, in New York City, where Yivo (*yidisher visnshaftlekher institut*, the current Yivo institute for Yiddish research) had transplanted itself from Vilna, its advocates not only researched the humanities but also devoted themselves to the applied social science concerns of their language.

By the time Uriel Weinreich was forming an academic program of study and research on Yiddish at Columbia University in the 1950s, the nationalistic goals of the East European Jews were not on the agenda – not the political nor the academic ones – after the destruction of most of those Jews and the repression of Jewish culture in the Soviet Union. Weinreich fit Yiddish Studies into the disciplines of most languages and cultures taught within humanities departments in the United States at the time. The base was language and literature; folklore, if present, represented additional literary genres, not an ethnographically process-related field such as exists today. By the 1980s, literary criticism became the only focus of language departments that had earlier embraced language area studies (including linguistics, literature and folklore of the language and culture under study). New researchers of Yiddish were largely attracted to Yiddish literary criticism from that time on.

Fishman's Approach to Yiddish Research

Joshua Fishman, who has researched Yiddish language and culture for more than 50 years, has contributed to Yiddish research in a more concentrated fashion in recent years. Although this is exactly the period when more and more researchers of Yiddish have turned their attention to Yiddish literary criticism, Fishman has chosen to specialize in the sociology of the Yiddish language and contributes to our understanding of how Yiddish functions in its varied social settings. At a time when the academic confines of the humanities have narrowed and there is not necessarily an academic berth to study specific languages and cultures within their social environment, Fishman's work on Yiddish represents a lone voice that constitutes a subfield unto itself in Yiddish Studies. Although his writings on Yiddish are a minor chord when contrasted with his main work, the voluminous nature of his writings, which reflects his agility in writing, in general, includes extensive publications on Yiddish. These works constitute a major contribution to Yiddish Studies. In fact, Fishman's work on Yiddish as a sideline is more substantial than the work of most Yiddish researchers who only work on Yiddish.

I will review the work of Fishman on Yiddish from the vantage point of the field of Yiddish Studies, and will ascertain its impact in terms of the areas of inquiry that he has opened up. This endeavor is based on my reading of the books and articles he has written and my familiarity with the current state of Yiddish Studies. I have not located critiques of the work by other Yiddish researchers. I have decided to cluster the research results according to topic and format. After evaluating the methods followed and the results that emanated, I will position the contribution within the field of Yiddish. Despite the fact that the work clearly reflects, in several instances, the chronological developments by which research projects in their design normally respond to earlier studies, I would rather fit them into our grasp of the needs of the field of Yiddish. The identified research areas are home to work written at different times during Fishman's career.

The Special Needs of Research on Minority Languages in Their Social Contexts: The Case of Yiddish

As everyone familiar with the sociology of language will attest, Joshua Fishman's research and publications stand as a testament to the advocacy of the vitality and contribution of minority languages and their cultures in their multiplicity the world over.

Rarely, however, is the spotlight put on the needs for higher levels of research and training, from the perspective of the minority language and its community, for post-graduate education and the funding and organization of scholarly research and publication. Yet, even in many areas of special interest to the sociology of language, such as language planning and bilingual education, these social processes themselves depend, at least in part, on scholarly activity. Most scholars, however, view themselves as members of academic disciplines, whose goals, hierarchies, practices and rituals are perceived as being constituted at a level of societal and intellectual organization far above and free from the local and specific social concern. Nevertheless, as an investigator who has been trained within the highest constituted levels of formal education and research of several disciplines and disciplinary interfaces, and whose motivation for entering Yiddish Studies was to meet the needs of this minority group and its scholarly enterprise, as identified by its own priorities, I recognize a blatant imperative to address such needs. Since such an effort is akin to the approach of Fishman in his own work in the sociology of language, be it in his research to identify the ethnic language resources in the United States and other societies, or to analyze minority community endeavors to reverse language shift, the framework I have chosen in which to present and critique Fishman's research on Yiddish is shaped by the parameters developed in Yiddish Studies.

During the 1990s, I was charged with redesigning the graduate curriculum in Yiddish Studies at Columbia University. One might have thought, given the burgeoning Jewish Studies programs in the United States in the 1980s, including many with full-fledged doctoral components, that Yiddish would have been provided for in that rubric. But as researchers of minority languages and cultures know too well, the neglect and oftentimes derision demonstrated towards vernacular languages and cultures reach from within the ethnic group to *di hoykhe fentster* (high society, the higher echelons). Academicians often share in the discriminatory attitudes toward the languages and cultures that nurtured them in their youth. Yiddish, the main spoken language and culture in the Jewish world during the past millennium, was relegated within the new American academic Jewish Studies programs to a single elementary course at the undergraduate level, if at all. Only a few institutions offered a second or third year at this level, and Columbia University was the only institution in the United States that had in its roster a complement of courses leading to a masters or doctoral degree in Yiddish.

Having completed the very same doctoral program in the preceding decade and with a penchant for broad-based training in any discipline and for concurrent interdisciplinary training (I had learned this proclivity with alacrity in my earlier career and training in cell and molecular biology), I set out to reform the graduate Yiddish Studies Program. My goals and targets were manifold, including a series of courses for graduate students that would encompass the broad social and cultural achievements of Yiddish throughout its history, as well as the diverse research subjects, traditions and methods that characterized the history of investigation of the language, culture and society. I was fortunate to have developed such interests and to have been exposed to the history of Yiddish research in my own training. With pride and in recognition of the deeply sensitive and well-educated graduates of the program, I can state with confidence that at that period in history Yiddish experts could be successfully trained in a program that stressed the social history of Yiddish culture over the long history of its speakers' experience, when studied through the lens of that life experience and the students' immersion in speaking and hearing Yiddish. I also worked hard at establishing linkages with other professors and researchers of Yiddish in New York to guarantee that graduate students in this small program would be exposed to the multiple perspectives of various investigators of Yiddish. Moreover, I was convinced that I must introduce Yiddish as the language of instruction in all advanced courses.

Within this framework, in my first year at Columbia, I designed a new introductory graduate course, Introduction to Yiddish Studies. It was the only offering that carried graduate credit and was designed both for students in the Yiddish Studies Program and for students in other programs. The content of the course was two-fold, to present the role of Yiddish in its social setting over its history and the history of Yiddish scholarship, the ways Yiddish has been studied, including language, literature, folklore, music, education, press and theater. There were several books and many articles required for reading, but as the main text I selected Fishman's (1981a) *Never Say Die! A Thousand Years of Yiddish in Jewish Life and Letters*. His introduction to the volume, 'The sociology of Yiddish: A forward,' 63 pages of text and 34 pages of references, constitutes the only comprehensive scholarly presentation on the history of the role of Yiddish in society that has been published up until today. It constituted the student's first introduction to Yiddish Studies and is divided into seven parts, a division that is recapitulated in the readings in the book that Fishman selected and edited: Sociohistorical perspective; Orthodoxy: Then and now; Modernization movements and modern attitudes; Historic moments; Formal institutions of language: The press, literature, theater, schools; Maintenance and shift; and Sociolinguistic variation and planning. All of Fishman's discussion and the articles in the anthology put Yiddish in center stage. The articles include academic research reports, popular essays and public addresses. Fishman (1991a: 9) himself later described the book as an attempt at popularization. But from its application and utility in the graduate course, we can see how an author cannot foresee his audience, especially at a time when the institutional settings for Yiddish were changing drastically.

The volume was quite ambitious in many of its features. Published by a major European press that featured language and linguistics, indeed the very same press that sponsored Fishman's *Contributions to the Sociology of Language* (of which this volume was the 30th in the series), no fewer than 22 of the 45 anthologized articles were reprinted from the Yiddish originals in the Yiddish alphabet. I am not familiar with another text aimed at a general audience that is divided into Yiddish and English. The format is large-dimension, coffee-table style, tallying at 763 pages and presents those features that interest Fishman, including cartoons and illustrations, along with tables of numbers that present aspects of Yiddish culture in quantitative terms. For example, Fishman's introduction contains statistics relating to Jewish libraries in Poland in the 1920s and the history of the Jewish press the world over from 1557–1920.

In a book of his anthologized essays about Yiddish that appeared ten years later, Fishman (1991b) included no fewer than 84 statistical tables. He was here meeting the demands of some members in the Jewish community who desire numbers and have difficulty finding them. A most common contemporary question is, 'how many speakers of Yiddish are there?' The downside of this statistical collection (other than the ubiquitous reservation that when '1 million French people' tell you this or that, their response to a question actually indicates the methodological quirks relating to the asking and the French attitudes to yet other issues) lies in the absence of a presentation of details or analysis of the methods that generated these numbers about Yiddish. Nevertheless, it is only Fishman who shows concern for assembling quantitative information having to do with the macrosociology of Yiddish.

For our present purposes, let it be said that Fishman has provided the field of Yiddish Studies with an exquisitely, integrated essay based on a voluminous bibliography on the changing functions of Yiddish throughout its history and within its myriad niches. His oeuvre on the sociology of Yiddish that he published at different stages of his career filled a void in the research plan for Yiddish that few even approached, and certainly not with as sustained an effort as Fishman's. These studies, as I will discuss, outline the macrosociological functions of the language, namely the appearance and uses for Yiddish in various institutions during its history in several societies, the public discourse on the role of Yiddish as outlined by several intellectual and political leaders (both religious and secular) in modern times, public events that focused on the language, and attempts to change the corpus of the language in order to meet new functions.

One may assume, although I am not certain that this should be uncritically accepted, that dominant Western languages and cultures (supported as they are by governments with budgets, legal codes and schools, and societies with media, commerce, the arts and populations that exhibit some residential continuity) can rest assured that all aspects of their existence will be examined in one way or other by social critics, students and researchers. For Yiddish and many other minority languages within Western societies, this is not necessarily the case. Being undervalued and neglected often both by agencies of the major co-territorial languages and cultures and those of its own ethnic group, it is not surprising to find that many aspects that are salient to the structure, history and function of minority languages remain unexamined. It is difficult to define the factors that determine whether a topic is researched or not. This is a question that is integral to the history of science and ideas. One generation may find a research question central to the understanding of a subject while the next generation may deem the same question obsolete, exhausted or trivial. Such determinations may depend on aesthetic, monetary or stylistic preferences of the contemporary research professionals and students within a field, to enumerate only three contingencies. Minority languages, and most especially the vernacular variants, attract only small numbers of advanced level students and researchers. Always looking over their shoulders toward the academy of the majority culture and its conventions, methods and theories, the researcher of the minority culture seldom constructs an independent list of preferred research topics. Consequently, topics that are vital to the minority community are often overlooked. Fishman, vis-à-vis Yiddish, is the exception to the rule.

Yiddish has attracted at various times advocates, *filologn,* as denoted by Borokhov, who worry that the full complement of research fields concerning language and culture is not being fulfilled. In that spirit, Max Weinreich (1923), the leading researcher of Yiddish language in the 20th century and Fishman's (1991c: 110) chief mentor in Yiddish studies, takes stock at the beginning of his first book of '*Vos mir hobn un vos undz felt*' ('what we have and what is missing'). Contemporary scholars of Yiddish limit their concerns to their own research area, and very few express alarm that vital sectors of Yiddish Studies are left fallow. Although the field of Yiddish has attracted hundreds of researchers to its ranks, it is Fishman who almost single-handedly has filled in the area of the sociology of language. Generations to come of Yiddish scholars will be indebted to him for investigating the role of Yiddish in society, for establishing theoretical constructs for asking research questions in this area, for setting standards for such research, and for opening the doors for reciprocal interests that are shared with the general discipline of the sociology of language.

Without a stable home in academia or in Jewish communal research institutions, Yiddish Studies, despite a plethora of young researchers working in the field, is ironically in greater disarray as an organized field than at any time since World War II. For example, from 1979 through 1992, four world congresses were convened to report research results in all areas of Yiddish research. During the past 13 years, no new congresses have been convened. Yivo, a community-supported library, archives and research institute devoted to Yiddish and east European Jewish Studies, no longer sponsors its own research and advanced training programs. Most alarming is that the past few years have witnessed a downturn in the opportunities to pursue advanced graduate studies in Yiddish. There is not a single graduate course on Yiddish culture in the United States today that uses both Yiddish texts and Yiddish as the language of classroom discourse. Within the world of Yiddish culture, this absence is overlooked. The cultural world of this minority language cannot muster the energies to be concerned with the lack of unified initiative and standards at these rarified levels of higher academic studies. In such a time, it comes as little surprise to find whole areas of Yiddish culture absent from the investigatory microscope.

Therefore, this current state of affairs makes the research record of Fishman on the sociology of Yiddish deserving of widespread recognition. Although other researchers have contributed isolated studies here and there, it is the more than half century experience of Joshua Fishman that has shed light on the mechanisms that operate to situate Yiddish within its social environment. Many of Fishman's analyses also provide hints to the applied workers of language within social institutions on guidelines for increasing the opportunities for Yiddish use and how to effect changes within the corpus of the language.

As far as I am aware, Fishman is the only researcher of Yiddish after World War II to articulate a research agenda for Yiddish (Fishman, 1980a, reprinted in 1981a). These research areas within the sociology of language beg for an empirical approach and remain largely untouched today, a quarter of a century later. In this project, Fishman dwelled on questions of micro-sociolinguistics – projects that he has yet to research on his own. However, his sensitivity to the needs of Yiddish within its speech community and to the gaps that remain within the research endeavors brought him to point to topics of face-to-face interaction within small groups, mechanisms for accommodation when members of different subgroups of Yiddish speakers come into contact, attitudinal expressions of beliefs and feelings within networks of religious Orthodox speakers as their world undergoes change, documentation of an altering world view of Yiddishist intellectuals, and the flux in the multilingualism and language shift of

Yiddish speakers. In the above-mentioned intellectual exercise, Fishman displays his creativity as well as his concern for a research field that he recognizes is potentially much larger and more diverse than the one that he himself dominates within the sociology of Yiddish. To date, the only book-length micro-sociolinguistic study to have appeared, since his call for new empirical evidence relating to spoken Yiddish and attitudes toward Yiddish expressed by its speakers, is my own (Peltz, 1998).

The small size of the Yiddish research world and the vulnerability of its structure and organization to deliver in a consistent and continuous fashion new generations of well-informed scholars, who are knowledge-able about the history of Yiddish scholarship and who can explore and teach the wide world of culture, thought and behavior that have accompa-nied Yiddish throughout its history, stand out when compared to the dependable and ever-changing innovative efforts of Joshua Fishman in his explorations within the realm of the sociology of Yiddish. Fishman's work can be appreciated in recent years to a greater extent since it is in starker contrast with the rest of the field of Yiddish, which sets its gaze largely on the written literature of Yiddish, the culture that can be located within the covers of books, rather than in the streets, the kitchen, the study hall, the synagogue or the nursery.

Although the reviews we possess about the history of Yiddish scholar-ship in its breadth have largely overlooked or minimized Fishman's contri-bution (cf. Althaus, 1972; Katz, 1986; Novershtern, 1989), in 1999 he was the recipient of the prestigious Yiddish literary Manger Prize in Tel-Aviv. The jury specifically stated that he was awarded the prize in recognition of 'his outstanding contribution to research on Yiddish and its status amongst Jews over the generations.' However, only one of the five undersigned members of the jury was an academically-trained scholar. Very few of the Manger laureates over the years were researchers. This award represented recognition of Fishman from the world of contemporary Yiddish literati.[1]

While reviewing the writings of Fishman that relate to Yiddish, I must also point to the looming influence he has wielded on Yiddish research by his support of publications on Yiddish by other researchers, especially younger ones, in the journal he edits, as well as in the books that he and his colleagues edit. He is always looking for opportunities that juxtapose Yiddish with other languages and cultures in such a manner that benefits all the relevant research efforts. I have profited from such opportunities, as have countless others. This contribution of Fishman to the field of Yiddish research is more difficult to measure than the lessons that have been learned from his diverse and numerous publications on Yiddish, but is just as significant.

Fishman's Yiddish Research Oeuvre

The research results I have chosen to review are scattered through a complexity of publications. What should I consider as material that focuses on Yiddish, that reveals an understanding of processes involved within the Yiddish speaking, reading, writing, acting and praying communities, and that constitutes a research report? I will outline the sources I have selected and point to ones that I have overlooked for one reason or other.

In a class by itself is Fishman's intellectual biography of Nathan Birnbaum, a study that is not only book length, but also one that contains the facets of scholarship and evaluation that characterize Fishman's attraction to language ideology vis-à-vis Yiddish. There are so many subjects here that uncover Fishman's fascination with theory and ideological loyalty as he traces Birnbaum's pilgrimages in social activism in the Jewish community. Issues of politics and religion dominate Birnbaum's life, but Fishman never takes his eye off of Birnbaum's language advocacy. There are unavoidable parallels to be drawn between the two lives, that of the language ideologue and his biographer. In this discussion, I will also introduce the research on the first Yiddish conference in Tshernovits, a study to which Fishman keeps returning and which led him to Birnbaum. At this point I will also make comparisons with Fishman's other biographical studies.

The second class of studies is the larger research projects on language resources in the United States that Fishman (1966, 1985a) executed and in which the collection of data on Yiddish was an integral part. For the field of Yiddish it is valuable to place Yiddish in the comparative context of other languages and cultures. With its emphasis on institutions and language, I would include here the monograph on *Yiddish in America* (Fishman, 1965).

Although a smaller context for Fishman's research on Yiddish, I would also want to discuss his approach of seeing Yiddish as only one of many Jewish languages. He is not the primary investigator of Jewish inter-linguistics, the comparative study of languages other than the Hebrew and Aramaic of the prayer book, Bible and Talmud, that Jewish communities evolved locally the world over (cf. Weinreich, 1973/1980; Wexler, 1981). But Fishman's view of the whole lot, his collection of comparative data within Israeli society, his theoretical grasp of the subtleties of diglossia and origins, all render his analysis of Yiddish, as one among other post-exilic Jewish languages, a significant contribution to Yiddish Studies and to the study of diglossia as a rich source for all linguistic investigation.

A less pervasive topic throughout Fishman's more than half century of Yiddish research is the relation between language and religion. Although the pre-history of his Yiddish research, starting even before his doctoral research, is situated in secular Jewish settings, much of the early data for analysis of Yiddish comes from the examination of language resources in religious schools (Fishman, 1965a). Eventually this focus meanders through the diglossic relationships of the secular and religious roles of Yiddish vis-à-vis other languages, explorations of Yiddish within the worlds of ultra-Orthodox and modern Orthodox religious communities, the anchor for the spiritual and communal religious adherence of Birnbaum, and ultimately leads to the possible implications of these observations for a full-blown analysis of holy languages.

The pivotal point in Fishman's careers, both in the sociology of language and the sociology of Yiddish, was the three years during which he resided in Jerusalem in the early 1970s and directed the Ford-Foundation-sponsored International Research Project on Language Planning Processes (Fishman, 1991c: 116–17). I would argue that Fishman as polymath, if pinned down to one subspecialty, should be identified as the student of language planning. The theoretical and methodological underpinnings of this applied field divide the processes into non-analogous but overlapping divisions of status and corpus planning, as well as into discrete stages of planning, implementation and evaluation. With regards to Yiddish, Fishman's work involves itself largely with early status planning stages, the first congress and aquisition of new functions that are viewed with respect in a changing modern society. However, he does not divorce himself from the corpus that he loves and uses daily. I will visit his rarer analyses of corpus planning, most specifically orthography.

As I introduce the publications, let me tackle right off the dimensions of language choice and style. To paraphrase the *bal-yoyvl* ('the jubilee celebrant himself'), 'what language does Joshua Fishman write to whom, when, where and about what, as he writes about Yiddish?' I have included Fishman's oeuvre on Yiddish research in all languages. If it is a significant part of the research literature on Yiddish, it belongs here. Popular accounts that do not reflect rigorous empirical or theoretical investigation, or do not present references to the research literature are omitted. Still, it is noteworthy that Fishman has been a regular contributor in Yiddish to two publications based in New York City, the quarterly *Afn shvel* (*On the Threshold*) where he writes a column *'Ume veloshn'* (*'Peoplehood and Language'*) and the weekly tabloid newspaper *Forverts* (*Forward*). The writings in *Afn shvel* are largely popular distillations of research results, most often replete with references. In the *Forverts*, the treatments are shorter and without references. Although this body of Fishman's sustained writing in and about Yiddish will on the whole be overlooked, in a few instances the unique view Fishman presents on sociolinguistic issues and the outlet provided for his research results seems significant enough. His desire is to influence directions within the Jewish community he is researching, by speaking to this minority about minority-language issues within minority-language publications. When it seems important to do so, I include selected analyses from this literature in my discussion.

Readers of Fishman's voluminous writings in English on the sociology of language are familiar with his recognizable language style, which engages the reader in a way that sociological or linguistic treatments fail to do. The techniques he uses create suspense, challenge the reader, often by means of neologisms and new phrase combinations that are intriguing and mark the issue at hand as far from pedestrian. Fishman's writing style brands the ideas as uniquely his, but also signals a non-typical academic felicity that attracts the reader's attention and respect. His articles written in Yiddish may in many cases be characterized as popular science. He treats his audience to short treatises on the societal applications of research into myriad languages and cultures, their legal status, their political struggles to reverse language shift, the similarities and differences that are experienced by their speakers in situations that are comparable to those in Jewish societies, as well as explorations of the cultural repercussions of linguistic questions that have largely been neglected. Even more than his writing in English, Fishman's Yiddish style is engaging and attractive and peculiarly recognizable as his own. Perhaps influenced by his mentor Max Weinreich, who had a masterful Yiddish style that was folksy and colloquial even in its academic garb, Fishman surpassed Weinreich in becoming a supreme stylist of the Yiddish essay. In the post-World War II realm of Yiddish literature, there is no one who can match this. Long sentences laden with conceptual complexity appeal to an intellectual reader in a fashion to which the lay Yiddish reader is unaccustomed. During this period of history, literary criticism was still preoccupied with belles-lettres, poetry and prose, to the neglect of the essay. For the record, I deem Fishman a master stylist of the Yiddish essay. A collection of his Yiddish essays in book form would serve as a corrective to the current neglect of this genre of Yiddish literature. To the credit of the editor of the 100-volume Yiddish language set *Musterverk fun der yidisher literatur* (*Exemplary Works of Yiddish Literature*), an essay by Fishman was included in the single volume devoted to the essay (see Fishman, 1982, reprinted in Rozhanski, 1984).

Ales in eynem iz nito ba keynem
('No one person can embody all attributes,' Yiddish proverb)

The centrality of the Birnbaum study

The Yiddish reader caught an early glimpse of the odyssey of Nathan Birnbaum, as chronicled by Fishman (1983a, 1985b, 1985c) a few years before the book-length study appeared. Although not a well-known historical figure in Jewish circles, Birnbaum's role as the architect of the first Yiddish conference, known as the *Tshernovitser konferents* (The Tshernovitz

Conference), was familiar to Yiddish readers. Fishman was of course taking a new look at that historic milestone, but he was going to jolt his readers' knowledge of history by pointing to Birnbaum's other incarnations – first as a founder of modern cultural Zionism before Herzl in the late 19th century, and his later third phase as a leader of the non-Zionist religious Orthodox Right. For the typical Yiddish reader, these intricate transformations could certainly be confusing. The readers in the Yiddish publications for which Fishman writes are largely secular Jews. It could be difficult for them to imagine the ideological and life-style switches that Birnbaum made in less than 20 years. But in his matter-of-fact style, propped up by facts, figures and documents, Fishman can surprise his Jewish audience while he educates them and gently nudges them with a historical sensitivity mixed with a contemporary flavor.

For his English readership, scholars of the sociology of language and Jewish intellectual history, the messages received and interpreted from the book (Fishman, 1987a) can only be more complex and challenging. Even the Jewish cultural historians who study Eastern Europe at the beginning of the 20th century had neglected Birnbaum, the man who coined the term 'Zionism,' launched the first Yiddish conference, and was the first leader of the post-World War I politically organized Jewish Orthodoxy (*Agudes yisroel*, 'Union of Israel'). In this single work, we find almost all aspects of Fishman's interests in issues relating to Yiddish, minority languages and language sociology. On the other hand, clearer than in any other work, we see the turning to spiritual issues, the implication that, if not through religious creed, then at least through weapons of the spirit, the language crusader seeks to point society on a path leading to a just and equitable society. Keeping his compass on language, Fishman is searching through history and biography to explain the credo of the language nationalist, the elite leader who brings the minority group to a position of self-respect and cultural equity and creativity. The figure of Birnbaum is cast in the mold of the language idealogue that Borokhov called a language nationalist, a leader of the nation. Despite his admission that there are similarities between himself and Birnbaum, Fishman (1987a: 133-34) underscores the differences. However, the reader cannot avoid the likeness shared by Birnbaum, the minority language advocate and activist, and Fishman. Fishman is the scholar par excellence who studies such languages from a vantage point that argues for the societal advantages reaped from cultivating a multiplicity of languages and cultures.

In this single work on Birnbaum, I located almost all the topics Fishman has studied that relate to Yiddish: the early stages of language planning, the function of language elites, the interrelation between language and organized politics, between language and organized religion, between language and ideological commitment in general, and between language and matters of religious faith. The historical time and place Fishman chose for this signature study, the years preceding and immediately following World War I in Eastern Europe, were home to the most variegated and concentrated cultural change processes to occur within world Jewry's largest community. The first years of this period witnessed a Jewish leadership that was turning away from political, revolutionary activity in Russia because the government's forces had reacted strongly to the revolution of 1905 with repressive recrimination. The young revolutionary leaders put energies instead into education and cultural construction for the masses. Towards the end of this period, the Russian Revolution and the Treaty of Versailles gave hope that Eastern Europe would arise in the form of new political entities that would constitute its minorities into well-organized autonomously functioning subunits. Throughout these years, Jews were migrating out of the traditional *shtetl* ('townlet') into the big city, accompanied by secularizing influences that would shake and test the well organized, traditional Jewish life that was regulated by religion. It was against this panorama that Nathan Birnbaum unfolded his beliefs and convictions.

There can be no question but that Fishman's volume on Birnbaum is a major addition to Jewish Studies scholarship. This is a volume of intellectual history, the presentation of one man's ideas in a social and historical context. Birnbaum is a leader who deals with big ideas that serve to solve the problems of the nation, in this case, of the Jewish people. Fishman (1987a: 8) calls his work socio-biography, ' a biography that stresses the social and historical circumstances that shape a person's life.' Furthermore, he asks whether a biography can be:

> Written almost entirely in societal terms, exploring societal issues and processes as much as or even more so than individual ones. Can an individual's life inform our understanding of his or her time and place, as much as the latter are often invoked in order to inform the former? (Fishman, 1987: 8)

I still view biography as a genre that treats the whole life, built on the pivotal influence of family of origin, the relations developed through family and friendship and the self-examination by the subject. Fishman (1991c: 123) has called his Birnbaum book 'a full-blown biography of a "language leader."' But he also questions whether the genre can be legitimately fulfilled without any psychological analysis (Fishman, 1987a: 8). No one will find the full-bodied Birnbaum in the biography, not his sighs nor his smiles, not his intimate moments nor the private drama that accompanies public appearances, not his lusts nor his revulsions. I would nevertheless encourage the reader to perform a content analysis of the text from cover to cover. Each section illustrates the ambitious goals of the author, and be it true biography or not, these essays are all recognizably Fishmanesque.

The structure of the volume

Opening the volume on Birnbaum is a foreward by two of the world's leading sociolinguists, Charles A. Ferguson and Shirley Brice Heath, who literally stood with Fishman and his wife Gella at Birnbaum's gravesite in the Netherlands. Inviting readers to learn about their own stance on issues of 'ideology, society and language' by becoming familiar with Birnbaum's ideas, these eminent participants underscore Fishman's talent for making the greater world and specifically its academy take notice of Jewish society, its issues and heroes. Following this, in the first half of the book Fishman describes Birnbaum's ideological formulations (especially those having to do with language) during his three periods of divergent but continuous leadership of European Jewry. The second half of the biography includes 15 articles by Birnbaum, translated from German and Yiddish into English. They were published over a span of 45 years (1886–1931). These all have to do with language ideology, the preference of both Birnbaum and Fishman and certainly a uniting theme, but do not reflect the entire universe of Birnbaum's concerns in those years. But to deal with the whole Birnbaum, *mit ales in eynem* (all together in one) would be too much for any one book.

In addition, Fishman painstakingly identified pictures, including photographs of Birnbaum, from the same years that the early Birnbaum articles were written (see Fishman 1987a: pp. 142–44). The emphasis on the visual, including symbolic and esthetic elements through the analysis of cartoons, has been an instructive aspect of Fishman's research on modern Jewry. The biography ends with 31pages of a glossary, composed of paragraph-length entries on sociolinguistic terms, Jewish and non-Jewish leaders and political parties, and terms in German, Hebrew and Yiddish. It is here that we see the grandest accomplishment of Fishman's research on Yiddish, his outreach to audiences: those who know nothing of Yiddish and those who do, those who know nothing of Jewish history, customs and beliefs and those who do, those who know no sociolinguistics and those who do. Which other researcher casts such a wide net? Accordingly, in analyzing Fishman's work on Yiddish, the brilliance of his approach becomes evident when we witness the range of readers to whom he is addressing his work on certain subjects at any given instance.

Birnbaum's phases

The progression of Birnbaum's ideological positions becomes clear as he moves through his three phases, the divisions that Fishman followed in the original separate articles he published before he wrote the book. But the transition phases between stages and the overlapping elements that linger from stage to stage show that Birnbaum had contemporaries who espouse the same positions as his. This holds for the early period of Zionism before political Zionism took over in 1897, as well as for the years before World War I when architects of Jewish cultural autonomy advocated for Yiddish and Yiddish culture. Birnbaum was also not alone after World War I, when he ascribed to an organized Orthodoxy that did not embrace Zionism. But he was the only leader to embrace all three positions. And although there were Zionist leaders other than Birnbaum who became advocates of Yiddish-based nationalism, there were no leaders of the secular Yiddishist position to transform themselves into leaders of European religious Orthodoxy.

As Fishman traces Birnbaum's views on Jewish languages, we follow Fishman at his strongest. In the early days of cultural Zionism, Birnbaum was like other Zionist activists, convinced that European Jews could retrieve their nationalist sentiments by way of Hebrew, the language of the Bible and of biblical times, not through Yiddish, the more recent language of European Jews, called by Fishman (1987a: 19), 'that hoarse child of the ghetto.' Yet even when he advocated for Hebrew, he recognized that the Zionist movement was unsuccessful at teaching its followers the language, and that included the few European masters of Hebrew who were assimilationists and those who opposed Zionism's nationalist goals (Fishman, 1987a: 21).

Consistently, Birnbaum stood out for his ability to recognize and speak about the weaknesses in his own camp. Having been a cultural Zionist, from 1898 Birnbaum ceased being involved in the movement led by Theodore Herzl that became increasingly engaged in world politics. In Birnbaum's second phase, until World War I, he familiarized himself with the mass of East European Jews and worked for Jewish cultural autonomy and the appreciation of the role of Yiddish. In those years, he was one of many intellectual and cultural leaders doing the same. However, Birnbaum was the initiator of the first Yiddish language conference in Tshernovits in 1908 and of the organization to implement a program of action on its behalf in subsequent years. He remained in the Austro-Hungarian Empire (Tshernovits and Vienna), where there was much scholarly, political and publishing effort in Yiddish directed at the masses in the Russian Empire, since such work was prohibited at that time in Russia. It was during these years that language issues dominated Birnbaum. From one angle, working for Yiddish heralded a Jewish future in Eastern Europe based on cultural autonomy for all minorities. From another viewpoint, the cultivation and expansion of roles for Yiddish inevitably raised the level of education and cultural awareness amongst the masses. Birnbaum was in good company in this work, including in the struggle for listing Yiddish as a language in the census, to represent the largest concentration of Jews in Austria, those within the former Polish and adjacent regions of Galicia (Fishman, 1987a: 211–17). The language and culture nationalists had their eyes on a future time when, after all the empires would be gone, the Jews and their neigh-boring minorities would be administering their own affairs in their own language within newly constituted multi-ethnic states organized on the premise of cultural autonomy. With regard to the competing linguistic ideologies that supported either Yiddish or Hebrew as the dominant national Jewish language, Birnbaum managed to make room for both – Hebrew in its non-vernacular forms and Yiddish as the creative vernacular that provided for the new cultural autonomy. Both languages, according to him, served as a bulwark against assimilation (Fishman, 1987a: 32-34).

The most unique transformation was Birnbaum's move into the third phase. This is not simply an ideological move, or a new conviction relating to the needs of the Jewish people. It required a personal faith, but also a substantial transformation for him and his family in their behavior and practices. As an observant Jew, he must eat, dress and pray in a distinctive manner, on a daily basis (Fishman, 1987a: 73). Fishman (1987a: 35) cannot help us trace the transition to phase three, other than to recognize that in 1912 Birnbaum wrote about 'the absolute Jewish idea' and that his reaction to the destructive world war brought him closer to belief in the Almighty. Rejecting both the establishment of a Zionist state and the idea of cultural autonomy in the diaspora, he called for (1) the establishment of small settle-ments of Orthodox Jews devoted to their uniquely Jewish habits and beliefs, and (2) later the political organization of Orthodox Jews (Fishman, 1987a: 74, 77). Although Fishman agrees that this third phase is the least language-focused of the three, he brings us only three writings for this phase, all discussing language. Birnbaum argues in 1919 that Jews need their holy tongue, Hebrew, and the language of hundreds of years of life in Eastern Europe, Yiddish, which is infused with Jewishness. But another factor of greater importance appears:

> We love both languages, Hebrew and Yiddish, each with a different love. But we also realize that before this love comes the love of 'You shall love the Lord, your God.' We realize that 'He has lifted us above all languages,' indeed, that He has made us higher than language *per se* (Fishman, 1987a: 234–35).

In the other texts, Birnbaum even more clearly identifies that advocacy of Yiddish alone is not enough. In his retrospective analysis of the Tshernovits Conference (1931), he reveals that Jewish tradition and religion are the incubators of Yiddish. He warns against the attempts of the radical Yiddishist secularists to ignore the contributions of religious life. He refers to his transformation, to finding the way to the foundations of Jewish belief and observance and to those Jews who are religious, the sector of Jewish life he deems most authentic and most responsible for the origin and creativity of the Yiddish language:

At the time of the Conference, I did not foresee (nor could I have fore-seen) this. But today, as a result of my return to the Torah and to the Jews who cannot live without it, I observe with mounting apprehen-sion how the radical parties attempt to monopolize the Yiddish language for their own purposes. In so doing, they have driven a wedge between Yiddish and the mass of religious Jews – the original and truthful creators of Yiddish – and, thereby, they have placed Yiddish in jeopardy of being sundered from its life-giving sources, of losing its own linguistic authenticity, its true Jewish nature, its vivid colors. (Fishman, 1987a: 243)

Birnbaum goes even further, writing in the same year in the journal of his movement's schools for girls. Turning the phrase 'dark forces,' on its head, a term usually used to refer to reactionary religious forces, he applies it to the non-believing scholars. Birnbaum managed to reject the defenders of Jewish languages at that time, who had not swayed much from the posi-tions he himself had once held, the secular Yiddishists and the secular Hebraists. Yiddish is valuable, according to Birnbaum, in his third phase:

> because it is saturated with the very essence of the Jewish soul. Further-more, what a difference between their Yiddish and our Yiddish, the Yiddish that is saturated with Jewish soul! Without *yidishkayt* the very flavor of Yiddish is lost, just as the holiness of the Holy Tongue is evap-orated. (Fishman, 1987a: 245)

Birnbaum's work, Fishman's work

In the texts that Fishman selected and from his attempts to comprehend Birnbaum's life and thought, we find themes for many of Fishman's writ-ings in English and Yiddish in future years – themes such as the connection between language and faith, concepts of authenticity of language, and the necessity of Jews to maintain primary institutions that nurture their ethnic mother tongue on a daily basis. But the conclusion that Fishman comes to from the model of Birnbaum as language architect is more telling. Birnbaum, in all his phases, was up to something more than just advocating for language, for his people and for himself. He did not switch haphazardly from one ideology to the next. Rather, he was always searching for deeper, broader meaning.

Fishman sees this trend, of goals grander than those that are just language-based, as part of the fate of most language ideologists:

> The majority of language ideologists ... are early and easily 'led astray' into philosophy, politics or culture-planning more generally. For most of them language is no more than a symbol, an index and a part of a far greater and more fundamental *something else*, often something more

tangibly instrumental than language alone. It was definitely usually so for Birnbaum. His constant quest, both in terms of underlying ideology and as an expression of basic personality, was for Jewish ethno-religious self-determination and continuity. Language was an important aspect of this more general and never-ending quest, sometimes highlighted and sometimes in the background, but always only part of the story. (Fishman, 1987a: 125–26)

I would expand this beyond the case of the language ideologist to all connections to ethnic mother tongue. Those who study the subject and those who feel the draw to the subject in their private lives know that on all levels, from unit to universe, or from individual to ethnic group, language is keyed to identity, personal identification and group solidarity. Those of us who study language planning, for example, know well that these processes are tied to all of social planning and social change. And those of us who help awaken ethnic language revitalization in individuals are told that we have stirred up fundamental processes of self-identification (*'Di host zey dermant vus zeym gehat, in zey hobm dus nisht yetst. Dus iz zeyer harts,'* 'You reminded them of that which they had, and they don't have now. That is their heart') (Peltz, 1998: 182). Birnbaum cared about language, but he also cared about the continuity of Jewish life in Europe. They were linked. It is not surprising that he was a deeply spiritual individual who eventually saw that religious faith and observance were necessities for group survival. Fishman's devotion to the fate of minority languages and cultures stems from his passion for his mother tongue, Yiddish, and his concern for Jewish survival. His work is rich precisely because his in-depth study of language phenomena leads him to the social linkages of religion, politics, cultural expression and myriad institutions. His fascination with Birnbaum reflects the premise that his own research results have revealed for years, that language is inherently enmeshed in society. Therefore, the language advocate and the language researcher must always be committed to language plus something more.

The Tshernovits Conference

It was Fishman's research on the first Yiddish language conference that actually led him to the study of Birnbaum, its architect. However, the biography also uncovered for Fishman a deeper knowledge of all aspects of the conference. At this point, I will take the opportunity to evaluate the gleanings from all his work on the Tshernovits Conference. For the past quarter of a century, what we might call the 'second phase' of Fishman's research on Yiddish, the conference has been the most recurring theme in his writings. It was not Fishman who claimed the discovery of the topic for Yiddish research and letters. From the historical moment of the conference onwards, there was wide coverage in the press, and the symbolic strength of the first conference was recognized by those concerned about the fate of Yiddish, both supporters and opponents, as well as those occupied with Yiddish scholarship. To this day, journal issues and conferences are organized to mark its anniversary. For example, following the twentieth anniversary, Yivo, the Yiddish Research Institute in Vilna, published a volume of various documents and commentaries related to the conference (*Di ershte* ... 1931). A book-length study in English, organized as an evaluation of the four leaders of the conference (Birnbaum, Mieses, Perets, and Zhitlovski) appeared before Fishman's first article (Goldsmith, 1976). Fishman, as journal editor, invited a young scholar to publish his research on the conference in the *International Journal of the Sociology of Language* (Rothstein, 1977). But in the words of Schaechter, the eminent Yiddish language planner and historian of Yiddish language planning, and himself a native of the city of Tshernovits:

> Fishman's paper ... touched me profoundly. I can't remember ever having read a scholarly paper that so completely changed my outlook as did Fishman's on the Tshernovits Conference. The fact that this paper also addressed general sociolinguistic concerns further intensified my high regard for it. (Schechter, 1991: x)

Fishman's (1980b, reprinted in 1981, 1982, 1991) first paper interprets the conference within the schemata of diglossia and language planning. Detractors would point to the lack of success and absence of any palpable change that resulted from post-conference planning by working groups to engineer the tools of corpus planning and standardization: dictionaries, grammars, terminologies, orthographic rules. Fishman, on the other hand, underlined the perceived achievements in status planning. The conference helped bring to the fore and legitimize new H functions (high status and more formalized societal functions) for Yiddish, positions that would be shared with Hebrew and Aramaic, which had monopolized such functions throughout European Jewish history. Those functions largely involved Yiddish as a language of diverse publications and of public spoken forums for a new secular Jewish culture, including the growing Yiddish press and theater. In addition, Yiddish had never before been perceived and described publicly as a bona fide linguistic structure that is a vehicle for all aspects of culture. Such status was dignified by the participation of the assembled intellectual and cultural elite. Fishman clearly underscored the achievement of 'attracting a following to high culture functions' for a language that had heretofore been perceived strictly as 'a language of everyday life.' Those high culture functions had been struggled over during the previous half-century, but this historic public conference in 1908 made manifest the conviction that those high positions that were fought for would not disappear.

Fishman, moreover, besides having achieved a more complete understanding of the symbolic significance and history of the conference and its leaders, was able to home in on aspects of the conference that helped to clarify for him the role of that conference particularly and of first conferences in general in the forward march of minority languages within their political and cultural surroundings. *'Oyb me ken nit di mamoshes fun an inyen, ken men oykh di simbolik derfun beemes nit masig zayn'* ('If one does not understand the nitty-gritty facts of a subject, one will also not be able to grasp its symbolism') (Fishman, 1994a: 1). These studies appeared in both Yiddish and English for Fishman's diverse audiences. The role of the city of Tshernovits itself had to be explained. For Birnbaum, at first, it was the local group of young university students who became his proponents and promoters in the pre-conference years that encouraged him. But, in the years following the conference before World War I, Tshernovits became Birnbaum's site of dejection and failure. Here he became materially and financially impoverished, and here he failed to set up a functioning headquarters for a world-wide Yiddishist movement. His detailed agenda of practical goals was full, but the movement had no mode of achieving them (Fishman, 2003). This multilingual, multi-bordered provincial town in Bukovina could attract the attention of both Eastern and Western European Jews in a way that the larger Jewish population centers of the Austro-Hungarian Empire, Kruke (Cracow) and Lemberik (Lviv) could not.

Fishman's (1988a) research also identified Tshernovits as the site for two other 'conferences' in which Birnbaum participated. As early as 1905, Birnbaum came from Vienna to Tshernovits by invitation and, in German, actually outlined all the goals for Yiddish that would occupy the later conference of 1908. The third 'conference' in Tshernovits was the protest march of 1910 before the implementation of the census, which was constructed so as to disallow the Jewish declaration of Yiddish as *Umgangssprache* (language of everyday use). Birnbaum organized and led the march, reported in the press to have attracted 10,000 marchers, to this day still the largest public manifestation for Yiddish in its millennial history. But the symbolic moment that remained prevalent in Jewish collective consciousness was the 1908 conference, even though it did not lead to immediate enhancement of status or corpus for Yiddish in Birnbaum's post-conference years in Tshernovits.

As a supplemental study, Fishman (1988b) was the first to analyze the response to the conference in the Hebrew-language press. Hebrew was the competitor language in the Jewish world then, a period known as the war of the languages. Both languages were competing to fill the relatively new H functions created by secularization of a traditional society. Linked to this war were the complex political struggles of the Jewish diaspora nationalist parties and the Zionist nationalist parties, together with those with overlapping interests. Fishman showed that some of the Hebrew-language response to the 1908 conference was positive, whereas another sector reacted with the familiar denigrating attitude regarding the upstart vernacular.

Fishman's deliberations on the conference for more than 20 years have been especially fruitful for his Yiddish research and for the sociology of language. As a social critic of Jewish historical development in the 20th century, Fishman's is a lone voice, but the strongest one regarding changing roles for Yiddish in Jewish society.

Fishman's ruminations over the Tshernovits Conference have also led to his comprehension of broad trends in Jewish societal development, politics and history in the 20th century. Poised as the chronicler of a language and culture whose center was practically erased from the face of the earth by Hitler's Germany, his reflections on the conference have brought us a poetry that paints the conference and its symbolic value into the tapestry of history:

> Many of the leading figures who attended the conference ultimately lost their lives as victims of Hitlerism or of Stalinism and the masses on whose behalf they labored were burned, gassed or otherwise scattered to the four corners of the world. Thus, the conference is reminiscent of a time when the world was still whole and when millions still spoke, read, wrote and dreamed in Yiddish. (Fishman, 1993a: 329)

Within Fishman's writings, seldom is the reader left mired in the feeling of dejection that a minority-language activist like Fishman must often experience. Such an emotional state did peek through in the understated conclusion he tendered upon evaluating the conference achievements from an 85-year perspective: 'In the Yiddish case, history has proved to be much more punishing than an ineffective conference alone could ever be' (Fishman, 1993a: 330).

For the general sociology of language, Fishman's (1993b) research on Birnbaum and the Tshernovits Conference led directly to his introducing the comparative study of first language conferences into the discipline. Fishman has acknowledged the general influence of his intimate involvement from birth, not only in an everyday Yiddish-language environment but also in an ideologically-committed Yiddishist family. Moreover, his trajectory, from Tshernovits Conference to Birnbaum, back to the Tshernovits Conference, to the general first congress phenomenon, clearly illustrates the way that the discipline of the sociology of language is indebted to Fishman's life-long sensitivity to the state of Yiddish and to his research on Yiddish. From the vantage point of the reviewers of his life-long contributions to the sociology of language and to Yiddish Studies, the editors of the current volume can trust Fishman's (1991c: 115) words, that 'hardly a day has passed during the past half-century that I have not re-examined the world of Yiddish in order to help me formulate an hypothesis or scrutinize an idea.'

Fishman's (1993c: 4–5, 1993d: 343–344) experience in carefully studying Tshernovits, as a place and time in Jewish and European history, led him to apply the quantitative approach he values and practices to construct graphs and tables that illustrate the context for first conferences, such as their continental distribution and convening dates. It is singularly characteristic of him to correlate and display such data in this manner. Although he calls these congresses 'the pre-stage,' his earlier, fuller analysis of the Tshernovits Conference has shown this actually to be the end of the pre-stage. If the early stages of Yiddish language planning occurred within organized commissions involved in both corpus and status planning after World War I, then the conference of 1908 culminates a pre-stage that extends back a half-century through many examples of cultural innovations in Yiddish, involving unorganized groups of writers, actors, researchers and educators, before there was a public conference or manifestation for Yiddish. This is evident from the nuanced, historical research of Fishman (1993a) and others.

For the sociologist of language I would add a reminder that organized, self-conscious, societal language planning usually comes after a long period of unorganized activation within the speech and culture community. These innate processes of standardization in ways stretching over long histories are themselves part of the history of language and culture and not just the narrower history of language and social planning. The interrelationship between the indigenous process and the deliberate procedure is a fascinating subject to explore. Fishman's work on the Tshernovits Conference and related topics points to the value of this approach, looking both back and forward in history from 1908.

I will quote from Fishman (1993c: 7) to summarize the motivations and agendas that unite the first mothers and fathers and congresses of language planning. The language illustrates his skill with words and the subtleties of connotation; he encapsulates processes in a nutshell and finds similarities even in situations such as these that in some cases were hardly congresses at all, and in congresses such as Tshernovits that manifested more dissension than consensus. In Fishman's words:

> They have organized to provide their vernaculars with greater longevity and to assure them the most prestigious functions (or co-functions) of their respective sociocultural establishments. In order to discharge these functions appropriately, these people and peoples have organized to make their vernaculars more all encompassing, more standardized in grammar, spelling and even pronunciation, freer

of influences or 'contamination' from other languages (particularly, from historically contra-indicated languages), more in accord with a model of the language characteristic of a particularly favored geographic region, social stratum or historical period. (Fishman, 1993c: 7)

If Tshernovits provided Fishman with the specific case that led to the general, an approach he follows in his research, he deserves credit for being able to extract usable generalizations from the comparison of disparate phenomena. He does not cover up the fact that after the work was done, the 'First Congresses' proved to be more diverse than in his initial conception of the project (Fishman, 1993d: 333). Language variation studies have become the mainstay of sociolinguistics. Fishman (1980a) has helped to put such analysis on the agenda of Yiddish research. Referring to these congresses, he writes:

> I, for one, being accustomed to the study of variation in social and in language behavior, am neither surprised nor disappointed ... For the first time, we now have enough papers on different first congresses so that these kinds of variance can be analyzed rather than either simply ignored (out of ignorance) or merely bemoaned. (Fishman, 1993d: 333–34)

Biography

Although I have addressed the kind of biography writing Fishman engaged in when he published his Birnbaum study, this is an opportunity to examine other articles that are essentially biographic. In writing about Zhitlovski, a Yiddish language ideologue who was a contemporary of Birnbaum, Fishman (2001a: 145) states, 'the sociology of Jewish languages has far too few heroes who have successfully made the transition to the general sociology of languages.' Fishman's goal is, accordingly, to introduce the larger academic field to the Jewish language leaders. Without a doubt, the primary hero and leader is Fishman, himself.

His article on Zhitlovski does not go further than his book on Birnbaum. We learn little of the private Zhitlovski. In fact the major generalization from his analysis of Zhitlovki is that here too we find advocacy, not of a language alone, but language together with something else and part of something larger, in this case, socialism. When Zhitlovski developed his Yiddishism in 1904, such advocacy was revolutionary in socialist circles. For Zhitlovski, 'national ... equality for Jews required recognition, utilization and cultivation of their mother tongue, Yiddish' (Fishman, 2001a: 148). But Fishman (2001a: 152), although admiring Zhitlovski's consistent devotion to Yiddish and socialism, in actuality is critical of the limitations of his 'single prism' of socialism plus Yiddish. The lesson that we learn from this study is that the language advocates of Jewish languages and of languages in general need to make room for many ideologies and philosophies.

Fishman's oeuvre demonstrates this because he presents language as extensively embedded in society.

Although we are treated only to the ideas of Zhitlovski and not to Zhitlovski the man, as with Birnbaum, we search for the broader understanding that Fishman must have about the personalities of language advocates. We find this briefly in his 'sociolinguistic appreciation' of Uriel Weinreich (Fishman, 1997a: 312), where he links their shared approach in which they 'intellectualized ... (their) initial interest in Yiddish ... (and) our involvement with Yiddish never ceased.' However, the only critical eye on the motivation for the work of language activist or scholar is found in his reflection on his own career. It is here that Fishman (1991c) traces his sociolinguistic interest to his family environment when he was growing up, including his involvement and ease with writing. His proclivity towards multidisciplinary approaches is connected to his training and is reflected in his evaluation of the life and work of language activists. Moreover, his focus on the periphery and minor languages in much of his work grows from his dominating involvement ideologically and practically with Yiddish. It is evident that when involved in his own autobiography Fishman is ready to delve into private moments, but not so in his look at language ideologues, such as Birnbaum and Zhitlovski.

Language Resources in the United States

Although quite accomplished in myriad facets of the sociology of language, Fishman (1966) may be best remembered for his first major study in the field, *Language Loyalty in the United States*. This landmark study established the comparative field of language maintenance of immigrants and their descendants. For a minority, such as the Jews, and for a minority vernacular, such as Yiddish, it is possible that history will judge this research to be the most significant of all Fishman's contributions. Minorities want to be included in the story of the larger society, not written out of history. The worst situation is that of being neglected. For the peoples on the periphery, even if their numbers are low, it is a consolation to know that they are counted. For American Jews who had largely 'forgotten' to give public recognition to their mother tongue, Yiddish, and for researchers of Yiddish and American Jewry, Fishman provided numbers relating to mother tongue maintenance that could be compared with that of other groups. I will not enumerate all the relevant investigations, but amongst other things they revealed that Yiddish was in the 'big six' claimants both in the census of 1940 and that of 1960. However, in those 20 years it experienced a 45% loss of claimants, while Spanish, for example, experienced an increase of 73% (Fishman, 1966: 44). Second- and third-generation claimants decreased for most languages, but Fishman suspected that psychosocial forces are especially at play here and influence both claiming and underclaiming (Fishman, 1966: 43). Data were also provided on such topics as the number of mother tongue newspapers of different sorts, minority-language broadcasts and ethnic group schools that teach the mother tongue. The study goes on to investigate ethnic organizations and their leaders and the use of ethnic languages in the family.

The same research grant resulted in Fishman's (1965a) monograph on Yiddish in America. In this volume, although also presenting quantitative data on many societal situations that depended on Yiddish-language resources, Fishman was able to paint a broader history onto the history of Jewish immigration to the United States and the development of Yiddish language use. Here we see his division of societal language use into secular and religious, a division that would be attracting his attention 40 years later. The data describe language use in the Yiddish secular schools, Orthodox religious day schools, periodical press, literature and publishing, theater and radio. When he wrote about survival of the language, Fishman (1965a: 76) raised the issue of the perpetuity of literature and the role of scholars in maintenance of the language and culture.

Twenty years later, Fishman (1985a) wrote a volume on *The Rise and Fall of the Ethnic Revival*. Analyzing mother tongue claiming between 1960 and 1970, he found dramatic increases in claiming, which he interpreted as reflecting the psychological and social factors alluded to earlier. For Yiddish, for example, the reported increase was 65%. The estimated change for 1970–1979, however, was a decrease of 24%, according to Fishman (1985a: 130, 147). Thus, the implications support the title of his book. In this study, too, there are details on various community resources and rich qualitative sections based on interviews of language activists, including Yiddish activists, and quantitative data on periodicals, including Jewish periodicals in English and Yiddish. In the background to the study, Fishman (1985a: 77–103) includes a wonderful retelling of an early 19th century Enlightenment historical account of the reaction to Mendl Lefin's revolutionary Bible translations into modern Yiddish. The above volumes (Fishman 1965a, 1966, 1985a) contain a treasure trove of information that is relevant to Yiddish in America.

Yiddish, One of Many Jewish Languages

The years 1970 to 1973 constituted a turning point in Fishman's work with Yiddish. Many changes took place in his life in those years. He and his family lived in Israel while he co-directed an international research team that focused on language planning in different societies. In addition, during those years, he became an observant, religious Jew. One of Fishman's main tasks then was to assist Shlomo Noble, a linguist at Yivo in New York, who had served as editor and translator of research reports from Yiddish to English. Max Weinreich, Fishman's mentor with regard to Yiddish research, had died in 1969 after completing his *magnum opus*, the 4- volume *Geshikhte fun der yidisher shprakh* (*'History of the Yiddish Language'*) (Weinrich, 1973), and Noble and Fishman were charged with translating the *Geshikhte* into English. The *Geshikhte*, although containing large sections on topics such as historical phonology and documenting phonological change across time and space, is actually a discourse on Ashkenazic Jewish civilization as reflected in Yiddish language structure, function, meaning and change. Scholarly notes constitute half the published materials and reward the advanced student with a veritable history of Yiddish Studies and its sources. Fishman (1991c: 116) admits that his delving into the depths of Yiddish scholarship served as a retooling period and gave him the confidence and know-how with which to carry out independent research on Yiddish. Before that time, having pursued only a minimal amount of advanced Jewish study, Fishman did not deem his knowledge of Yiddish Studies sufficient for doing Yiddish research. Besides noting this turning point, I want to underscore the influence of Weinreich's opening sections devoted to the history of Jewish languages in Jewish society.

Fishman adopted Weinreich's focus on comparative Jewish languages and fitted the study of Yiddish, the big sister of the group, into this framework. He developed a shorthand notation, including CT (co-territorial language), LK (*loshn koydesh* 'the holy tongue' – Hebrew and Aramaic), and JL (Jewish language, especially the previous Jewish language at the time of genesis of a new Jewish language in a new area of settlement). Fishman's (1981b) comparison of the different Jewish languages, their histories, and structures through a unifying theoretical frame became a powerful stimulus for uniting and defining the field. His introduction of the concepts and relationships afforded by use of the theory of diglossia strengthened these studies. Thus, Fishman was able to open a window on a linguistic phenomenon that had largely been relegated to individual studies of small languages. Outsiders to Jewish Studies with an eye on diasporas, as well as researchers of Jewish societies who had never realized how unifying these Jewish societies could seem, benefited from the application of diglossia to their studies. Max Weinreich had grasped the intricacy of multilingual relationships in Ashkenaz, vis-à-vis both non-Jewish and Jewish languages and cultures. Fishman, perhaps because of his early exposure to the Yiddish situations, could distinguish between individual bilingualism and societal diglossia. This synthesis by Fishman helped to establish a research field. He demonstrated his support for the field in the issues of the *International Journal of the Sociology of Language* that he devoted to the sociology of Jewish languages, Yiddish and Judezmo, and in his edited volume, *Readings in the Sociology of Jewish Languages,* (Fishman, 1985d).

Yiddish in Israel

Fishman is a language activist for Yiddish. He grew up in a family that advocated for Yiddish at a time when few did so. His commitment was expressed in his private life through practice every day, by speaking Yiddish with his wife and children, at a time and place when few did so. He attended events that were manifestations of such advocacy and other events that demonstrated appreciation of public Yiddish cultural expression when few did so. He spoke out at so many of these events and published his thoughts in countless publications, when few did so. Yet in his academic publications, he reined in the emotions of advocacy, of fighting for the life of something that is near and dear to him. If Yiddish was to be considered alongside other languages, all were to be treated evenhandedly. Even when he devoted an entire monograph to *Yiddish in America*, a scene in which he was an active participant, there was no tone of special pleading or promotion. Fishman (1965a) helped normalize Yiddish as a subject of academic investigation. But this is not the case in his treatment of Yiddish in Israel (Fishman & Fishman, 1978; see also Fishman's views in Yiddish publications, 1974, 1983b). The statistics on mother tongue claimants are present, and here alongside comparable statistics for the USA. But the quantitative information is complemented by examples of communiqués, letters to the editor, and anecdotes that reveal the author's active protest of the denigrating attitude and policy toward Yiddish on the part of the government and institutions, as well as identifiable individuals.

The 'Yiddish in Israel' study is replete with information on radio and television broadcasts, governmental shortwave broadcasts targeted at overseas populations, theater performance, the press and book production. The authors present someone's critical response to Prime Minister Golda Meir's declaration that she intended to speak Yiddish to her grandchild, but they also pointed the finger at the leading professor of Yiddish at Hebrew University for not adding his voice when it was needed to support Yiddish initiatives within Israeli society and for not nurturing in institutions a collegial spirit that would encourage the growth of Yiddish Studies at other Israeli universities (Fishman & Fishman, 1978: 238, 242-43). Fishman and Fishman's detailed, extensive presentation has remained the main source on Yiddish in Israel.

One might think that the impact of the outspoken judgments of a professor of sociology of language would be minimal, but the lasting effects did not disappear easily. I was on the organizing committee for the last world conference on research on Yiddish language, literature and culture, which was held in Jerusalem in 1992. Although Chone Shmeruk, the former Hebrew University professor, was no longer part of the committee, he attempted to ensure that, as retribution for his past sins and in accord with a policy of exclusion that had obviously been in effect since the first conference in the series in Oxford, England, in 1979, Joshua Fishman would not be invited to participate. My protest to Shmeruk's successor finally prevailed, although the invitation to Fishman arrived only after great delay. Contemporary universities are perceived as being bastions of free exchange of ideas, not as harbors for dark, medieval forces of excommunication.

There are many lessons to learn here. A professor who fights for inclusive multilingualism and multiculturalism in society should be ready to be the victim of the exclusionary forces that oppose such goals. The destructive agents may be found in the very sectors that are constructed to educate about the discriminated language and culture. We are privy to a bit of what Fishman has endured by choosing to cross the line from academics to advocacy.

In the original study, effective comparisons were made between the situation of Yiddish in the USA and non-Jewish languages in Israel. There was little discussion of other Jewish languages, even though Israeli society provided the main historical testing ground for the way that different Jewish languages and cultures interact with each other. For several reasons, the data on these languages could not be teased out from the data on non-Jewish languages. Only for radio broadcasting was there information given on Mugrabi and Judezmo, which also do not fare well. However, some 15 years later, Fishman (2000), revisited the Israeli scene to look specifically at the language-planning needs and practices for the Jewish language communities. He found Yiddish to be the strongest, with its ultra-Orthodox religious sector as the only growing community amongst those he looked at. Ladino (Judezmo) is reported to boast a cadre of prominent young language leaders, whereas Judeo-Arabic (Mugrabi) and Judeo-Persian lack the leadership, the identification of a recognized, autonomous spoken or written variety, or any organized institutional efforts. The absence of effective planning may doom these languages (other than Yiddish in the Orthodox circles that do not depend on societal planning) at a time when Israeli society and culture are open to the appreciation of a Jewish heritage that is expressed by Jewish languages other than Hebrew.

Holiness and Yiddish

Since language is linked in many ways to all thought and human social organization, almost every psychological and social issue can be scrutinized in its relation to language expression, structure and regulation. The history of European Jewry up until modern times was that of an ethnic and religious group whose members believe its principles and practice its rituals. Along with the harbingers of modernity in Europe came opportunities to leave the system of beliefs and practices. Alongside this process of secularization, up until today, the remnants of European Jewry after the

Holocaust in communities across the globe have also maintained traditional life, in some instances also adapting it to modernity. Fishman has studied secularized Jewish expression in Yiddish, as well as Yiddish in traditional ultra-Orthodox and in modern Orthodox life. Although his treatment of US census data has certainly dealt with the majority of Jews, his qualitative analysis has not dwelled on these Jews who, on the surface, do not in practice or ideology connect with Yiddish. Our discussion will move to the area of attitude toward language, namely how the different sectors identify Yiddish with being holy, if they do at all deal with Yiddish in their public expression.

In Fishman's overall research work, the interplay of the specific case study with the general trend, behavior and theory carries significant weight. He harbors a particular distaste for the accumulation of what he sees as useless observations if they cannot be linked to theory. Yiddish as practiced on the ground and the theoretical issues related to Yiddish have stimulated much of his research, and, in turn, he has applied his more general findings to scrutinizing and explicating the Yiddish scene. When it comes to Yiddish and questions of religion, Fishman has, starting in the 1980s, stressed the necessity that secular positions that value Yiddish should replicate the insular fortification of primary and everyday institutions and rituals characteristic of groups such as the Amish and the Hasidim, in order to maintain Yiddish. Turning to the Orthodox sector of Jewish society, within the realm of attitudes, he has searched the pronouncements of rabbis and religious leaders that may speak to the lifting of the status of the vernacular to holiness. Moreover, he has integrated the lessons from these empirical revelations from the Jewish communities into a scheme for the sociology of language of what it means to sense language as being holy (Fishman, 2002a).

In his treatment of Yiddish as an immigrant tongue in his 'first phase' of Yiddish Studies and in his later analyses of Yiddish as one of many Jewish languages, the connection of Yiddish to holiness was not a major subject in Fishman's work. Earlier he did not foresee that religious life might serve as a bulwark against language shift, although he identified the 'Great Tradition' as not protecting Yiddish:

> The vast majority of the immigrants arrived *without* either a symbolically elaborated Great Tradition overtly protective of Yiddish *or* an unshaken Little Tradition that might have unconsciously provided Yiddish with security within an inviolable pattern of daily rounds. (Fishman, 1965b: 155)

Later on, Fishman noted that the displacement of one Jewish vernacular by another was 'totally unmarked and unlamented in rabbinic sources':

> The major Jewish cultural survival mechanism was doubtless the fact

that rabbinic culture did not depend on a vernacular but, rather, on a religious classical language, *loshn koydesh*. ... Its stability derived from its sanctification, its restricted networks of active users, and its diglossic detachment from everyday vernacular functions. (Fishman, 1994b: 92–93)

But Fishman (1994b: 93) continues by charging that rabbinic sources, those who equate the 'Great Tradition' with all of Jewish culture, did not recognize 'the different degrees and areas of mutual interpenetration' of the vernacular (Little) tradition and the rabbinic (Great) tradition. Two exceptions from Orthodox circles who recognized the religious value of both Yiddish and *loshn koydesh* were the pre-World War II leaders, Birnbaum and Sore Shenirer (for elaboration of their positions, see Birnbaum in Fishman, 1987a: 245, and Shenirer in Fishman, 1981a: 173–176).

One of the specializations of Fishman in his Yiddish-language articles has been to inform his secular readers of the extensive involvement of the Orthodox Jewish world with Yiddish. He attempts to educate them about the differentiated Orthodox world. For example, he surveys the history, content and Yiddish language style of the Orthodox press in New York City (Fishman, 2002c); he reports on a new ultra-Orthodox Yiddish journal in Monsey, New York that enthusiastically defends the role of Yiddish (Fishman, 1987b); and he acquaints his readers with the modern Orthodox world that cannot entirely run away from Yiddish and in all ways clings to markers of traditional life more than the mass of secularized American Jews (Fishman, 1994c).

Aimed at the Yiddish secularists, the ideological defenders of Yiddish who do not lead a religious life, Fishman (1982) in Yiddish, exhorted that sector to secure Yiddish in its primary institutions and to effect physical and ideological separation in order to guarantee continuity of language and culture. Fishman would repeat this call up until today. The Yiddish secularists who spend their energies on monthly Yiddish concerts or yearly literary prizes will not form any foundation for intergenerational continuity, he warned. Only the way of the observant and believing sector will work, according to Fishman. Those Orthodox circles, especially the ultra-Orthodox, must live close together to support the neighborhood religious institutions. Thus, in addition to speaking Yiddish within the household, which serves as a barrier to assimilation to the major non-Jewish language and culture, people can also speak the language with their neighbors. The cultural activity of the secularists does not provide for this kind of contact and support. Fishman's repeated advice to the secular Yiddishists derives from his general findings on ethnic language resources in the United States (Fishman, 1985a), namely, that only those communities that ensure stable residential and cultural segregation can maintain their ethnic mother tongue beyond the second generation. To his Yiddish readers, who are largely secular, he described the situation of Gaelic activists in Ireland who have in recent years, albeit to a limited extent, reversed language shift by establishing neighborhoods of Gaelic speakers (Fishman, 1989). Fishman reminded his secular Yiddish readers in 1983 that census data predict that in 2000 the children in the United States with Yiddish as their first language and perhaps their only language will number 26,000 (Fishman, 1982: 4). More recently, in his review of secular and ultra-Orthodox Yiddish activities during one year in New York City (mostly through press reports and publicity), Fishman (2001b: 90) estimated the ultra-Orthodox Yiddish speakers as approaching 300,000 and the secular ones at 3000. In the ultra-Orthodox lifestyle, the efforts that reverse and resist language shift are firmly based in the home and neighborhood, with community schools and inroads into businesses conducted in Yiddish. The secular Yiddishists concentrate their efforts, on the other hand, mostly on senior citizens and on occasional performance and entertainment (Fishman, 2001b: 97, 85).

Fishman's second approach in identifying the intersection of Yiddish language and religious life was to analyze over history the pronouncements of rabbis and Yiddish writers on the value of Yiddish. Fishman (1997b, 2002b) accepted the appellations of this group, when they referred to the Yiddish words for 'holy' (*heylik, koydesh, kedushe*). This kind of presentation, therefore, is open to the criticism that the writers may be utilizing different criteria to judge what is holy. Fishman showed that these writers were on all continents, were secularists as well as religious spokespeople, and wrote both before and after the Holocaust. The secular writers refer their concepts of holiness to the long history of *kiddush hashem* ('sanctification of the name of God'), of Yiddish-speaking Jews going to their forced death, from medieval times to the Holocaust. The rabbinic leaders use the argument that Yiddish derives its associated holiness from its connection to holy and revered books and people, spiritual and legendary leaders and guides. Such leaders, claiming consciously a chain of religious tradition, include the leader, the *Khsam soyfer*, in Pressburg at the beginning of the 19th century, and the authoritative rabbinic arbiter of Modern Orthodoxy in 20th century America, Rabbi Joseph Soloveitchik.

These observations and correlations of Fishman beg for a social-psychological investigation of a sample of Jews, Yiddish speakers and non-Yiddish speakers, religiously observant and secular, to examine their associations of sanctity and their identification of those relationships with Yiddish. The significance of the issue is placed in broader terms by Fishman (2002b: 124, 2002a: 19–20), who reports that some three quarters of today's languages are reported as being sanctity-linked. He views this need for associating language and holiness, together with the need for local rituals and traditions, as well as spirituality in general, as counterweights to the pressures of globalization and modernization. Fishman underscores the relationship between more than one holy language and sanctity, thus:

> The staying power of sanctified languages with bilingual repertoires is also noticeable in yet another way: they do not come and go the way quotidian vernaculars do. They wax and wane and have a seemingly phoenix-like capacity to arise again out of their own ashes. This later capacity too is a reflection of the sanctity attributed to them. (Fishman, 2002b: 22)

Coming together here are many of Fishman's main interests: diglossia, language and religion, the interplay of secular and religious sectors, revitalization and reversing language shift.

Corpus Planning for Yiddish

Although most of Fishman's work on Yiddish deals with its status in Jewish society and within the larger non-Jewish social and political stratifications, this prolific researcher and publicist has also tackled corpus planning for Yiddish. Two examples will illustrate how devoted Fishman is to the language itself, its letters and words as spoken and written.

Although inter-war Eastern Europe was fertile ground for organized Yiddish language planning, the post-World War II scene was a shadow of the earlier efforts. Yet Fishman (1983c), at the end of his own intense period of involvement in general concerns of language planning, chose to illustrate the rationales presented by normative arbiters with examples from planning recommendations for Yiddish after World War II. This article (Fishman, 1983c) is full of Yiddish items, such as an appeal to the rationale for a composite noun structure that is both widespread historically and productive in the corpus. Another example of a recommended composite sounds like a neologism, but actually was used in the late 19th century by a classic Yiddish author (Fishman, 1983c: 113).

Additionally, in a historical treatment, Fishman reports on the development in the early 19th century of a single typeface for Yiddish in print, *oysyos merubos* ('square type') that had previously been reserved for *loshn koydesh* (Hebrew and Aramaic). Up until then, Yiddish had been printed in *vayber taytsh* ('script of translations for women'), also called Rashi script, because it had been used in the widely accepted commentaries of the 11th century rabbi, Rashi (Fishman, 2001c). Fishman reviews this transition with comparative historical information on Ladino/Judezmo. The inclusive use of the *oysyos merubos* for all Yiddish printing allowed for the rapid take-off of a popular print culture. Once again, Fishman introduces the world of sociologists of language to the detail in the history of the Yiddish corpus and in its regulation.

Conclusions: Fishman the *Filolog*

At the beginning of the 20th century, Borokhov called for a generation of researchers of the Yiddish language who would be *'filologn'* – national leaders who would meet the cultural needs of the Jewish people by researching the history of the Yiddish language, the vernacular of the East European masses, and by providing for the people's knowledge of their culture and for the myriad linguistic applications that a culturally autonomous minority would need in the Europe of the future. Research into Yiddish language and culture had a broad burden to carry in the process of educating the people, but also in establishing a cultural pedigree, and in guaranteeing that the Yiddish language could function culturally within the Jewish and non-Jewish environs. Research on Yiddish after World War II, without the base of mass speakers and readers, fit into the scheme of the disciplines of the humanities at the time: linguistics, literature and folklore. By the end of the 20th century, Yiddish researchers were largely devoted to the academic conventions of the day, solely literary analysis. Yiddish is a vernacular of a minority in all the societies in which it is found. Minority languages and cultures have their own societal agendas and research agendas.

Joshua Fishman was born in 1926. His family microcosm was a Yiddishist one, which took on the cause of Yiddish, cultivating a language and culture that was largely rejected by his American-born contemporaries and their immigrant families. This son of immigrants in Philadelphia grew up reading Yiddish books from his family's shelf. For him, Jules Verne was a Yiddish author; he did not realize he was reading the literature of the world in translation, so pervasive was the cultural influence of Yiddish in his family. Yet his cultural world of reference was not pre-World War II Jewish Philadelphia. Even in those years, he reports that he was learning about the Yiddish culture and Jewish life in Eastern Europe on paper, by reading about that center of the Jewish world.

> *Mikh hot men dertsoygn, i intelektuel i emotsyonel, zikh tsu bateylikn in a kultur vos kh'hob milekhatkhile gekent nor fun bikher un fun di farbenkte oygn fun di vos hobn zikh dermont in ir.* (I was raised, both intellectually and emotionally, to participate in a culture that I only knew from books and from the longing eyes of those who remembered it.) (Fishman, 1999: 17)

That world was more alive for him than Jewish life in Philadelphia. By 1945, when Fishman was only 19, it was evident that the cultural center of world Jewry had been extinguished.

Under the influence of his mentor in Yiddish matters, Max Weinreich, himself a *filolog* of the East European generation that followed Borokhov, Fishman decided to pursue a career in social science research. Eventually, in the 1960s, he became the founder of the sociology of language. From his earliest research, Yiddish has been both a setting and a subject for his research. Starting in the 1970s, he devoted increasing effort to Yiddish research, although this is only a fraction, albeit an important and impassioned part, of his research agenda.

From the 1980s on, Fishman became a regular columnist for Yiddish periodicals, writing essays on sociolinguistics in general and on the sociology of Yiddish in particular. A prolific writer from his youth, Fishman's published research work on Yiddish, although a mere fraction of his oeuvre, is greater than that of most full-time Yiddish researchers.

Fishman's research and writing have analyzed the societal roles for Yiddish over its history. In contemporary times, he has focused on the linguistic needs that this vernacular provides for various sectors within the Jewish community. Relatively few researchers venture into the sociology of Yiddish, a wide area of interest that analyzes much of modern Jewish cultural expression. Fishman's contributions to Yiddish have not received the attention they deserve. Although he has pursued his work doggedly at a time in history after the heartland of his culture was torn out from under him, other researchers do not sense the same cultural imperative as Fishman.

Both Fishman and Borokhov set a wide field of view in their research telescope. Both are *filologn* and are motivated by the cultural and research needs of the Jewish people. The general field of the sociology of language benefits from Fishman's analysis of Yiddish, just as the field of Yiddish research profits from Fishman's insights and approaches that derive from the sociology of language. A day will come when the field of Yiddish research will once again have a far reach, as in the vision of Borokhov. At that time, the many research niches filled by Fishman's Yiddish work will be duly appreciated by researchers in Jewish Studies, as well as by a broader Jewish public. In the meanwhile, Fishman will continue to be admired and respected by those of us who fight for a deservedly rich future for minorities and their languages and cultures.

Acknowledgements

This essay was written while I was the Miles Lerman Center for the Study of Jewish Resistance Research Fellow and Visiting Scholar at the Center for Advanced Holocaust Studies of the United States Holocaust Memorial Museum, Washington, DC. I am always indebted to the Friends of Judaic Studies at Drexel University who support all the academic projects in Judaic Studies that I organize.

Notes

1. In Yiddish the resolution of the jury reads, *'Der prayz vert im tsugeteylt far zayn oysnemikn baytrog tsu der forshung fun yidish un ir maymed bay yidn in meshekh fun doyres.'* Signed June 10, 1999 by Sholem Rozenfeld, Rivke Basman Ben-Khayim, Avrom Novershtern, Avrom Sutzkever and Mordkhe Tsanin. (Copy provided to R.P. by Gella Schweid Fishman.) For a fascinating response by Fishman to receiving the Manger Prize, that includes an evaluation of the influence of his family environment and a review of some of the highpoints of his research on Yiddish, see Fishman (1999).

References:
Joshua A. Fishman works cited

Fishman, J.A. (1965a) *Yiddish in America*. Bloomington, IN: Indiana University Research Center in Anthropology, Folklore and Linguistics.

Fishman, J.A. (1965b) Language maintenance and language shift in certain urban immigrant environments: The case of Yiddish in the United States. *Europa Ethnica* 22, 146–158.

Fishman, J.A. (1966) *Language Loyalty in the United States* (with V.C. Nahirny, J.E. Hofman, R.G. Hayden *et al.*) The Hague: Mouton.

Fishman, J.A. (1974) Vos ken zayn di funktsye fun yidish in yisroel? [What can the function of Yiddish in Israel be?] *Yidisher kemfer* (April), 40–46.

Fishman, J.A. (1978) Yiddish in Israel: A case study of efforts to revise a monocentric language policy (with D.E. Fishman). In J.A. Fishman (ed.) *Advances in the Study of Societal Multilingualism* (pp. 185–262). The Hague: Mouton.

Fishman, J.A. (1980a) The sociology of Yiddish after the Holocaust: Status, needs and possibilities. In M.I. Herzog, B. Kirshenblatt-Gimblett, D. Miron and R. Wisse (eds) *The Field of Yiddish* 4, 475–498.

Fishman, J.A. (1980b) Attracting a following to high-culture functions for a language of everyday life: The role of the Tshernovits Language Conference in the rise of Yiddish. *International Journal of the Sociology of Language* 24, 43–74.

Fishman, J.A. (1981a) (ed.) *Never Say Die! A Thousand Years of Yiddish in Jewish Life and Letters*. The Hague: Mouton.

Fishman, J.A. (1981b) The sociology of Jewish languages from the perspective of the general sociology of language: A preliminary formulation. *International Journal of the Sociology of Language* 30, 5–18.

Fishman, J.A. (1982) Yidish, modernizatsye un re-etnifikatsye: An emeser un faktndiker tsugang tsu der itstiker problematic [Yiddish, modernization and re-ethnification: A true and factual approach to the current problem]. *Afn shvel* 248, 1–6 (reprinted in Rozhanski, 1982).

Fishman, J.A. (1983a) D'r Nosn Birnboyms ershter peyrek: Afn veg tsu yidish un tsum mizrekh-eyropeishn yidntum [Dr Nosn Birnboym's first chapter: On the road to Yiddish and East European Jewry]. *Afn shvel* 255, 13–16.

Fishman, J.A. (1983b) Shprakhikeyt in hayntikn yisroel [The language scene in contemporary Israel]. *Afn shvel* 252, 5–8.

Fishman, J.A. (1983c) Modeling rationales in corpus planning: Modernity and tradition in images of the good corpus. In J. Cobarrubias and J.A. Fishman (eds) *Progress in Language Planning: International Perspectives* (pp. 107–118). Berlin: Mouton.

Fishman, J.A. (1985a) *The Rise and Fall of the Ethnic Revival: Perspectives on Language and Ethnicity* (with M.H. Gertner, E.G. Lowy and W.G. Milan). Berlin: Mouton de Gruyter.

Fishman, J.A. (1985b) D'r Nosn Birnboyms tsveyter peyrek: Der kemfer far yidish un yidisher kultur-oytonomye [Dr Nosn Birnboym's second chapter: The fighter for Yiddish and Jewish cultural autonomy]. *Afn shvel* 257, 2–6.

Fishman, J.A. (1985c) D'r Nosn Birnboyms driter peyrek: Di derheybung un fartifung fun yidisher kedushe [Dr Nosn Birnboym's third chapter: The elevation and deepening of Jewish sanctity]. *Afn shvel* 258, 10–13.

Fishman, J.A. (ed.) (1985d) *Readings in the Sociology of Jewish Languages*. Leiden: E.J. Brill.

Fishman, J.A. (1987a) *Ideology, Society and Language: The Odyssey of Nathan Birnbaum*. Ann Arbor, MI: Karoma.

Fishman, J.A. (1987b) A naye farteydikung fun yidish in di khareydishe krayzn [A new defense of Yiddish in the ultra-Orthodox circles]. *Afn shvel* 266, 3–6.

Fishman, J.A. (1988a) Nosn Birnboyms dray tshernovitser konferentsn [Nosn Birnboym's three conferences in Tshernovits]. *Di tsukunft* 95 (1), 85–90.

Fishman, J.A. (1988b) Der hebreyisher opruf af der tshernovitser konferents [The Hebrew reaction to the Tshernovits Conference]. *Afn shvel* 271, 8–13.

Fishman, J.A. (1989) Far vos zol undz ongeyn der matsev fun irlendish? [Why should we care about the condition of Gaelic?]. *Afn shvel* 274, 3–7.

Fishman, J.A. (1991a) Preface. In J.A. Fishman. *Yiddish: Turning to Life* (pp. 1–9). Amsterdam: John Benjamins.

Fishman, J.A. (1991b) *Yiddish: Turning to Life*. Amsterdam: John Benjamins.

Fishman, J.A. (1991c) My life through my work: My work through my life. In K. Koerner (ed.) *First Person Singular II: Autobiographies by North American Scholars in the Language Sciences* (pp. 105–124). Amsterdam: John Benjamins.

Fishman, J.A. (1993a) The Tshernovits Conference revisited: The first world conference for Yiddish, 85 years later. In J.A. Fishman (ed.) *The Earliest Stage of Language Planning: The 'First Congress' Phenomenon* (pp. 321–332). Berlin: Mouton de Gruyter.

Fishman, J.A. (1993b) (ed.) *The Earliest Stage of* Language *Planning: The 'First Congress' Phenomenon*. Berlin: Mouton de Gruyter.

Fishman, J.A. (1993c) Introduction: Exploring an overlooked sociolinguistic phenomenon (The First Congress for Language X). In J.A. Fishman (ed.) *The Earliest Stage of Language Planning: The 'First Congress' Phenomenon* (pp. 1–9). Berlin: Mouton de Gruyter.

Fishman, J.A. (1993d) The 'First Congress' phenomenon: Arriving at some general conclusions. In J.A. Fishman (ed.) *The Earliest Stage of Language Planning: The 'First Congress' Phenomenon* (pp. 333–348). Berlin: Mouton de Gruyter.

Fishman, J.A. (1994a) Vos far a min konferents iz geven di tshernovitser konferents fun 1908? [What kind of conference was the Tshernovits Conference of 1908?]. *Afn shvel* 293, 1–5.

Fishman, J.A. (1994b) The truth about language and culture (and a note about the relevance of the Jewish case). *International Journal of the Sociology of Language* 109, 83–96.

Fishman, J.A. (1994c) Di 'moderne ortodoksye' un yidish ['Modern Orthodoxy' and Yiddish]. *Afn shvel* 294, 2–5.

Fishman, J.A. (1997a) Uriel Weinreich (1926–1967): A Sociolinguistic Appreciation. In C.B. Paulston and G.R. Tucker (eds) *The Early Days of Sociolinguistics: Memories and Reflections* (pp. 307–313). The Summer Institute of Linguistics.

Fishman, J.A. (1997b) Kedushe shebeyidish [Sanctity that is in Yiddish]. *Afn shvel* 307, 3–8.

Fishman, J.A. (1999) Baym bakumen di Manger-premye [Upon receiving the Manger Prize]. *Forverts,* June 11, 17.

Fishman, J.A. (2000) Language planning for 'the other Jewish languages' in Israel: An agenda for the beginning of the 21st century. *Language Problems and Language Planning* 24 (3), 215–231.

Fishman, J.A. (2001a) Introducing Khayem Zhitlovski. In R. Cooper, E. Shoshamy and J. Walters (eds) *New Perspectives and Issues in Educational Language Policy* (pp. 145–154). Amsterdam: John Benjamins.

Fishman, J.A. (2001b) A decade in the life of a two-in-one language: Yiddish in New York City (secular and ultra-Orthodox). In J.A. Fishman (ed.) *Can Threatened Languages Be Saved?* (pp. 74–100). Clevedon: Multilingual Matters.

Fishman, J.A. (2001c) Digraphia maintenance and loss among east European Jews (intertextual and interlingual print-conventions since 1800). *International Journal of the Sociology of Languages* 150, 27–41.

Fishman, J.A. (2002a) 'Holy languages' in the context of societal bilingualism. In L. Wei, J-M. Dewaele and A. Houston (eds) *Opportunities and Challenges of Bilingualism* (pp. 15–24). Berlin: Mouton de Gruyter.

Fishman, J.A. (2002b) The holiness of Yiddish: Who says Yiddish is holy and why? *Language Policy* 1, 123–141.

Fishman, J.A. (2002c) Di frume prese af yidish in Nyu-york [The Yiddish-language Orthodox press in New York]. *Forverts*, October 4, 11.

Fishman, J.A. (2003) Birnboym in Tshernovits [Birnboym in Tshernovits]. *Afn shvel* 329/330, 10–11 and 19.

Other works cited

Althaus, H.P. (1972) Yiddish. *Current Trends in Linguistics* 9 (2), 1345–1382.

Borokhov, B. (1913a) Di bibliotek fun yidishn filolog [The library of the Yiddish researcher]. In Sh. Niger (ed.) *Der pinkes* (pp. 1a–68a). Vilna: Kletskin.

Borokhov, B. (1913b) Di ufgabn fun der yiddisher filologye [The tasks of Yiddish research]. In Sh. Niger (ed.) *Der pinkes* (pp. 1–22). Vilna: Kletskin.

Borokhov, B. (1917) Di geshikhte fun der yidisher literatur [The history of Yiddish literature]. In R. Ayzland and M. Leyb (eds) *Literatur in lebn* [Literature in life]. New York (reprinted in B. Borokhov (1966) *Shprakh-forshung un literatur-geshikhte* [Language research and literary history] (pp. 178–221) ed. N. Mayzl. Tel-Aviv: Perets-farlag.

Di ershte yidishe shprakh-konferents: barikhtn, faktn, opklangen fun der tshernovitser konferents [The first Yiddish language-conference: Reports, facts, reactions to the Tshernovits Conference] (1931). Vilna: Yiddish Research Institute, Yivo.

Goldsmith, E.S. (1976) *Architects of Yiddishism at the Beginning of the Twentieth Century: A Study in Jewish Cultural History.* Rutherford, NJ: Farleigh Dickinson University Press.

Katz, D. (1986) On Yiddish, in Yiddish and for Yiddish: 500 years of Yiddish scholarship. In M.H. Gelber (ed.) *Identity and Ethos: A Festschrift for Sol Liptzin on the Occasion of His 85th Birthday* (pp. 23–36). New York: Peter Lang.

Novershtern, A. (1989) From folk to the academics: Study and research of Yiddish after the Holocaust. In *Encyclopedia Judaica Year Book* (pp. 14–24). Jerusalem: Keter Publishing.

Peltz, R. (1998) *From Immigrant to Ethnic Culture: American Yiddish in South Philadelphia.* Stanford, CA: Stanford University Press.

Rothstein, J. (1977) Reactions of the American Yiddish press to the Tshernovits Language Conference of 1908 as a reflection of the American Jewish experience. *International Journal of the Sociology of Language* 13, 103–120.

Rozhanski, Sh. (ed.) (1984) Memuarn – filosofye – forshung in der yidisher literatur [Memoirs – philosophy – research in Yiddish literature] (Vol. 97, *Musterverk fun der yidisher literature*). Buenos Aires: Literatur-gezelshaft baym yivo in argentine.

Schaechter, M. (1991) Foreward. In J.A. Fishman. *Yiddish: Turning to Life* (pp. ix–xii). Amsterdam: John Benjamins.

Weinreich, M. (1923) *Shtaplen* [Levels]. Berlin.

Weinreich, M. (1973) *Geshikhte fun der yidisher shprakh* [History of the Yiddish language] 4 vols. New York: Yivo Institute for Jewish Research [(1980) *History of the Yiddish Language*, Eng. transl. of vols 1 & 2, by Sh. Noble, with the assistance of J.A. Fishman. Chicago: University of Chicago Press].

Wexler, P. (1981) Jewish interlinguistics. *Language* 57, 99–149

Part 2

Concluding Sentiments

A Week in the Life of a Man from the Moon

JOSHUA A. FISHMAN

I write these few reflections about the past week in my life not because I consider it to be overly exemplary nor because the last week has been so characteristic of others. I do so partly because I have been asked to and partly because those of us who live mostly cloistered, private, indoor lives make it hard to know what we are really like. We get to know very few of even those who have contributed most to our thinking, partly because getting to know someone takes time and effort that we are loathe to interrupt what we are doing. And, besides, how can one get to really know anyone who is at his/her desk (reading/writing) most of the time?

Just recently, quite by accident, I discovered that a once-student and now-(distinguished) colleague of mine is a fine operatic singer and gives public concerts from time to time. What a surprise, and what a voice! Even on our cases, the cases of sheltered and self-sheltered isolates, our work is far from being the complete 'story' of our lives, not even of our intellectual lives. The two are closely related, of course, and at many levels of temperament and personality, but they are not the whole story by any means at any level. So I turn to this essay, which I expect to be a rather free-flowing account, partly because I promised to and partly because, at the moment, I have nothing else on my plate of a higher priority to keep me from doing so. There are at least a dozen other people from whom I would really like to receive a counterpart essay, but I am afraid to ask them for fear of being thought to be 'nosy.' We reveal so much of our lives indirectly, that we are doubly hesitant about doing so directly, claiming our right to privacy in self-defense.

Sunday: Summertime

I am writing in the middle of the doldrums of August (2005), and the weather has been beastly for weeks. Summer used to be my favorite season, but in the past few years it has become too hard for me to take with equanimity, even in my air-conditioned study. The endless, lazy summers of my childhood are only a hazy memory, as is Wildwood-by-the-Sea (NJ), the ocean-side resort town at which they were spent. My mind slides back to them with ease. I remember that I would be the first one out on the beach in the morning (except for the beach clean-up crew and the praying mantises) and among the very last to return 'home' in the evening. My mother would bring lunch at around noon and stay for an hour or so, together with my baby sister. My father would come out from Philadelphia only on the weekends. He was so fair skinned that he didn't enjoy the beach at all. Any sunburn could be extremely painful for him so he rarely joined me there even on the weekends. My days at the beach were spent alone, my sister (nine years my junior) still being far too small to be entrusted to me there. I busied myself building sandcastles, swimming, getting a slow, careful tan, dozing, reading a Yiddish children's book (I read Robert Louis Stevenson's *Treasure Island*, Louisa May Alcott's *Uncle Tom's Cabin* and, later, Knut Hamsun's *The Song of the Valley*), talking to myself, imagining the about-to-come evening's outing on the boardwalk.

The boardwalk was the joy of my life. The beach was in a neighborhood that my parents preferred, because it was so quiet and lightly populated. The boardwalk was full of life, including not only amusement-park 'rides,' ice cream, saltwater taffy (what a misnomer for sweet, chewy, multi-flavored delights), but, as the evening turned into night, my parents' friends would congregate at one of the piers for their regular nightly '*shmues*' (conversation), conducted in Yiddish of course. I was the only child who attended (while others were still gallivanting on the boardwalk) and got my first introductions to Jewish socialism, Zionism, anti-Zionism, Yiddishism, Jewish secularism and religious Judaism, the American labor movement, the New Deal, the gathering war clouds overseas, etc. Kathy Bateson has written, somewhere, that as a child she had the notion that going to conferences and giving lectures was the way adults 'thought.' I definitely imagined that the evening 'shmues' was the way vacation-time evenings ended. I never actually participated in them, and still am not likely to join into a general discussion, but I definitely soaked them up, even remembering when I heard specific terms for the first time and who introduced them into the discussion.

Monday: Grandchild

Age around 80 is a little late in life for one's grandchildren still to be making their first appearances in this world, but yesterday I accepted the latest one, the sixth, with both alacrity and tenderness. How innocent! How helpless! How beautiful ('objectively speaking' of course)! Actually, I was afraid to touch him, for fear that I would not match those sterling qualities and might even harm or detract from them. For some reason I was afraid of feeling too elated, of feeling too much of anything. I couldn't help remembering that I had already 'lost' two grandchildren whom I had considered to be as children of my own, and thinking to myself that I couldn't take any possible future losses.

When does one lose a dear one who is still alive and well? When they are lost emotionally; when the tender connections of love, attachment, fondness, mutual involvement, concern and connectedness that were formerly there are destroyed and replaced by nothingness: passivity, formality, avoidance. The children themselves were not to blame for this transformation. This is part of the price that was paid (by them, by me, by my wife Gella) for something that none of us were responsible for: the divorce of their parents. Time does not heal all wounds just because life goes on. It goes on without the irreplaceable ties that formerly constituted it. Those ties are the stuff of life itself and one is not the same 'afterwards,' even if all parties to a break go on acting civilly toward one another.

What weird and unfortunate thoughts to have when viewing one's newest grandchild for the first time! In all likelihood this incomparably lovely little boy would never cause me any grief or hurt. May God grant that I never give him anything but joy. I make that resolution to myself and pray. My Yiddish patrimony for the fourth generation is still on hold. Language maintenance within the modern family hangs on a very slender thread.

Tuesday: *Tishe-bov*

Yesterday, the ninth day of the Hebrew month of Ov (hence, *tishe-bov*) is the traditional day for mourning all major Jewish tragedies throughout history (the destruction of the First Temple in 586 B.C.E. by the Babylonians, the destruction of the Second Temple in 70 B.C.E. by the Romans, the expulsion from Spain in 1492, and many Jews even observe the Nazi-conducted Holocaust on this date too). It is a solemn fast-day and, coming as it does in the midst of the summer's heat, is one that is often uncomfortable and difficult to bear. At my age, any number of health reasons may be seized upon to excuse non-observance of the required sundown to sundown fast. Indeed, many rabbis go out of their way to urge the elderly not to overdo the fast and to take some nourishment at any time that they feel weak, but one is surrounded by fasting men, women and even children and it ultimately feels as difficult to partake of food or drink as to fast. The mind races on...

So many tragedies; the survivors of the Holocaust are still well represented in the synagogue itself. The imminent withdrawals from Gaza with the abandonment of homes, gardens, synagogues, gravesites and self-created surroundings, also elicit feelings and expressions of mourning from many congregants, many of whom are sitting on the floor, as if in mourning and in actual mourning. The rabbi has opposed the pull-out from

Gaza, but he has also opposed disobeying the government's democratic decision-making authority and its military enforcement. My father had been an advocate of the 'dual-nationality state,' even way back in the 1930s, well before the State of Israel was created, precisely because he worried about possible Arab–Jewish confrontations in the Holy Land. He later became a territorialist (a seeker of some neutral place for organized Jewish – and, in his case, Yiddish – concentration) immediately after World War II and largely because of the same worries. I myself have always tried to combine 'here-ism' and 'there-ism,' not being willing to grant Israel the status of be all and end all of modern Jewish existence, but not being willing to deny it the support it needed to exist and prosper. The anti-Yiddish sentiment that I myself experienced there, both from the Hebrew University and from the government's Office of Statistics, during the years 1970–1973 when I had brought the entire family there in order to conduct the International Research Project on Language Planning Processes (Rubin *et al.*, 1977), made it impossible for me to settle there (despite ample governmental efforts to sweeten the pill for me personally).

How strange of inscrutable Jewish fate to bring all this together on one day: the Holocaust, the pull-back from Gaza ('the beginning of a new Holocaust,' as some fear), the arrival of a new grandchild. In my mind all of the above are sociolinguistically heightened by their interconnections with each other and with Yiddish. Yiddish is everywhere. Sadness is everywhere. The drive to overcome depression is everywhere. Who will get the upper hand? The descent to the grave is too much on my mind, but that's life too. I guess.

Tuesday: The Holocaust

I hesitate to write in this personal mode about the Holocaust, which *tishebov* has brought so strongly to mind. So much that has been written about the Holocaust, particularly by outside commentators 'who were not there' themselves – and even by some of those who have been – cannot help being or bordering upon the trivial and the maudlin. Who can really understand what occurred then?

As an adolescent I didn't really expect that the Holocaust would impact on me personally. I had no relatives 'over there,' but my emotional and intellectual ties to 'Yiddishland' were far stronger than I knew or expected.

Throughout every winter of the 30s, I was accustomed to collect small change from people on the street and from neighbors nearby for the 'poor children at the Medem Sanitarium' in Poland (an institution maintained by the Jewish Workers' Bund in order to give children who lived in the abject poverty of urban ghettos a fleeting taste of summer in a self-governing children's commune). Yankev Patt (pronounced 'pot') would come from

Warsaw every fall, as a representative of the Sanitorium's Board of Directors, to kick off the campaign and to remind us, children of the Workmen's Circle Yiddish Schools, that the children we were helping where our brothers and sisters and that we must not, could not let them down. A few years after his last visit (in the fall of 1938), the children and their teachers were carted off to be shot, burned or gassed. Not a single one of those then 'in residence' survived the war, and I did feel their loss quite personally, although it was years until we knew about it for sure.

But the loss was far more extensive. Our enculturation, at home, in school, at camp and in the Yiddish cultural circles that supported all the books, plays, films, dances, concerts and literary events – poetry and song recitals, lectures, club sessions, park outings, boat trips etc. – that constituted the noteworthy bulk of our daily lives, aimed to prepare us to be citizens of, participants in (even from afar) and contributors to a Yiddish Camelot in Eastern Europe and its immigrant colonies abroad. When I finally realized that Camelot no longer existed and that it was irrevocably gone, I experienced an emptiness that has lasted in part until this very day. I was as American as anyone that I knew or encountered (even though my father had convinced me that a democratic American government owed us Yiddish public schools because this was a multicultural country), but a huge chunk of my total identity no longer had any counterpart in reality. My identification with the languages of Amerindians and other indigenous peoples throughout the world, an identification that is even stronger than that with immigrants who usually have homelands that they could return to if they so wanted, stems from my sensing our joint-void created by the cruel disappearance of a reality that they, and I, had a right to count on and that the world has stolen from us.

Can such a loss ever be recouped, repaired or rectified? Much of my work on language maintenance, reversing language shift, and language planning more generally stems from the intellectualization of that loss. 'What once existed is gone and can no longer be,' a Yiddish theater-song laments, but even efforts to bring it back, to revive it in part, can be constructive, healing or both. Such efforts build community ('*gemeinschaft*') and provide purpose for those who might otherwise be largely if not totally bereft of both. Nevertheless, it is incumbent upon us to recognize the need to do so even if successful. Reconstituted communities may not be exactly like the originals that inspired them (just as cooking by following directions in a cookbook does not fully reproduce the original taste and aroma of 'what grandma used to make'). Also the reconstituted language, speech networks and speech communities do not really fully recapture the ethos of the originals. The 'beloved language' (Fishman, 1997) is now the second language (and later on, the co-language) of the community of revivalists and RLSers (language activists who are involved in efforts to Reverse

Language Shift). As such, it cannot but have a substratum that is derived from the first language or/and the more widely functional co-language of its speakers.

Both social change and language change are ongoing everywhere, and had the cataclysm not caused such change it would have gone on anyway (more controllable, to be sure), so that neither would have been exact duplicates in Time 2 (post-cataclysm) of what they had been in Time 1 (pre-cataclysm). Had it succeeded, even Ghandi's nativism would not have resulted in a carbon copy of Indian rural life in Time 1 because in Time 2 those who wove their own clothing (in order not to buy British manufactured cloth) undoubtedly realized that they could do so if they needed or preferred to. So, though I still struggle 'against the apocalypse' (Roskies, 1984), for without that struggle I would indeed be despondent, I know that what I lost is irretrievable. My fascination with Ultra-Orthodox Jewry stems from its ability to reinstate its pre-War reality with as much fidelity as it has, actually making it into a virtual carbon-copy of its remembered and still-largely-rural 'paradise-lost' – in behavior, belief, attitude and language – a return that every fundamentalism is committed to pursuing. But my 'paradise lost' was a modern secular one (and in an urban setting to boot) and the chances that it would have remained essentially unchanged even during a peaceful half-century are nil. It is not the reality of the dream that determines its power, but, rather, the pent-up needs of the dreamer. The heart seeks what the heart needs, no matter how real or unreal that may be.

Wednesday: The Perils of Intellectualization

My good friend the sociolinguist Bonifacio Sibayan, of Manila, has written tellingly of the 'intellectualization' of Filipino (Sibayan, 1999). By that he meant the corpus planning efforts to render Filipino (originally referred to as 'Pilipino') capable of discharging all the modern functions of an increasingly technological and modernizing world-linked nation state. But my reference to 'intellectualization' in the previous paragraph has at least a somewhat different (though related) meaning. When I was a graduate student, my major mentor was Max Weinreich, the 20th century's most outstanding Yiddish linguist – I became a co-translator of his crowning work, *The History of the Yiddish Language* (1980), as an expression of the deep admiration that I felt for him. Weinreich's major admonition to me was that, if research on Yiddish-related topics was to have any resonance in the 'outside academic world,' it would have to be intellectualized so as to address general academic interests, needs and theories. 'If Margaret Mead can do so when she writes about coming of age in Samoa,' he was fond of saying, 'then why can't we do so when writing about the modernization of *Shnipishok* (the proverbial shtetl)?' The world attributes to Weinreich the aphorism that 'A language is a dialect with an army and a navy' (1945) (an attribution that I once amended slightly), in his reply to the then-common view that Yiddish was only a mangled dialect of German. This aphorism, now widely quoted throughout the world in connection with weaker languages that live in the shadow of much stronger and structurally very similar 'big brothers,' is itself an example of 'intellectualization' in the Weinreichian sense. I have for many years tried to practice what I preach and have insisted that my students try to reformulate their research problems without even mentioning the names of the specific languages or cultures from which these problems were initially derived in the minds of the students themselves.

Thursday: Public Relations

I have encountered both success and resistance in trying to follow this maxim, and I do not recommend it to everyone as a *modus operandi* with all speech networks. It renders difficult my own attempts to communicate with others, and even my own children have accused me of unnecessary theorizing in the midst of an ordinary conversation. A conversation ostensibly focusing on congratulating my recent grandparental attainment unfortunately got detoured by an innocent comment of one interlocutor that the trouble with the Democrats was that their PR ('public relations') was so inferior to that of the Republicans. I reacted, equally innocently, that 'PR cannot be the major determinant in influencing change among holders of ideologized positions.'

I didn't mean to impugn my neighbor's intelligence nor his deepest convictions, but that is exactly what I seemed to have done by converting an everyday exchange of pleasantries into an examination of a general proposition. The fact that I then pointed out that all of the putatively excellent and presumably heavily-financed Republican PR had changed very few minds once the campaign was well underway, only added oil to the fire. Everything I said thereafter (e.g. that by the time campaigns are well advanced, most people generally only attend to the ads they already agree with; therefore, perhaps PR might best be stressed early in a campaign and then efforts should be switched to admittedly-more-expensive in-person persuasion, small-group discussions, etc.) only made a bad scene worse. All this went over like a lead balloon and was actually viewed as a confusion of fact with fancy, something 'so typical of self-styled intellectuals.'

Friday: The Pleasures of Intellectualization

One of the major pleasures that I have experienced in my academic work is when I have been able to theoretically restructure an 'old chestnut.' My recent efforts with the hidden status agenda in corpus planning (Fishman,

2000) represented such an undertaking. So did my work on the difference between weak and strong levels of the Whorfian hypothesis at the beginning of the 60s (Fishman, 1960), the distinction that I drew between ethnicity and nationalism (i.e. ethnicity rendered conscious and mobilized –Fishman, 1972) in the early 70s, and perhaps two or three other instances, such as putting 'language maintenance' on the sociolinguistic map in the late 60s (Fishman,1968). Like the worldclass photographer who felt that he had taken only 10 'really good photos' over an entire lifetime, I feel that I have made real theoretical contributions only about half a dozen times in 50 years. And who knows how long even these will abide? Academia is in the business of tearing down its own forefathers – indeed, of tearing down more and more readily than it builds up.

I still hang on to being General Editor of *IJSL*, an honor almost without 'perks' of any kind, having founded it and guided it since 1973. I do so perhaps not so much because it needs me (I have no doubt that there are several others, much younger than I, who would do as good job at it as I do), but because I need it now more than ever, my teaching loads having disappeared as American higher education has entered a new period of financial stringency vis-à-vis 'part-timers in the humanities,' in order to feel intimately connected to sociolinguistics. I rejoice in bringing out issues every year that focus on forgotten or even unknown corners of the world. Each issue has a local editor, so that *IJSL* cannot become a handmaiden of the 'Americanization of everything.' I am enough of a Whorfian to greatly regret that I cannot persuade most issue editors to provide much publishable material in any of the four 'languages other than English' (LOTEs) – French, German, Spanish and Italian – in which *IJSL* easily publishes. I consider this to be a general malady of academic publishing today, rather than just an *IJSL* problem. Unless we publish in those languages, sociolinguists who consider this a particular challenge to their own honor will never succeed in convincing their increasingly Anglophone students to read seriously in other languages. Perhaps we need to permit subsequent republication (after a 3–5 year hiatus) in English, because many academic regimes do not permit articles to count toward tenure unless they are published in English. This may lead to a two-tiered publication system (journals of first publication and journals of re-publication) but, at least, the LOTEs will have a better 'shot at it,' at least among their own constituencies, than they do now.

Saturday: Sabbath

Gella and I have engaged in the practice of reading to each other in Yiddish on *sha'bes* (the Jewish sabbath) from even before we were married. It gives us a regular exposure to the literary style that has lately become rarer and rarer, not only among writers but, even more so, among educated speakers. We generally read newly-published novels and short stories situated in Eastern Europe (pre-Holocaust, Holocaust and post-Holocaust), but we have also read new books in which the plots are situated in Israel and America. Our major selection criterion is that the author is a living creating contributor to Yiddish literature, rather than one whose work is translated into Yiddish or was popular long ago. It is a part of our Sabbath experience that we particularly look forward to, in addition to the more obligatory resting, sleeping, newspaper reading (in both Yiddish and English), eating and praying.

We have both added Modern ('Open') Orthodoxy to our basic Yiddish secularism, doing so out of our longing for the world that vanished and our desire to enrich an approach to Jewishness that had become enfeebled through no fault of its own. Socialism and secularism alone seem to have lost their moral imperatives. Therefore, being syncretistic rather than rejectionist or exclusionist by inclination and preference, the combination of Yiddish secularism and modern Orthodoxy works well for us. It also partially replenishes the ranks of those friends who have passed on and shows us that there are thousands of young Jews who live fully involved and normatively Jewish lives. That being said, I must admit (speaking entirely for myself here) that I find a steady diet of prayer (in Hebrew), classics-derived solutions to any and all modern Jewish problems and relying on rabbinic *obiter-dicta* to be oppressive and often stultifying. Although I remain reasonably Orthodox in all daily behavioral rounds, I cannot claim to be a paragon of virtue when judged by these standards, but the moral basics, I believe, remain inviolable nevertheless. I consider the no-working, no-traveling, no-writing, no-cooking, no-smoking Sabbath to be God's greatest gift, and I would not trade it or infringe upon it for the world. I fervently hope that my children and grandchildren will follow this path as well (Yiddish plus modern orthodoxy), and have faith that they will find their ways to it by their own designs.

That's Life

When friends, colleagues, students or acquaintances ask me (as some of them have) what I consider to be my favorite published 'work' I struggle to give them an answer of the kind they want: a title. After I do so, they generally remain surprised or even disappointed. They expected me to name a more major opus. Actually, however, if it were entirely up to me, I would not name any title at all. I do not expect any of them to outlive me by many years. Max Weinreich, Irving Lorge, Paul Lazersfeld, Robert Thorndike and the other giants of my graduate student years, are hardly ever mentioned today, except in a bibliographic review in which they are no more than one name among scores of others. In an age in which even Sigmund Freud and Karl Marx have been toppled from their exalted pedestals, it would be sheer folly to think otherwise about myself. To the extent that I am at all content with my accomplishments it is primarily because I have maintained and even cultivated the multidisciplinarity of my approach to sociolinguistic topics.

I was bilingual and bicultural from birth. I received both a fine public school education (every year we studied a book of the Bible, a book of Shakespeare, a book of great English literature, a course in mathematics, a course in a natural science, a course in a foreign language, and a course in American or world History) and a very stimulating exposure to Jewish history, Yiddish language and literature, and Jewish 'freedom movements' via a 10-year after-school program. In undergraduate school I majored in 'social studies' (primarily history) and minored in Spanish. In my graduate school I majored in (social) psychology and minored in history (studying Jewish history as well, most semesters, with the incomparable Silo W. Baron – who refused to accept me as a doctoral student in Jewish studies because my Hebrew fluency was deficient). At the postgraduate level, I studied quantitative methods with Irving Lorge, linguistics with Charles Ferguson and Jewish folklore with Max Weinreich. I have been a multiple causationist throughout life, and I reject all reductionism and determinism, be it economic, psychological or spiritual, while recognizing the importance of all of them as co-influences among others. I attribute my preference for factor analysis and multiple correlation to the simultaneous expectations of complexity and to the need for parsimony in any explanatory efforts. I have never lost my conviction that 'the history of...' is a necessary place to begin any investigation.

All in all, it is the above tolerance of complexity, diversity (a more diverse world is inherently more complex) and ambiguity (there are no good, clear answers to many problems in life, in research or in theory) that I consider my greatest attainment. Like a veritable 'man in the moon,' I always try to keep some distance between myself and my research topics and to yearn for a broader perspective. Perhaps the world is my oyster, but, even if I am not a pearl in that oyster, I am often quite a good irritant.

References

Fishman, J.A. (1960) A systematization of the Whorfian hypothesis. *Behavioral Science* 8, 323–339.

Fishman, J.A. (1968) *Language Loyalty in the United States*. The Hague: Mouton.

Fishman, J.A. (1972) *Language and Nationalism*. Rowley: Newbury House.

Fishman, J.A. (1997) *In Praise of the Beloved Language*. Berlin: Mouton de Gruyter.

Fishman, J.A. (2000) The status agenda in corpus planning. In R.D. Lambert and E. Shohamy (eds) *Language Policy and Pedagogy* (pp. 43–52). Amsterdam: Benjamins.

Roskies, D. (1984) *Against the Apocalypse: Responses to Catastrophe in Modern Jewish Culture*. Cambridge: Harvard University Press.

Rubin, J., Ferguson, C.A., DasGupta, J. and Jernudd, B. (1977) *Language Planning Processes*. The Hague: Mouton.

Sibayan, B. (1999) *The Intellectualization of Filipino*. Manila: Linguistic Society of the Philippines.

Weinreich, M. (1945) Der yivo un di problemen fun undzer tsayt. *Yivo-bleter* 25, 1–13.

Weinreich, M. (1980) *History of the Yiddish Language* (S. Noble and J.A. Fishman, trans.). Chicago: University of Chicago Press (original work published in 1973 in Yiddish).

Part 3

Bibliographical Inventory

Joshua A. Fishman's Bibliographical Inventory

COMPILED BY GELLA SCHWEID FISHMAN

The following is an inventory of Joshua A. Fishman's prolific body of work, from 1947 to current literature in press. The bibliography was compiled by Gella Schweid Fishman and is organized into five general sections:

- Books, Monographs and Reports;
- Articles and Book Chapters;
- Reviews, Prefaces, Comments and Notes;
- Popular Articles;
- Interviews.

In each section, works are listed under year of publication and then arranged alphabetically, with parenthetical notes regarding reprints and translations. Those works listed in the Popular Articles section were published primarily in the Yiddish press, under Joshua A. Fishman's Yiddish name, Shikl Fishman.

Most of the literature provided here, together with their related drafts, notes, research materials, audio/videocassettes, etc., from the early 1940s through 1992 (approximately 180 linear feet), are available in *The Joshua A. Fishman and Gella Schweid Fishman Family Collection* at Stanford University Libraries Department of Special Collections. From 1992 on, all materials pertaining to the Joshua A. Fishman bibliographical listings (including some from former years that cannot be found at Stanford) are presently in the possession of Joshua A. Fishman and Gella Schweid Fishman. The processed collection in New York (approximately 90 linear feet) continues to grow, and is waiting for a hospitable recipient.

Between 1938 and 1947, several dozen Yiddish articles were published in journals for children and young folks, primarily in *Ilpik* and *Yugntruf*, on a variety of Jewish topics. These articles are not listed in this bibliography, nor are a few additional articles of a similar nature, authored before 1950.

With the assistance of Zeena Zakharia, we have combed through the extensive bibliography prepared by Gella Schweid Fishman, and have added and/or revised items. Despite our arduous efforts, we know that some of Joshua A. Fishman's extensive work may have eluded us, especially that which has been translated into many languages. We ask you, the readers, then, to send us corrections and additions to this bibliographical inventory. You may also send your queries directly to the Fishman family.

Acknowledgement

Special appreciation is expressed to Evagelia Bakoulis, personal archival assistant, and to Eric Heath, Stanford University Libraries Librarian, for their helpful assistance to Gella Fishman in the preparation of the bibliography. We also wish to thank Zeena Zakharia and Leah Mason of Teachers College, Columbia University, for their assistance in preparing the bibliography for publication in this volume.

Books, Monographs and Reports

1949 Bilingualism in a Yiddish school: Some correlates and non-correlates. Unpublished manuscript, Yiddish Scientific Institute.

1953 Negative stereotypes concerning Americans among American-born children receiving various types of minority-group education. PhD thesis, Columbia University.

1955 The acceptance of new reference groups, exploratory phase (R.E. Hartley, principal investigator). Annual Technical Report 1, National Office of Naval Research (01). Unpublished manuscript, The City College.
Negative stereotypes concerning Americans among American-born children receiving various types of minority-group education. *Genetic Psychology Monographs* 51, 107–182.
A Review of the Research Activities of the College Entrance Examination Board, 1952–1955. New York: College Entrance Examination Board.
Supplement (1955–56) to the Review of the Research Activities of the College Entrance Examination Board. New York: College Entrance Examination Board.

1957 The acceptance of new reference groups (R.E. Hartley, principal investigator). Annual Technical Report 2, National Office of Naval Research (01). Unpublished manuscript, The City College.
The 1957 Supplement to College Board Scores 2. New York: College Entrance Examination Board.

1958 *The Research Activities of the College Entrance Examination Board, 1952–1957.* New York: College Entrance Examination Board.

1964 Language loyalty in the United States. Three-volume report to Language Research Section, United States Office of Education. Unpublished report, Yeshiva University.

1965 *For Max Weinreich on His Seventieth Birthday* (ed. with L. Dawidowicz, E. Ehrlich and S. Ehrlich). The Hague: Mouton.
Toward Integration in Suburban Housing: The Bridgeview Study (with M. Deutsch and E. Leacock). New York: Anti-Defamation League.
Yiddish in America. Socio-linguistic Description and Analysis. Bloomington, IN:

Indiana University Research Center in Anthropology, Folklore and Linguistics.

1966 *Hungarian Language Maintenance in the United States.* Bloomington, IN: Indiana University Press and The Hague: Mouton.
Language Loyalty in the United States. The Maintenance and Perpetuation of Non-English Mother Tongues by American Ethnic and Religious Groups (with V.C. Nahirny, J.E. Hofman, R.G. Hayden *et al.*). The Hague: Mouton.

1968 Bilingualism in the barrio (with R.L. Cooper, R. Ma *et al.*). Final Report to United States Department of Health, Education and Culture under Contract No. OEC-1-7-62817-0297 (2 vols). Unpublished manuscript, USDHEW.
Expanding Horizons of Knowledge About Man (ed.). New York: Yeshiva University.
Language Problems of Developing Nations (ed. with C.A. Ferguson and J. Das Gupta). New York: Wiley.
Readings in the Sociology of Language (ed.). The Hague: Mouton.

1970 *Sociolinguistics: A Brief Introduction.* Rowley, MA: Newbury House.
Taalsociologie. Brussels: Labor and Steppe, and Netherlands: Ninove (translation into Dutch of *Sociolinguistics: A Brief Introduction, 1970*).

1971 *Advances in the Sociology of Language I* (ed.). The Hague: Mouton.
Bilingualism in the barrio (with R.L Cooper, R. Ma *et al.*). *Language Science Monographs* 7. Bloomington, IN: Indiana University Press.
Sociolinguistique. Brussels: Labor and Paris: Nathan (translation into French of *Sociolinguistics: A Brief Introduction, 1970*).

1972 *Advances in the Sociology of Language II* (ed.). The Hague: Mouton.
Hasotziyologiya shel yidish be-artsot habrit. Pirsumey Hug Leyidiot Am Yisrael Batfutsot. Jerusalem: *Presidential Lecture Series* 6 (3).
Language and Nationalism. Rowley, MA: Newbury House.
Language-Behavior Papers I. Jerusalem: Language-Behavior Section, The School of Education of the Hebrew University and the Ministry of Education and Culture.
Language in Sociocultural Change: Essays by Joshua A. Fishman. Stanford, CA: Stanford University Press.
The Sociology of Language: An Interdisciplinary Social Science Approach to Language in Society. Rowley, MA: Newbury House.
Studies in Modern Jewish Social History (ed.). New York: Ktav.

1973 *Advances in Language Planning* (ed.). The Hague: Mouton.
Hasotsiologia shel yidish beartsot habrit: Avar, hove veatid. Jerusalem: The Institute of Contemporary Jewry, Sprinzak Division.
Language-Behavior Papers II. Jerusalem: Language-Behavior Section, The School of Education of the Hebrew University and the Ministry of Education and Culture.

1974 The sociology of bilingual education. Final Report, under Contract OECO-73-0588 for the Division of Foreign Studies, DHEW, OE. Unpublished manuscript, Ferkauf Graduate School, Yeshiva University.
Gengo shakaigaku nyumon. Tokyo: Taishukan shoten (translation into Japanese of *The Sociology of Language: An Interdisciplinary Social Science Approach to Language in Society, 1972*).
Studies on Polish Jewry, 1919–1970: The Interplay of Social, Economic and Political

Factors in the Struggle of a Minority for its Existence (ed.). New York: YIVO Institute for Jewish Research.

1975 Bilingualism in the barrio (with R.L Cooper, R. Ma *et al.*). *Language Science Monographs* 7. Bloomington, IN: Indiana University Press (revised edition of 1971).

Soziologie der Sprache. Munich: Hueber (translation into German of *The Sociology of Language: An Interdisciplinary Social Science Approach to Language in Society,* 1971).

La sociologia del linguaggio. Roma: Officina Edizioni (translation into Italian of *The Sociology of Language: An Interdisciplinary Social Science Approach to Language in Society,* 1971).

1976 Advances in the sociology of language I (ed.). *Language Science Monographs* 7. Bloomington, IN: Indiana University Press (revised edition of *Advances in the Sociology of Language I,* 1971).

Bilingual Education: An International Sociological Perspective. Rowley, MA: Newbury House.

1977 Bilingual education: A perspective. *IRCD Bulletin* 12 (2).

Bilingual Education, Current Perspectives: Social Science. Arlington, VA: Center for Applied Linguistics.

Language Maintenance. Washington, DC: The National Institute of Education.

Language Planning Processes (with J. Rubin, B. Jernudd, J. Das Gupta and C.A. Ferguson). The Hague: Mouton.

The Spread of English: The Sociology of English as an Additional Language (with R.L. Cooper and A.W. Conrad). Rowley, MA: Newbury House.

1978 *Advances in the Creation and Revision of Writing Systems* (ed.). The Hague: Mouton.

Advances in the Study of Societal Multilingualism (ed.). The Hague: Mouton.

Istruzione Bilingue: Una Prospetiva Sociologica Internazionale. Bergamo: Minerva-Italien (translation of *The Sociology of Bilingual Education,* 1974).

Language Loyalty in the United States (with V.C. Nahirny, J.E. Hofman, R.G. Hayden *et al.*). New York: Arno Press (reprint of 1966).

Sociolingüística del Lenguaje. Madrid: Cátedra (translation of *The Sociology of Language: An Interdisciplinary Social Science Approach to Language in Society,* 1971).

Sociologija Jezika. Sarajevo: Svjetlost (translation into Serbocroatian of *The Sociology of Language: An Interdisciplinary Social Science Approach to Language in Society,* 1971).

Yiddish in America. Bloomington, IN: Indiana University Research Center in Anthropology, Folklore and Linguistics (reprint of 1965).

1979 The ethnic mother tongue school in America: Assumptions, findings and directory (with B.R. Markman). Final report under Grant NIE G-78-0133, Project No. 8-0860. Unpublished manuscript, Ferkauf Graduate School, Yeshiva University.

1980 *Max Weinreich's History of the Yiddish Language* (co-translated from the Yiddish edition, with S. Noble). Chicago, IL: University of Chicago Press.

Non-English language resources of the United States: A preliminary return visit (with assistants/associates). Final report under G-00-79-01816,

Research Section, Washington, DC: International Studies Branch, Department of Education.

1981 Guide to non-English-language print media (with E.G. Lowy, M.H. Gertner and W.G. Milán). *Language Resources in the United States 1*. Rosslyn, VA: National Clearinghouse for Bilingual Education.
Never Say Die! A Thousand Years of Yiddish in Jewish Life and Letters (ed.). The Hague: Mouton.
Sociology of language. *Sociolinguistische Studies* 2 (translation into Dutch of *The Sociology of Language*, 1972).

1982 The acquisition of biliteracy: A comparative ethnography of minority ethnolinguistic schools in New York City (with C. Reidler-Berger, P. Koling and J.M. Steele). Final reports to National Institute of Education under Grant G-79-0122 (first part, February; second part, August). Unpublished manuscript, Ferkauf Graduate School, Yeshiva University.
Bilingual Education for Hispanic Students in the United States (ed. with G. Keller). New York: Teachers College Press.
Guide to Non-English Broadcasting (with E.G. Lowy, W.G. Milán and M.H. Gertner). *Language Resources in the United States* 2. Rosslyn, VA: National Clearinghouse for Bilingual Education.

1983 *Progress in Language Planning: International Perspectives* (ed. with J. Cobarrubias). Berlin: Mouton.

1985 *Ethnicity in Action: The Community Resources of Ethnic Languages in the United States* (with M.H. Gertner, E.G. Lowy and W.G. Milán). Binghamton, NY: Bilingual Press.
Readings in the Sociology of Jewish Languages (ed.). Leiden: E.J. Brill.
The Rise and Fall of the Ethnic Revival: Perspectives on Language and Ethnicity (with M.H. Gertner, E.G. Lowy and W.G. Milán). Berlin: Mouton de Gruyter.

1986 *The Fergusonian Impact: In Honor of Charles A. Ferguson on the Occasion of his 65th Birthday* (ed. with M. Abdulaziz, M. Clyne, B. Krishnamurti and A. Tabouret-Keller) (2 vols). Berlin: Mouton de Gruyter.

1987 *Ideology, Society and Language: The Odyssey of Nathan Birnbaum*. Ann Arbor, MI: Karoma.

1989 *Language and Ethnicity in Minority Sociolinguistic Perspective*. Clevedon: Multilingual Matters.
Studies in Modern Jewish Social History. New York: Ktav (reprint of 1972).

1991 *Reversing Language Shift: Theoretical and Empirical Foundations of Assistance to Threatened Languages*. Clevedon: Multilingual Matters.
Yiddish: Turning to Life: Sociolinguistic Studies and Interpretations. Amsterdam: John Benjamins.

1993 *The Earliest Stages of Language Planning: The 'First Congress' Phenomenon* (ed.). Berlin: Mouton de Gruyter.

1996 *In Praise of the Beloved Language: A Comparative View of Positive Ethnolinguistic Consciousness*. Berlin: Mouton de Gruyter.
Post-Imperial English: Status Change Since the End of Colonial Rule (1940–1990) (ed. with A. Conrad and A.R. Lopez). Berlin: Mouton de Gruyter.

1997 *The Multilingual Apple: Languages in New York City* (ed. with O. García). Berlin: Mouton de Gruyter.

1999 *Handbook of Language and Ethnic Identity* (ed.). New York: Oxford University Press.

2001 *Can Threatened Languages Be Saved?* (ed.). Clevedon: Multilingual Matters.
      Llengua i Identitat. Valencia: Bromera (includes translation into Catalan of nine articles and an interview).

2003 *Introduction to Test Construction in the Social and Behavioral Science: A Practical Guide* (with T. Galguera). Lanham, MD: Rowman & Littlefield Publishers.

Works in progress and accepted for publication (as of 2005)
      Along the Routes to Power: Explorations of Empowerment Through Language (with M. Pütz and J. Neff-van Aertselaer). Berlin: Mouton de Gruyter.
      Developing Minority Language Resources: Spanish for Native Speakers in California (with G. Valdés). Clevedon: Multilingual Matters.
      Do Not Leave Your Language Alone: The Hidden Status Agenda in Corpus Planning. Mahwah, NJ: Lawrence Erlbaum Associates.
      The Sociology of Language and Religion (with T. Omoniyi). Amsterdam: John Benjamins.
      A yidisher yid in amerike (a selection of Joshua A. Fishman's articles in Yiddish, with sectional introductions).

Articles and Book Chapters

1947 Vegn dem proyekt tsu transkribirn af english yidishe nemen. *Yidishe shprakh* 7, 36–46.

1949 Der oytser fun yidishn folklor. *Yivo-bleter* 33, 195–204.

1951 Testing: Its relationship to teaching and learning. *Jewish Education Committee Bulletin* 76, 8–10.
      Tsveyshprakhikeyt in a yidisher shul. *Bleter far yidisher dertsiyung* June–September 4, 32–42.
      A verterbukh fun folklor, mitologye un legende. *Yivo-bleter* 35, 264–272.

1952 Degree of bilingualism in a Yiddish school and leisure time activities. *Journal of Social Psychology* 36, 155–165.
      How long should the lesson be? (Massed vs. spaced learning in the classroom). *The Synagogue School* 10 (3), 5–9.
      How safe is psychoanalysis? *Jewish Education* 231, 45–48.

1954 Evaluation of results in current American Jewish education. *Jewish Education* 24 (3), 22–29.
      Patterns of American self-identification among children of an American minority group: Preliminary exploration of hypotheses via interview data. *YIVO Annual of Jewish Social Science* 10, 212–266.
      Sekulere yidishkeyt. *Yidisher kemfer*, Peysekh issue 35, 35–40.

1955 Negative stereotypes concerning Americans among American-born children receiving various types of minority-group education. *Genetic Psychology Monographs* 51, 107–182.

1956 An examination of the process and function of social stereotyping. *Journal of Social Psychology* 43, 27–64.

The MTAI in an American minority-group school setting I: Differences between test characteristics for norm and non-norm populations. *Journal of Educational Psychology* 48, 41–51.

A note on Jenkins' 'Improved method for tetrachoric r.' *Psychometrika* 21, 305.

1957 New directions in College Board research. *College Board Review* 33, 9–12.

Social science research relevant to American Jewish education: First annual bibliographic review. *Jewish Education* 28 (2), 49–60.

Some current research needs in the psychology of testimony in witnesses and testimony at trials and hearings (with R.E. Morris). *Journal of Social Issues* 13 (2), 60–67.

The use of quantitative techniques to predict college success. *Admissions Information* 1, 49–61.

The use of tests for admission to college: The next 50 years. Long range planning for education. In A. Traxler (ed.) *American Council for Education* 74–79.

1958 Educational evaluation in the context of minority-group dynamics. *Jewish Education* 29 (1), 17–24.

The MTAI in an American minority-group school setting II: Indirect validation as a test of pupil directedness. *Journal of General Psychology* 59, 219–227.

Remarks of the Chairman: Improving criteria for educational and psychological measurement. *Proceedings of the 1957 Invitational Conference on Testing Problems.* Educational Testing Service 11–12 and 30–32.

Unsolved criterion problems in the selection of college students. *Harvard Educational Review* 28, 340–349.

1959 The American dilemmas of publicly subsidized pluralism. *School and Society* 87, 264–267.

The American Jewish family today. *The Jewish Family* (pp. 2–6). Anti-Defamation League.

American Jewry as a field of Social Science research. *YIVO Annual of Jewish Social Science* 12, 70–102.

The Bridgeview study: A preliminary report (with E. Leacock and M. Deutsch). *Journal of Social Issues* 15, 30–37.

The influence of judges' characteristics on item judgments and on Thurstone Scaling via the method of ranks (with I. Lorge). *Journal of Social Psychology* 49, 187–205.

Non-intellective factors as predictors, as criteria and as contingencies in selection and guidance of college students. *Field Service Center for the Study of Higher Education* (pp. 55–73). Los Angeles, CA: University of California Press.

Publicly subsidized pluralism: The European and the American contexts. *School and Society* 87, 246–248.

Separatism and integrationism: A social-psychological analysis of editorial context in New York newspapers of three American minority groups (with G.S. Fishman). *Genetic Psychology Monographs* 59, 219–261.

Social Science research relevant to American Jewish education: Second annual bibliographic review. *Jewish Education* 29, 64–71.

1960 American higher education in current social perspective. *Teachers College Record* 62, 95–105.

College admission-selection studies (with A. Passanella). *Review of Educational Research* 30, 298–310.

The emerging picture of modern American Jewry. *Journal of Jewish Communal Service* 37, 21–34.

Home–school relations as reciprocal influences in a minority group context. *The Synagogue School* 18 (3), 13–20.

New York's non-English dailies and the deliverymen's strike. *Journalism Quarterly* 37, 241–254.

Social change and student values (with P.E. Jacob). *Educational Record* 41, 338–346.

A systematization of the Whorfian hypothesis. *Behavioral Science* 5, 323–339.

1961 Childhood indoctrination for minority group membership. *Daedalus* 90 (2), 329–349.

Flies in the psychometric ointment. *Teachers College Record* 62, 595–601.

Social-psychological theory for selecting and guiding college students. *American Journal of Sociology* 66, 472–484.

Some social and psychological determinants of intergroup relations in changing neighborhoods. *Social Forces* 40, 42–51.

Some social-psychological theory for selecting and guiding college students. In N. Stanford (ed.) *The American College* (pp. 666–689). New York: John Wiley.

Southern City. *Midstream* 7 (3), 39–56.

1962 Amerikaner yidntum vi an obyekt fun sotsial-visnshaftlekher forshung: Dergreykhungen un problemen. *Yivo-bleter* 42, 35–67.

Higher education in Megalopolis. *Journal of Higher Education* 33, 72–76.

How have Franco-Americans fared in preserving the French language in the United States? *Les Conferences de l'Institut Franco-Americain de Bowdoin College*, Deuxieme series, 44–77.

Safot zarot b'artsot habrit. *Hachinuch* 34, 274–278.

Yiddish in America. *Heritage* Fall, 5–12.

1963 The administrator in higher education as an educational leader. *School and Society* 91, 304–306.

Change in emphasis needed in schools of education. *GSE Newsletter* (Yeshiva University) 11 (3), 2.

The impact of testing programs on college preparation and attendance (with P.L. Clifford,). In W.A. Findley (ed.) *The Impact and Improvement of School Testing Programs* (pp. 82–102). Chicago, IL: University of Chicago Press.

Moving to the suburbs: Its possible impact on the role of the Jewish minority in American community life. *Phylon* 24, 146–153.

Should teachers strike? *GSE Newsletter* (Yeshiva University) 11 (4), 2.

Yidish un andere natsionale shprakhn in amerike. *Tsukunft* 68, 212–216.

1964 The academic social compact. *School and Society* 92, 29–31.

The continuity of languages in the United States. *Freeland* 17, 1 (53), 7–9 and 15.

The ethnic group school and mother tongue maintenance in the United States (with V. Nahirny). *Sociology of Education* 37, 306–317.

Guidelines for testing minority group children (with M. Deutsch, K. Kogan, R. North and M. Whiteman). *Journal of Social Issues* 20 (2), 129–145.

The impact of exposure to ethnic mother tongues on foreign language teachers in American high schools and colleges (with R.G. Hayden). *Modern Language Journal* 48, 262–274.

Language maintenance and language shift as a field of inquiry. *Linguistics* 9, 32–70.

What can mass-testing programs do for-and-to the pursuit of excellence in American education? *Harvard Educational Review* 34, 63–79.

1965 American immigrant groups: Ethnic identification and the problem of generations (with V. Nahirny). *Sociological Review* 13, 311–326.

Bilingualism, intelligence and language learning. *Modern Language Journal* 49, 227–237.

Language loyalty: Its functions and concomitants in two bilingual communities (with P. Hesbacher). *Lingua* 13, 145–165.

Language maintenance and language shift: The American immigrant case within a general theoretical perspective. *Sociologus* 16, 19–38.

Language maintenance and language shift in certain urban immigrant environments: The case of Yiddish in the United States. *Europa Ethnica* 22, 146–158.

The status and prospects of bilingualism in the United States. *Modern Language Journal* 49, 143–155.

US census data on mother tongues: Review, extrapolation and prediction. In J.A. Fishman, L. Davidowicz, E. Ehrlich and S. Ehrlich (eds) *For Max Weinreich on His Seventieth Birthday* (pp. 51–62). The Hague: Mouton.

Varieties of ethnicity and language consciousness. *Georgetown University Press Monograph Series on Language and Linguistics* 18, 69–79.

Who speaks what language to whom and when? *La Linguistique* 2, 67–88.

1966 Bilingual sequences at the societal level. *Teaching English to Speakers of Other Languages* 2, 139–144.

The ethnic group school and mother tongue maintenance in the United States. In J.A. Fishman (ed.) *Language Loyalty in the United States* (pp. 92–126). The Hague: Mouton (reprint of 1964).

The historical and social context of an inquiry into language maintenance efforts. In J.A. Fishman (ed.) *Language Loyalty in the United States* (pp. 21–33). The Hague: Mouton.

The implications of bilingualism for language teaching and language learning. In A. Valdman (ed.) *Trends in Language Teaching* (pp. 121–132). New York: McGraw Hill.

Italian language maintenance efforts in the United States and the teacher of Italian in American high schools and colleges. *The Florida FL Reporter* 4 (3), 26.

Language maintenance and language shift as a field of inquiry. In J.A. Fishman (ed.) *Language Loyalty in the United States* (pp. 424–458). The Hague: Mouton (reprint of 1964).

Language maintenance in a supra-ethnic age: Summary and conclusions. In J.A. Fishman (ed.) *Language Loyalty in the United States* (pp. 392–411). The Hague: Mouton.

Methodological notes. In J.A. Fishman (ed.) *Language Loyalty in the United States* (pp. 414–423). The Hague: Mouton.

Mother tongue and nativity in the American population (with J.E. Hofman). In J.A. Fishman (ed.) *Language Loyalty in the United States* (pp. 34–50). The Hague: Mouton.

The non-English and the ethnic group press, 1910–1960 (with R.G. Hayden and M.E. Warshauer). In J.A. Fishman (ed.) *Language Loyalty in the United States* (pp. 51–74). The Hague: Mouton.

Organizational and leadership interest in language maintenance (with V. Nahirny). In J.A. Fishman (ed.) *Language Loyalty in the United States* (pp. 156–189). The Hague: Mouton.

Planned reinforcement of language maintenance in the United States: Suggestions for the conservation of a neglected national resource. In J.A. Fishman (ed.) *Language Loyalty in the United States* (pp. 369–391). The Hague: Mouton.

Some contrasts between linguistically homogeneous and linguistically heterogeneous polities. *Sociological Inquiry* 36, 146–158.

Ukrainian language maintenance efforts in the United States (V. Nahirny). In J.A. Fishman (ed.) *Language Loyalty in the United States* (pp. 318–357). The Hague: Mouton.

1967 Bilingualism with and without diglossia: Diglossia with and without bilingualism. *Journal of Social Issues* 23 (2), 29–38.

The breadth and depth of English in the United States. *University Quarterly* March, 133–140.

Childhood indoctrination for minority group membership. In M.L. Barron (ed.) *Minorities in a Changing World* (pp. 177–200). New York: Knopf (reprint of 1961).

Cross-cultural perspective on the evaluation of guided behavioral change. In *The Evaluation of Teaching* (pp. 9–13). Washington, DC: PI Lambda Theta.

Iz do a veg tsu dernentern di yidishe shtudirndike yugnt in amerike tsu yidishkeyt? *Tsukunft* July–August, 273–277.

The management of educational establishments (with N. Gross). In P. Lazarsfeld, W.H. Sewell and H.L. Wilensky (eds) *The Uses of Sociology* (pp. 304–358). New York: Basic Books.

Some contrasts between linguistically homogeneous and linguistically heterogeneous polities. *International Journal of American Linguistics* 33 (4), 18–30 (reprint of 1966).

Tsveyshprakhike dertsiyung in amerike. *Afn shvel* 179 (4), 8–10.

1968 The breadth and depth of English in the United States. In A.H. Marckwardt (ed.) *Language and Language Learning* (pp. 43–53). Dartmouth: The Dartmouth Seminar Papers (reprint of 1967).

The contextualization of school children's bilingualism (with M. Edelman and R.L. Cooper). *Irish Journal of Education* 2, 106–111.

Language loyalty: Its functions and concomitants in two bilingual communities. In *Georgetown University Round Table Selected Papers on Linguistics, 1961–1965* (pp. 91–101). Washington, DC: Georgetown University Press (reprint of 1965).

Language problems and types of political and sociocultural integration: A conceptual summary. In J.A. Fishman, C.A. Ferguson and J. Das Gupta (eds) *Language Problems of Developing Nations* (pp. 491–498). New York: Wiley.

Nationality-nationalism and nation-nationism. In J.A. Fishman, C.A. Ferguson and J. Das Gupta (eds) *Language Problems of Developing Nations* (pp. 39–51). New York: Wiley.

Problems of research collaboration and cooperation. *Journal of Social Issues* 24 (2), 235–241.

Semantic independence and degree of bilingualism in two Puerto Rican communities (with T.D. Berney and R.L. Cooper). *Revista Interamericana de Psicologìa* 2, 289–294.

Sociolinguistics and the language problems of the developing countries. In J.A. Fishman, C.A. Ferguson and J. Das Gupta (eds) *Language Problems of Developing Nations* (pp. 3–16). New York: Wiley.

Sociolinguistics and the language problems of the developing countries. *International Social Science Journal* 20, 211–225 (reprint of 1968 original; also translated for French edition of journal).

Sociolinguistics and national development. In *Language Development* (selected papers from a Ford Foundation Conference on the State of the Art) (pp. 3–14). New York: Ford Foundation.

Sociolinguistic perspective on the study of bilingualism. *Linguistics* 39, 21–50.

Some contrast between linguistically homogeneous and linguistically heterogeneous polities. In J.A. Fishman, C.A. Ferguson and J. Das Gupta (eds) *Language Problems of Developing Nations* (pp. 53–68). New York: Wiley.

What can mass-testing programs do for-and-to the pursuit of excellence in American education? *Problems and Issues in Contemporary Education* [vol/issue number missing], 150–166 (reprint of 1964).

1969 Alternative measures of bilingualism (with R.L. Cooper). *Journal of Verbal Learning and Verbal Behavior* 8, 276–282.

Bilingual attitudes and behaviors. *Language Sciences* 5, 5–11.

The description of societal bilingualism. In L.G. Kelly (ed.) *The Description and Measurement of Bilingualism* (pp. 275–284). Toronto: Toronto University Press (originally a paper given at International Seminar, University of Moncton, June 6–14, 1967).

Language maintenance and language shift: Yiddish and other immigrant languages in the United States. *YIVO Annual of Jewish Social Science* 16, 12–26.

Language switching and the interpretation of conversation (with J. Kimple and R.L. Cooper). *Lingua* 21, 127–134.

The multiple prediction of phonological variables in a bilingual speech community (with E. Herasimchuk). *American Anthropologist* [vol/issue number missing], 648–657.

National languages and languages of wider communication in the developing nations. *Anthropological Linguistics* 11, 111–135.

Puerto Ricans in our press (with H. Casiano). *Modern Language Journal* 53, 157–163.

Puerto Rican intellectuals in New York: Some intragroup and intergroup contrasts. *Canadian Journal of Behavioral Sciences* 1 (4), 215–226.

A sociolinguistic census of a bilingual neighborhood. *The American Journal of Sociology* 75, 323–339.

Some measures of the interaction between language domain and semantic dimension in bilinguals (with S. Fertig). *Modern Language Journal* 53, 244–249.

Some things learned: Some things yet to learn. *Modern Language Journal* 53, 255–258.

The validity of census data on bilingualism in a Puerto Rican neighborhood (with C. Terry). *American Sociological Review* 34 (5), 636–650.

Word naming and usage scores for a sample of Yiddish-English bilinguals (with J. Ronch and R.L. Cooper). *Modern Language Journal* 53, 232–235.

1970 Bilingual education in sociolinguistic perspective (with J. Lovas). *TESOL Quarterly* 4, 215–222.

Di yidishe svive un di internatsiyonale akademishe svive. In M. Shtarkman (ed.) *Khesed l'avrohom* (pp. 741–748). Los Angeles, CA: Avrom Golomb-yoyul-Komitet baym yivo in los-andzheles.

Intellectuals from the Island. *La Monda Lingvo-Problemo* 2 (4), 1–16.

The interrelationships and utility of alternative bilingualism measures. In W.H. Whiteley (ed.) *Language Use and Social Change* (pp. 126–142). London: Oxford University Press (revised reprint of Alternative measures of bilingualism, 1969).

Language attitude studies (with R. Agheyisi). *Anthropological Linguistics* 11, 137–157.

Max Weinreich, 1894–1969. *Jewish Book Annual* 27, 76–80.

National languages and languages of wider communication in the developing nations. In W.H. Whiteley (ed.) *Language Use and Social Change* (pp. 27–56). London: Oxford University Press (revision of Language problems and types of political and sociocultural integration, 1968).

The politics of bilingual education. *Georgetown University Press Monograph Series on Languages and Linguistics* 23, 47–58.

Situational measures of normative language views in relation to person, place and topic among Puerto Rican bilinguals (with L. Greenfield). *Anthropos* 65, 602–618.

Sociolinguistic perspective on internal linguistic tensions and their impact on external relations. In *Transactions of the Sixth World Congress of Sociology* 3 (pp. 281–289). Milan: International Sociological Association.

Subsequent written comment (on Haugen's paper). *Georgetown University Press Monograph Series on Languages and Linguistics* 23, 9–11.

1971 Alternative measures of bilingualism. In J.A. Fishman, R.L. Cooper, R. Ma *et al. Bilingualism in the barrio* (pp. 483–512). *Language Science Monographs* 7. Bloomington, IN: Indiana University Press (revised reprint of 1969).

Attitudes and beliefs about Spanish and English among Puerto Ricans. *Bulletin of the School of Education, Indiana University at Bloomington* 47 (2), 51–72.

Bilingual attitudes and behaviors. In J.A. Fishman, R.L. Cooper, R. Ma *et al. Bilingualism in the barrio* (pp. 105–116). *Language Science Monographs* 7. Bloomington, IN: Indiana University Press (revised reprint of 1969).

Bilingualism with and without diglossia: Diglossia with and without bilingualism. In J.A. Fishman, R.L. Cooper, R. Ma *et al. Bilingualism in the barrio* (pp. 539–555). *Language Science Monographs* 7. Bloomington, IN: Indiana University Press (revised reprint of 1967).

The contrastive validity of census data on bilingualism in a Puerto Rican neighborhood (with T. Terry). In J.A. Fishman, R.L. Cooper, R. Ma *et al. Bilingualism in the barrio* (pp. 177–197). *Language Science Monographs* 7. Bloomington, IN: Indiana University Press (revised reprint of 1969).

The description of societal bilingualism. In J.A. Fishman, R.L. Cooper, R. Ma *et al. Bilingualism in the barrio* (pp. 605–611). *Language Science Monographs* 7. Bloomington, IN: Indiana University Press (revised reprint of 1969).

Ein mehrfaktoren-und mehrebenenansatz zum studium von sprachplanung-sprozessen. In R. Kjolseth and F. Sack (eds) *Zur Soziologie der Sprache* (pp. 206–213). Opladen: Westdeutscher Verlag.

How I talk to my parents. In J.A. Fishman, R.L. Cooper, R. Ma *et al.* Bilingualism in the barrio (pp. 253–272). *Language Science Monographs* 7. Bloomington, IN: Indiana University Press.

Inter-state migration and subsidiary-language claiming: An analysis of selected Indian census data (with J. Das Gupta). *International Migration Review* 5, 227–249.

The impact of nationalism on language planning. In *Aspects Sociologiques du Plurilinguisme* (pp. 15–34). Bruxelles: AIMAV.

The impact of nationalism on language planning. In J. Rubin and B. Jernudd (eds) *Can Language be Planned?* (pp. 3–20). Honolulu, HI: University Press of Hawaii (expanded reprint of 1971).

Individual interview: Puerto Rican intellectual. In J.A. Fishman, R.L. Cooper, R. Ma *et al.* Bilingualism in the barrio (pp. 75–104). *Language Science Monographs* 7. Bloomington, IN: Indiana University Press.

Intellectuals from the Island. In J.A. Fishman, R.L. Cooper, R. Ma *et al.* Bilingualism in the barrio (pp. 57–74). *Language Science Monographs* 7. Bloomington, IN: Indiana University Press.

Jewish languages and Jewish identity. In Institute of Contemporary Jewry *The Study of Jewish Identity: Issues and Approaches* (pp. 18–21). Jerusalem: Hebrew University Press.

Life in the neighborhood (with G. Hoffman). *International Journal of Comparative Sociology* 12, 85–100.

Life in the neighborhood (with G. Hoffman). In J.A. Fishman, R.L. Cooper, R. Ma *et al.* Bilingualism in the barrio (pp. 13–42, 198–232). *Language Science Monographs* 7. Bloomington, IN: Indiana University Press (revised reprint of 1971).

Measurement and description of societal bilingualism. In J.A. Fishman, R.L. Cooper, R. Ma *et al.* Bilingualism in the barrio (pp. 3–10). *Language Science Monographs* 7. Bloomington, IN: Indiana University Press.

The multiple prediction of phonological variables in a bilingual speech community (with E. Herasimchuk). In J.A. Fishman, R.L. Cooper, R. Ma *et al.* Bilingualism in the barrio (pp. 465–482). *Language Science Monographs* 7. Bloomington, IN: Indiana University Press (revised reprint of 1969).

Puerto Ricans in our press (with H. Casiano). In J.A. Fishman, R.L. Cooper, R. Ma *et al.* Bilingualism in the barrio (pp. 43–56). *Language Science Monographs* 7. Bloomington, IN: Indiana University Press (revised reprint of 1969).

Puerto Rican intellectuals in New York: Some intragroup and intergroup contrasts. In J.A. Fishman, R.L. Cooper, R. Ma *et al.* Bilingualism in the barrio (pp. 57–74). *Language Science Monographs* 7. Bloomington, IN: Indiana University Press (revised reprint of 1969).

The relationship between micro- and macro-sociolinguistics in the study of who speaks what language to whom and when. In J.A. Fishman, R.L. Cooper, R. Ma *et al.* Bilingualism in the barrio (pp. 583–604). *Language Science Monographs* 7. Bloomington, IN: Indiana University Press.

Research outline for comparative studies of language planning (with J. Das Gupta). In J. Rubin and B. Jernudd (eds) *Can Language be Planned?* (pp. 293–305). Honolulu, HI: University Press of Hawaii.

Situational measures of normative language views in relation to person, place and topic among Puerto Rican bilinguals (with L. Greenfield). In J.A.

Fishman, R.L. Cooper, R. Ma *et al.* Bilingualism in the barrio (pp. 232–252). *Language Science Monographs* 7. Bloomington, IN: Indiana University Press (revised reprint of 1970;).

Societal bilingualism: Stable and transitional. In J.A. Fishman, R.L. Cooper, R. Ma *et al.* Bilingualism in the barrio (pp. 539–556). *Language Science Monographs* 7. Bloomington, IN: Indiana University Press.

A sociolinguistic census of a bilingual neighborhood. In J.A. Fishman, R.L. Cooper, R. Ma *et al.* Bilingualism in the barrio (pp. 157–176). *Language Science Monographs* 7. Bloomington, IN: Indiana University Press (revised reprint of 1969).

Sociolinguistic perspective on the study of bilingualism. In J.A. Fishman, R.L. Cooper, R. Ma *et al.* Bilingualism in the barrio (pp. 557–582). *Language Science Monographs* 7. Bloomington, IN: Indiana University Press (revised reprint of 1968).

Sociology of language. *Pensiero e Linguaggio Operazioni* 2, 99–112.

Some things learned: Some things yet to learn. In J.A. Fishman, R.L. Cooper, R. Ma *et al.* Bilingualism in the barrio (pp. 513–518). *Language Science Monographs* 7. Bloomington, IN: Indiana University Press (reprint of 1969; revised).

The uses of sociolinguistics. In G.E. Perren and S.L.M. Trim (eds) *Applications of Linguistics* (pp. 19–40). Cambridge: Cambridge University Press.

Who speaks what language to whom and when? In J.A. Fishman, R.L. Cooper, R. Ma *et al.* Bilingualism in the barrio (pp. 583–604). *Language Science Monographs* 7. Bloomington, IN: Indiana University Press (revised reprint of 1965).

Yiddish for the people! *Judaism* 20 (2), 218–222.

1972 Bilingual and bidialectal education: An attempt at a joint model for policy description. In *Language in Sociocultural Change: Essays by Joshua A. Fishman* (pp. 331–339). Stanford, CA: Stanford University Press.

Bilingual education in sociolinguistic perspective (with J. Lovas). In B. Spolsky (ed.) *The Language Education of Minority Children: Selected Readings* (pp. 83–93). Rowley, MA: Newbury House (reprint of 1970).

Bilingualism with and without diglossia: Diglossia with and without bilingualism. In *Language in Sociocultural Change. Essays by Joshua A. Fishman* (pp. 135–153). Stanford, CA: Stanford University Press (reprint of 1966).

The description of societal bilingualism. In *Language in Sociocultural Change. Essays by Joshua A. Fishman* (pp. 153–161). Stanford, CA: Stanford University Press (reprint of 1969).

Di sotsiyologye fun yidish in amerike, 1960–1970 un vayter. *Goldene keyt* 75, 110–127.

Domains and the relationship between micro- and macro-sociolinguistics. In J.J. Gumperz and D. Hymes (eds) *Explorations in Sociolinguistics* (pp. 435–453). New York: Holt, Rinehart and Winston.

Domains and the relationship between micro- and macro-sociolinguistics. In *Language in Sociocultural Change. Essays by Joshua A. Fishman* (pp. 244–267). Stanford, CA: Stanford University Press (reprint of 1972).

Historical dimensions in the sociology of language. *Georgetown University Press Monograph Series in Language and Linguistics* 25, 145–155.

The impact of nationalism on language planning. In *Language in Sociocultural Change: Essays by Joshua A. Fishman* (pp. 224–248). Stanford, CA: Stanford University Press (reprint of 1971).

Language maintenance and language shift as a field of inquiry. In *Language in Sociocultural Change: Essays by Joshua A. Fishman* (pp. 76–134). Stanford, CA: Stanford University Press (reprint of 1964).

Language maintenance in a supra-ethnic age: Summary and conclusions. In *Language in Sociocultural Change. Essays by Joshua A. Fishman* (pp. 48–75). Stanford, CA: Stanford University Press (reprint of 1966).

The multiple prediction of phonological variables in a bilingual speech community. In *Language in Sociocultural Change: Essays by Joshua A. Fishman* (pp. 162–178). Stanford, CA: Stanford University Press (reprint of 1969).

National languages and languages of wider communication in the developing nations. In *Language in Sociocultural Change: Essays by Joshua A. Fishman* (pp. 191–233). Stanford, CA: Stanford University Press (reprint of 1969).

Planned reinforcement of language maintenance in the United States: Suggestions for the conservation of a neglected national resource. In *Language in Sociocultural Change: Essays by Joshua A. Fishman* (pp. 16–47). Stanford, CA: Stanford University Press (reprint of 1966).

Problems and prospects of the sociology of language. In *Language in Sociocultural Change: Essays by Joshua A. Fishman* (pp. 268–285). Stanford, CA: Stanford University Press.

Problems and prospects of the sociology of language. In E. Scherabon Firchow, K. Grimstad, N. Hasselmo and W.A. O'Neill (eds) *Studies for Einar Haugen* (pp. 214–226). The Hague: Mouton.

Situational measures of normative language views in relation to person, place and topic among Puerto Rican bilinguals. In S.K. Gosh (ed.) *Man, Language and Society* (pp. 4–86). The Hague: Mouton (reprint of 1970).

Sociology of language. In P.P. Giglioli (ed.) *Language and Social Context* (pp. 45–58). Harmondsworth: Penguin Books (reprint of 1971).

Sociology of language. In *Language in Sociocultural Change: Essays by Joshua A. Fishman* (pp. 1–15). Stanford, CA: Stanford University Press (reprint of 1971).

The sociology of language: An interdisciplinary approach to language in society. *Socjolinwistyka*, 255–257.

The uses of sociolinguistics. In *Language in Sociocultural Change: Essays by Joshua A. Fishman* (pp. 305–330). Stanford, CA: Stanford University Press (reprint of 1971).

Varieties of ethnicity and language consciousness. In *Language in Sociocultural Change. Essays by Joshua A. Fishman* (pp. 79–190). Stanford, CA: Stanford University Press (reprint of 1965).

What has the sociology of language to say to the teacher? On teaching the standard variety to speakers of dialectal or sociolectal varieties (with E. Lueders-Salmon). In C.B. Cazden, V.P. John and D. Hymes (eds) *Functions of Language in the Classroom* (pp. 67–83). New York: Teachers College Press.

What has the sociology of language to say to the teacher? On teaching the standard variety to speakers of dialectal or sociolectal varieties. In *Language in Sociocultural Change: Essays by Joshua A. Fishman* (pp. 340–355). Stanford, CA: Stanford University Press (reprint of 1972).

1973 Bilingual education: What and why? *Florida FL Reporter* Spring/Fall, 13–14 and 42–43.

Enseignera–t–on encore les langues en l'an 2000? *Le Français dans le Monde*

100, 11–14 (translation into French of Bilingual education: What and why? 1973).

Language modernization and planning in comparison with other types of national modernization and planning. *Language in Society* 2, 23–43.

Lekoved yudl mark. *Goldene keyt* 78, 22–26.

Natsionalizm un shprakh: Sotsyiale protsesn in 19tn un 20tn y''h. *Yivo-bleter* 44, 207–216.

The phenomenological and linguistic pilgrimage of yiddish (some examples of functional and structural pidginization and depidginization). *Kansas Journal of Sociology* 9, 127–136.

The sociolinguistics of nationalism. In P. Watson (ed.) *Psychology and Race* (pp. 403–414). Chicago, IL: Aldine.

Sociology of language. In G.A. Miller (ed.) *Communication, Language and Meaning* (pp. 268–279). New York: Basic Books (reprint of 1971).

Sociology of language. *Revista Interamericana Review* 2, 465–477 (reprint of 1971).

The sociology of language and second language teaching (with R.L. Cooper). *Kritikon Litterarum* 2, 285–292.

The third century of non-English language maintenance and non–Anglo ethnic maintenance in the United States of America. *TESOL Quarterly* 7, 221–223.

Will foreign languages still be taught in the year 2000? *Materiales en Marcha* December, 12–15 and 21.

Yiddish in Israel: The press, radio, theatre and book publishing (with D.E. Fishman). *Yiddish* Fall (2), 4–23.

1974 The comparative dimensionality and predictability of attitudinal and usage responses to centralized language planning activity. Proceedings of the Association Internationale de Linguistique Appliquée. Third Congress, Copenhagen, 1972 (Vol. II). *Applied Sociolinguistics* (pp. 71–80).

The international journal of the sociology of language: Why? *International Journal of the Sociology of Language* 1, 5–7.

Introduction: The sociology of language in Israel. *International Journal of the Sociology of Language* 1, 9–14.

Language planning and language planning research: The state of the art. *Linguistics* 119, 15–34.

Minority resistance: Some comparisons between interwar Poland and postwar USA. In J.A. Fishman (ed.) *Studies on Polish Jewry, 1919–1970: The Interplay of Social, Economic and Political Factors in the Struggle of a Minority for its Existence* (pp. 3–11). New York: YIVO Institute for Jewish Research

The sociology of bilingual education. *Études de Linguistique Appliquée*, 112–124.

Sociology of language. In G.A. Miller (ed.) *Psychology and Communication* (pp. 303–314). Washington, DC: Voice of America Forum Series (reprint of 1971).

Some studies of language attitudes in Israel (with R.L. Cooper). *English Teachers Journal* 12, 38–39.

The study of language attitudes (with R.L. Cooper). *International Journal of the Sociology of Language* 3, 5–20.

A systematization of the Whorfian hypothesis. In L.W. Berry and P.R. Dasen (eds) *Culture and Cognition: Readings in Cross-Cultural Psychology* (pp. 61–85). London: Methuen (reprint of 1968).

The use of Hebrew loanwords in spoken German in two bilingual communities (with R.H. Kressel). *Linguistics* 140, 69–78.

Vos ken zayn di funktsiye fun yidish in yisroel? *Yidisher kemfer* April, 40–46.

Will foreign languages still be taught in the year 2000? *New Ideas in Language Teaching* 11, 1–2 (partial reprint of 1973).

Yiddish in Israel: A case-study of efforts to revise a monocentric language policy (with D.E. Fishman). *International Journal of the Sociology of Language* 1, 124–146.

Yiddish in Israel: A case-study of efforts to revise a monocentric language policy. *Yiddish* 1 (2), 4–23 (abbreviated reprint of 1974).

1975 Advances in the sociology of language I. *Current Trends in Linguistics* 12, 1629–1784 (reprint of *Advances in the Sociology of Language* I, 1971).

Bilingual education and the future of language teaching and language learning. *Association of Departments of Foreign Languages (ADFL)* 3, 5–8.

Conservación y desplazamiento del idioma como campo de investigación (reexamen). In P.L. Garvin and Y. Lastra de Suarez (eds) *Antología de etno-lingüística y sociolingüística* (pp. 375–423). Mexico: Universidad Nacional Autónoma de México (revision and translation into Spanish of Language maintenance and language shift as a field of inquiry, 1964).

Guidelines for testing minority group children (with M. Deutsch, L. Kogan, R. North and R. Whiteman). In D.A. Payne and R.F. Mc Morris (eds) *Educational and Psychological Measurement; Contributions to Theory and Practice* (pp. 297–307). Waltham, MA: Blaisdell Pub. Co (reprint of 1964).

The 'official languages' of Israel: Their status in law and police attitudes and knowledge concerning them (with H. Fisherman). In J.G. Savard and R. Vigneault (eds) *Multilingual Political Systems: Problems and Solutions* (pp. 497–535). Québec: Presses de l'Université Laval.

The study of language attitudes. In L. Palmer and B. Spolsky (eds) *Papers on Language Testing: 1967–1974* (pp. 187–197). Washington, DC: TESOL (revised reprint of 1974).

The uses of diversity. In G.C. Harvey and M.F. Heiser (eds) *Southwest Languages and Linguistics in Educational Perspective* (pp. 393–427). San Diego, CA: San Diego University Press.

What do we know about language planning? (A preliminary report). In R.K. Herbert (ed.) *Patterns in Language, Culture and Society: Sub-Saharan Africa* (pp. 1–2). Columbus, OH: Ohio State University Press.

Yiddish in Israel: A case study of efforts to revise a monocentric language policy. *Jewish Digest* 20 (9), 37–39 (partial reprint of 1974).

1976 Bilingual education and the future of language teaching and language learning (with R. Cooper). In *Bilingual Education: An International Sociological Perspective* (pp. 32–46). Rowley, MA: Newbury House (reprint of 1975).

Bilingual education: Hope for Europe's migrants. *Un Nuevo Día* 2 (3), 1 and 12.

Bilingual education: What and why? In A. Simoes (ed.) *TheBilingual Child* (pp. 229–235). [City: publisher missing] (reprint of 1973).

Bilingual education: What and why? In J.A. Fishman (ed.) *Bilingual Education: An International Sociological Perspective* (pp. 23–31). Rowley, MA: Newbury House (reprint of 1973).

Bilingual education: What and why? In *Sprachen und Staaten, Festschrift Heinz Kloss* (pp. 125–142). Hamburg: Stiftung Europa-Kolleg, 2 (reprint of 1973).

Comments on recent references. In J.A. Fishman (ed.) *Bilingual Education: An*

International Sociological Perspective (pp.136–149). Rowley, MA: Newbury House.

The future of ethnicity in America. In E.J. Friis (ed.) *The Scandinavian Presence in North America* (pp. 12–32). New York: Norwegian-American Historical Association.

How do terminological committees of the Hebrew language academy actually work? (with J. Fellman). *Comparative Interdisciplinary Studies Section, Working Paper* 81.

International socioeducational perspective on some uncomfortable questions about bilingual education. In J.A. Fishman (ed.) *Bilingual Education: An International Sociological Perspective* (pp. 108–125). Rowley, MA: Newbury House.

The international sociology of bilingual secondary education: Empirical findings and theoretical implications. In A. Juilland (ed.) *Linguistic Studies Offered to Joseph Greenber* (pp. 27–42). New York: Anna Ligri.

The international sociology of bilingual secondary education: Empirical findings and theoretical implications. In J.A. Fishman (ed.) *Bilingual Education: An International Sociological Perspective* (pp. 94–107). Rowley, MA: Newbury House (reprint of 1976).

Language and culture in the global community. In J.A. Fishman (ed.) *Bilingual Education: An International Sociological Perspective* (pp. 3–10). Rowley, MA: Newbury House.

The nations of the world: Some social and economic characteristics. In *Bilingual Education: An International Sociological Perspective* (pp. 77–93). Rowley, MA: Newbury House.

Problems and prospects of the sociology of language. *Zeitschrift fur Dialekt-ologie und Linguistik* 39 (1), 2–18 (translation into German of 1972).

The sociology of bilingual education. In *Sprachen und Staaten, Festschrift Heinz Kloss* (pp. 143–165). Hamburg: Stiftung Europa-Kolleg, 2 (reprint of 1974).

The sociology of language in Israel. *Language Sciences* 40, 28–31.

The spread of English as a new perspective for the study of language maintenance and language shift. *Studies in Language Learning* 1 (2), 59–104.

The third century of non-English language maintenance and non-Anglo ethnic maintenance in the United States of America. In J.A. Fishman (ed.) *Bilingual Education: An International Sociological Perspective* (pp. 11–22). Rowley, MA: Newbury House (reprint of 1973).

Thumbnail sketches of ten bilingual schools outside of the United States. In J.A. Fishman (ed.) *Bilingual Education: An International Sociological Perspective* (pp. 127–135). Rowley, MA: Newbury House.

Will foreign languages still be taught in the year 2000? In J.A. Fishman (ed.) *Bilingual Education: An International Sociological Perspective* (pp. 47–51). Rowley, MA: Newbury House (reprint of 1973).

Worldwide perspective on bilingual education. In J.A. Fishman (ed.) *Bilingual Education: An International Sociological Perspective* (pp. 52–77). Rowley, MA: Newbury House.

Yerusholayemer 'velt-konferents far yidisher kultur' fun a sotsio-lingvistishn kukvinkl. *Yidishe shprakh* 35, 1–3 and 16–31.

Yiddish and Loshn Koydesh in traditional Ashkenaz: The problem of societal allocation of macro-functions. In A. Verdoodt and R. Kjolseth (eds)

Language in Sociology (pp. 39–47). Louvain: Institute de Linguistique de Louvain.

Yudel Mark (1897–1975) *Jewish Book Annual* 34, 94–97.

1977 Bilingual education: Ethnic perspectives and response to panelists. In *Bilingual Education: Ethnic Perspectives* (pp. 1–15, 47–52). Philadelphia: Nationalities Center.

The bilingual education act: High time for a change. *Bilingual Review* 3 (1), 1–2.

The comparative study of language planning: Introducing a survey. In J. Rubin, J. Das Gupta, C.A. Ferguson, J.A. Fishman and B.H. Jernudd (eds) *Language Planning Processes* (pp. 31–39). The Hague: Mouton.

Conference on the methodology of sociolinguistic surveys: A subjective summary. *Vicus* 1, 161–167.

Der yivo in amerike: Problemen un dergreykhn in shaykhes mit zayn mehus. *Goldene keyt* 93, 111–122.

English around the world (with R.L. Cooper and Y. Rosenbaum). In J.A. Fishman, R. Cooper and W. Conrad (eds) *The Spread of English: The Sociology of English as an Additional Language* (pp. 77–107). Rowley: Newbury House.

English as a world language: The evidence (with A.W. Conrad). In J.A. Fishman, R. Cooper and W. Conrad (eds) *The Spread of English: The Sociology of English as an Additional Language* (pp. 3–76). Rowley: Newbury House.

English in Israel: A sociolinguistic study (with E. Nadel). *Anthropologica Linguistica* 19 (1), 27–53.

English in Israel: A sociolinguistic study (with E. Nadel). In J.A. Fishman, R. Cooper and W. Conrad (eds) *The Spread of English: The Sociology of English as an Additional Language* (pp. 137–167). Rowley: Newbury House (reprint of 1977).

English in the context of international societal bilingualism. In J.A. Fishman, R. Cooper and W. Conrad (eds) *The Spread of English: The Sociology of English as an Additional Language* (pp. 329–336). Rowley: Newbury House.

English on Keren Kayemet Street (with Y. Rosenbaum, E. Nadel and R.L. Cooper). In J.A. Fishman, R. Cooper and W. Conrad (eds) *The Spread of English: The Sociology of English as an Additional Language* (pp. 179–196). Rowley: Newbury House.

English the world over: A factor in the creation of bilingualism today. *Bilingualism: Psychological, Social and Educational Implications*, 103–139.

Knowing, using and liking English as an additional language. *TESOL Quarterly* 11 (2), 157–171.

Knowing, using and liking English as an additional language. In J.A. Fishman, R. Cooper and W. Conrad (eds) *The Spread of English: The Sociology of English as an Additional Language* (pp. 302–328). Rowley: Newbury House (reprint of 1977).

Language and ethnicity. In H. Giles (ed.) *Language and Ethnicity in Intergroup Relations* (pp. 16–53). London and New York: Academic Press.

Language planning in Israel: Solving terminological problems (with J. Fellman). In J. Rubin, J. Das Gupta, C.A. Ferguson, J.A. Fishman and B.H. Jernudd (eds) *Language Planning Processes* (pp. 79–95). The Hague: Mouton.

Language, ethnicity and racism. In *Georgetown University Round Table on*

Language and Linguistics (pp. 297–309). Washington, DC: Georgetown University Press.

Language, technology and persuasion (with R. Cooper, L. Lown, B. Schaier and F. Seckbach). In J.A. Fishman, R. Cooper and W. Conrad (eds) The Spread of English: The Sociology of English as an Additional Language (pp. 197–211). Rowley: Newbury House (reprint of 1977).

Language, technology and persuasion: Three experimental studies. In H. Giles (ed.) Language and Ethnicity in Intergroup Relations (pp. 83–98). London: Academic Press.

The link between language and ethnicity: Its importance for the language teacher. In W.C. Born (ed.) Language Acquisition, Application, Appreciation (pp. 97–101). [City: publisher missing.]

A model for bilingual and bidialectal education. In W.F. Mackay and T. Andersson (eds) Bilingualism in Early Childhood (pp. 11–18). Rowley, MA: Newbury House.

Per un educazione bilingue. Lingue et Civilta 3/4, 19–24.

Selected dimensions of language planning: A comparative analysis. In J. Rubin, J. Das Gupta, C.A. Ferguson, J.A. Fishman and B.H. Jernudd (eds) Language Planning Processes (pp. 195–214). The Hague: Mouton

The sociology of bilingual education. In B. Spolsky and R.L. Cooper (eds) Frontiers of Bilingual Education (pp. 94–105). Rowley: Newbury House (reprint of 1974).

The sociology of language and second language teaching (with R. Cooper). Min hasadne 3–4, 173–184 (translation into Hebrew of 1973).

The sociology of language, yesterday, today and tomorrow. In R. Cole (ed.) Current Issues in Linguistic Theory (pp. 51–75). Bloomington, IN: Indiana University Press.

The spread of English as a new perspective for the study of 'language maintenance and language shift'. In J.A. Fishman, R. Cooper and W. Conrad (eds) The Spread of English: The Sociology of English as an Additional Language (pp. 108–136). Rowley: Newbury House.

Standard vs. dialect in bilingual education: An old problem in a new context. Modern Language Journal 61, 315–325.

A study of language attitudes (with R.L. Cooper). Bilingual Review 4, 1–2, 7–34.

A study of language attitudes (with R.L. Cooper). In J.A. Fishman, R. Cooper and W. Conrad (eds) The Spread of English: The Sociology of English as an Additional Language (pp. 239–277). Rowley: Newbury House (reprint of 1977).

1978 Bilingual education and the future of language teaching and language learning. The Bilingual Journal 2 (4), 19–22 (reprint of 1975).

Bilingual education: What and why? In M.A. Lourie and N.F. Conkin (eds) A Pluralistic Nation: The Language Issue in the United States (pp. 407–416). Rowley: Newbury House (reprint of 1973).

Bilinguismo e insegnamento della lingue (with R.L. Cooper). Quaderni per la Promozione de Bilingualismo 17/18, 18–32 (translation into Italian of Bilingual Education: An International Sociological Perspective, 1976: Chapter 4).

Der yivo in amerike: problemen un dergreykhn in shaykhes mit zayn mehus. Buenos Aires: Instituto Científico Judío (reprint of 1977).

The history and future of language policy in the USA. EDC News 12, 3–4.

A gathering of vultures, the 'legion of decency' and bilingual education in the USA. NABE Journal 21, 13–16.

A graduate program in the sociology of language. In J. Fishman (ed.) *Advances in the Study of Societal Multilingualism* (pp. 795–798). The Hague: Mouton.

A graduate program in the sociology of language. In J.A. Fishman (ed.) *Advances in the Creation and Revision of Writing Systems* (pp. 471–474). The Hague: Mouton (reprint of 1978).

The Indonesian language planning experience: What does it teach us? A socio-historical reconstruction and projection. In S. Udin (ed.) *Spectrum Essays Presented to Sutan Takdir Alisjahbana on His Seventieth Birthday* (pp. 333–339). Jakarta: Dian Rakyat.

Language in society (with H. Giles). In H. Tajfel and C. Friseur (eds) *Introducing Social Psychology* (pp. 380–400). Hardmondsworth: Penguin.

Positive bilingualism: Some overlooked rationales and forefathers. In *Georgetown University Round Table on Language and Linguistics* (pp. 42–52). Washington DC: Georgetown University Press.

The phenomenological and linguistic pilgrimage of Yiddish (some examples of functional and structural pidginization and depidginization). In J.A. Fishman (ed.) *Advances in the Creation and Revision of Writing Systems* (pp. 293–306). The Hague: Mouton (reprint of 1973).

The sociolinguistic 'normalization' of the Jewish people. *Archibald Hill Festschrift* 3, 223–231.

The sociology of Yiddish after the Holocaust: Status, needs and possibilities. *Gesher* 6, 148–168.

The spread of English: A worldwide factor in the making and breaking of bilingualism. *CATESOL Occasional Papers* 4, 12.

Yiddish in Israel: A case study of efforts to revise a monocentric language policy (with D.E. Fishman). In J.A. Fishman (ed.) *Advances in the Study of Societal Multilingualism* (pp. 185–262). The Hague: Mouton.

1979 Bilingual education: What and why? In H. Trueba and C. Barnett-Mizrahi (eds) *Bilingual Multicultural Education and the Professional* (pp. 11–19). Rowley: Newbury House (reprint of 1973).

Linguistics: The scientific study of languages. In H. Trueba and C. Barnett-Mizrahi (eds) *Bilingual Multicultural Education and the Professional* (pp. 130–137) Rowley: Newbury House (reprint of *The Sociology of Language: An Interdisciplinary Social Science Approach,* 1972: Section X).

On going beyond kinship, sex and the tribe. In R. Pinxten (ed.) *On Going Beyond Kinship, Sex and the Tribe* (pp. 127–144). The Hague: Mouton.

Philosophies of bilingual education in societal perspective. In E.J. Brierre (ed.) *Language Development in a Bilingual Setting* (pp. 36–47). Los Angeles: National Dissemination and Assessment Center.

Some basic sociolinguistic concepts. In H. Trueba and C. Barnett-Mizrahi (eds) *Bilingual Multicultural Education and the Professional* (pp. 120–130) Rowley: Newbury House (reprint of *The Sociology of Language: An Interdisciplinary Social Science Approach,* 1972: Section III).

Standard vs. dialect in bilingual education: An old problem in a new context. In H. Trueba and C. Barnett–Mizrahi (eds) *Bilingual Multicultural Education and the Professional* (pp. 454–466) Rowley: Newbury House (reprint of 1977).

The dimensionality and predictability of responses to language planning activities. In W.C. McCormack and S.A. Wurm (eds) *Language in Society: Anthropological Issues* (pp. 703–723). The Hague: Mouton.

The significance of the ethnic community mother tongue school: Introduction to a study. *National Association of Bilingual Education Journal* 3 (3), 39–47.

Transition, maintenance or a third alternative. In *Proceedings of the Fourth National Portuguese Conference* (pp. 3–23). Providence, RI: National Association of Portuguese Bilingual Education.

1980 Attracting a following to high-culture functions for a language of everyday life: The role of the Tshernovits language conference in the rise of Yiddish. *International Journal of the Sociology of Language* 24, 43–74.

Bilingual education in the United States under ethnic community auspices. In *Georgetown University Round Table* (pp. 8–13). Washington, DC: Georgetown University Press.

Bilingual education, language planning and English. *English World-Wide* 1, 11–24.

Bilingualism and biculturalism as individual and as societal phenomena. *Journal of Multilingual and Multicultural Development* 1 (1), 3–15.

Ethnic community mother tongue schools in the USA: Dynamics and distributions. *International Migration Review* 14, 235–247.

Ethnocultural dimensions in the acquisition and retention of biliteracy. *Basic Writing* Fall/Winter (3), 48–61.

Language maintenance and ethnicity. *Harvard Encyclopedia of American Ethnic Groups* (pp. 629–638).

Language policy: Past, present and future. In C.A. Ferguson and S.B. Heath (eds) *Language in the USA* (pp. 516–526). Cambridge: Cambridge University Press.

Language spread: Implications of an international conference for the Southwest. In E.L. Blansitt and R.V. Teschner (eds) *Festschrift for Jacob Ornstein: Studies in General Linguistics and Sociolinguistics* (pp. 114–119). Rowley, MA: Newbury House.

Minority language maintenance and the ethnic mother tongue school. *Modern Language Journal* 64, 167–172.

The need for language planning in the United States. *AFDL Bulletin* 12 (2), 1–3.

New worlds to conquer in the sociology of language. *York Papers in Linguistics* 9, 99–104.

Social theory and ethnography: Language and ethnicity in Eastern Europe. In P. Sugar (ed.) *Ethnic Diversity and Conflict in Eastern Europe* (pp. 69–99). Santa Barbara, CA: ABC-Clio.

The sociology of Yiddish after the Holocaust: Status, needs and possibilities. In M.I. Herzog, B. Kirshenblatt-Gimblett, D. Miron and R. Wisse (eds) *The Field of Yiddish: Studies in Language, Folklore and Literature* (pp. 475–498). Philadelphia, PA: Institute for the Study of Human Issues.

The Whorfian hypothesis: Varieties of valuation, confirmation and disconfirmation 1. *International Journal of the Sociology of Language* 26, 25–40.

Theoretical issues and problems in the sociolinguistic enterprise. *Annual Review of Applied Linguistics* 1, 161–168.

1981 Attracting a following to high-culture functions for a language of everyday life: The role of the Tshernovits conference in the rise of Yiddish. In J.A. Fishman (ed.) *Never Say Die! A Thousand Years of Yiddish in Jewish Life and Letters* (pp. 369–394). The Hague: Mouton (reprint of 1980).

Cultural pluralism and the American school. *Plural Societies* 12, 5–12.

Epilogue: Contributions of the sociology of Yiddish to the general sociology of language. In J.A. Fishman (ed.) *Never Say Die! A Thousand Years of Yiddish in Jewish Life and Letters* (pp. 739–756). The Hague: Mouton.

Ethnic community mother tongue schools in the USA: Dynamics and distributions. In J.A. Fishman (ed.) *Never Say Die! A Thousand Years of Yiddish in Jewish Life and Letters* (pp. 369–394). The Hague: Mouton.

In defense of learning English and maintaining other languages (in the United States and elsewhere too). *English Around the World* 25, 1–3.

Language maintenance and ethnicity. *Canadian Review of Studies in Nationalism* 8, 229–248.

On-reservation residence and the survival of Native American languages. *Current Anthropology* 22, 580–582.

Sociology of language. In G. Geertz and A. Hagen (eds) *Sociolinguistiese Studies 2.* Groningen: Wolters-Noorhopp (translation into Dutch of 1971).

The sociology of Jewish languages from the perspective of the general sociology of language: A preliminary formulation. *International Journal of the Sociology of Language* 30, 5–18.

The sociology of Yiddish: A foreword. In J.A. Fishman (ed.) *Never Say Die! A Thousand Years of Yiddish in Jewish Life and Letters* (pp. 1–102). The Hague: Mouton.

Treci aspekt vorfove misili: Ethnolinguistica raznolikost kao dobrobit drustvenih azjednica sveta. *Zbornik Radova Instituta za Strane Jezike i Knjizevnosti* 3, 17–46.

Tsi iz nokh do a hofenung far yidish in amerike? Buenos Aires: *Davke* 82, 62–74.

1982 Attracting a following to high-culture functions for a language of everyday life: The role of the Tshernovits language conference in the 'rise of Yiddish'. In R.L. Cooper (ed.) *Language Spread* (pp. 291–320). Bloomington, IN: Indiana University Press (reprint of 1980).

Bilingual education. *World Book Encyclopedia* (Vol. B; p. 234). Chicago: World Book Childcraft International.

Bilingualism and biculturalism as individual and as societal phenomena. In J.A. Fishman and G. Keller (eds) *Bilingual Education for Hispanic Students in the United States* (pp. 23–36). New York: Teachers College Press (reprint of 1980).

A critique of six papers on the socialization of the deaf child. In J.B. Christian and R.W. Meisegeiser (eds) *National Research Conference on the Social Aspects of Deafness* (pp. 5–20). Georgetown: Gallaudet Press.

Language and identity: Keynote address. *Revista del Colegio Universitario del Turbo* 7 (1), 12–24.

Language maintenance, the ethnic revival and diglossia in the United States (with M.H. Gertner, E.G. Lowy and W.G. Milán). *Journal of Intercultural Studies* 3, 5–24.

Maintien des langues, 'renouveau ethnique' et diglossie aux États-Unis (with M.H. Gertner, E.G. Lowy and W.G. Milán). *La Linguistique* 18, 45–64 (translation into French of 1982).

Mother tongues as media of instruction in the United States. In K. Zondag (ed.) *Bilingual Education in Friesland* (pp. 263–273). Leeuwarden/Ljouwert: Franeker, Liber.

Sociolinguistic foundations of bilingual education. *Bilingual Review* 9, 1–35.

The Jewish daily *Forward* and non-English resources in the USA today. *The Forward* (English supplement) May 23, pp. 5 and 25.

The lively life of a 'dead language' or everyone knows that Yiddish died long ago. *Judaica Book News* 13 (1), 7–11.

The sociology of English as an additional language. In B. Kachru (ed.) *The Other Tongue: English Across Cultures* (pp. 15–22). Urbana, IL: University of Illinois Press.

Whorfianism of the third kind: Ethnolinguistic diversity as a worldwide societal asset (The Whorfian hypothesis: Varieties of validation, confirmation and disconfirmation 2). *Language in Society* 11, 1–14.

Yidish, modernizatsye un re-etnifikatsye: An emeser un faktndiker tsugang tsu der itstiker problematik. *Afn shvel* 248, 1–6.

1983 The Americanness of the ethnic community school. In B.A. Burch (ed.) *Minnesota's Ethnic Language Schools: Potential for the 80s* (pp. 5–15). St Paul, MN: Immigration Research Center.

Aménagement et norme linguistique en milieux linguistiques récemment conscientisés. In E. Bedard and J. Maurais (eds) *La Norme Linguistique* (pp. 383–394). Montreal: Conseil de la langue française.

Comments on Symmon-Symonolewicz' collective sentiments and their social hierarchies. *Canadian Review of Studies in Nationalism* 10, 283–287.

D'r nosn birmboyms ershter peyrek: Afn veg tsu yidish un tsum mizrekh-eyropeyishn yidntum. *Afn shvel* 255, 13–16.

Epistemology, methodology and ideology in the sociolinguistic enterprise. In A.Z. Guiora (ed.) *An Epistemology for the Language Sciences* (pp. 33–47). Detroit, MI: Wayne State University Press.

Ethnic activists view the ethnic revival and its language consequences: An interview study of three American ethnolinguistic minorities (with E.G. Lowy, M.H. Gertner, I. Gottesman and W.G. Milán). *Journal of Multilingual and Multicultural Development* 4 (4), 237–254.

Language and ethnicity in bilingual education. In W. McCready (ed.) *Culture, Ethnicity and Identity: Current Issues and Research* (pp. 127–137). New York, Academic Press.

Language and ethnicity in the periodical publications of four American ethnic groups (with M.H. Gertner, E.G. Lowy and W.G. Milán). *Multilingua* 2, 83–99.

Modeling rationales in corpus planning: Modernity and tradition in images of the good corpus. In J. Cobarrubias and J.A. Fishman (eds) *Progress in Language Planning: International Perspectives* (pp. 107–118). Berlin: Mouton.

Mother-tongue claiming in the United States since 1960. *International Journal of the Sociology of Language* 50, 21–99.

'Nothing new under the sun' (Ecclesiastes 1:9): A case study of early stages of the language and ethnocultural identity linkage. In A. Jacobson-Widding (ed.) Identity: Personal and socio-cultural (pp. 263–287), *Uppsala Studies in Cultural Anthropology* 5. Uppsala: Uppsala Acta Universitatis Upsaliensis.

On the peculiar problems of smaller national languages. In A. Gonzales (ed.) *Panagani: Essays in Honor Bonifacio P. Sibayan on His Sixty–Seventh Birthday* (pp. 40–45). Manila: Linguistic Society of the Philippines (simultaneous publication of 1983 below).

On the peculiar problems of smaller national languages. *Philippine Journal of Linguistics* 1983–1984, 2 (1), 40–45 (simultaneous publication of 1983 above).

Progress in language planning: A few concluding sentiments. In J. Cobarrubias and J.A. Fishman (eds) *Progress in Language Planning: International Perspectives* (pp. 381–383). Berlin: Mouton.

Reflections on ten years of *IJSL*. *International Journal of the Sociology of Language* 45, 5–7.

The rise and fall of the 'ethnic revival' in the USA. *Journal of Intercultural Studies* 4 (3), 5–46.

Shprakhikeyt in hayntikn yisroel. *Afn shvel* 252, 5–8.

Spanish language resources of the United States: Some preliminary findings (with W.G. Milán). In L. Elías-Olivares (ed.) *Spanish in the United States Setting: Beyond the Southwest* (pp. 167–179). Rosslyn, VA: National Clearing House for Bilingual Education.

Studies of language as an aspect of ethnicity and nationalism (A bibliographic introduction). *Sociolinguistics* 14 (2), 1–6.

The use of minority mother tongues in the education of children. *Prospects* 14 (1), 51– 61.

The use of minority mother tongues in the education of children. *Prospects* (French edition) 14 (1), 53–64 (translation into French of 1983).

The use of minority mother tongues in the education of children. *Prospects* (Spanish edition) 14 (2), 53–64 (translation into Spanish of 1983).

The use of minority mother tongues in the education of children. *Prospects* (Japanese edition) 14 (3), 43–52 (translation into Japanese of 1983).

The use of minority mother tongues in the education of children. *Prospects* (Arabic edition) 14 (1), 48–58 (translation into Arabic of 1983).

Yidish, modernizatsye un re-etnifikatsye: An emeser un faktndiker tsugang tsu der itstiker problematic. In S. Rozhansky (ed.) *Memuarn, filosofye, forshung in der yidisher literature* (pp. 315–330). Buenos Aires: Musterverk (reprint of 1982).

1984 Mother tongue claiming in the United States since 1960: Trends and correlates related to the revival of ethnicity. *The International Journal of the Sociology of Language* 50, 21–100.

Reflections on 10 years of *IJSL*. *International Journal of the Sociology of Language* 45, 5–8.

1985 'Am' and 'Goy' as designations for ethnicity in selected books of the Old Testament (with D.E. Fishman and R. Mayerfeld). In J.A. Fishman (ed.) *The Rise and Fall of the Ethnic Revival: Perspectives on Language and Ethnicity* (pp. 15–38). Berlin: Mouton de Gruyter.

Arabic language-maintenance efforts in the United States (with M. Sawaie). *Journal of Ethnic Studies* 13 (1), 33–49.

Bilingualism and biculturalism as individual and as societal phenomena. In J.A. Fishman (ed.) *The Rise and Fall of the Ethnic Revival: Perspectives on Language and Ethnicity* (pp. 39–56). Berlin: Mouton de Gruyter (reprint of 1980).

D'r nosn birnboyrns tsveyter peyrek: Der kemfer far yidish un yidisher kultur–oytonomye. *Afn shvel* 257, 2–6.

D'r nosn birnboyms driter peyrek: di derheybung un fartifung fun yidisher kedushe. *Afn shvel* 258, 10–13.

Demographic and institutional indicators of German language maintenance in the United States, 1960–1980. In F. Trommler and J. McVeigh (eds) *America and the Germans: An Assessment of a 300 Year History* (Vol. 1; pp. 251–269). Philadelphia, PA: University of Pennsylvania Press.

Ethnic activists view the ethnic revival and its language consequences: An interview study of three American ethnolinguistic minorities. In J.A. Fishman (ed.) *The Rise and Fall of the Ethnic Revival: Perspectives on Language and Ethnicity* (pp. 283–302). Berlin: Mouton de Gruyter (reprint of 1983).

The ethnic revival in the United States: Implications for the Mexican-American community. In W. Conner (ed.) *Mexican-Americans in Comparative Perspective* (pp. 309–335). Washington DC: Urban Institute.

Ethnocultural dimensions in the acquisition and retention of biliteracy: A comparative ethnography of four New York City schools. In J.A. Fishman (ed.) *The Rise and Fall of the Ethnic Revival: Perspectives on Language and Ethnicity* (pp. 377–442). Berlin: Mouton de Gruyter.

The Hispanic press in the United States: Content and prospects (with O. García, S. Burunat and M.H. Gertner). In J.A. Fishman (ed.) *The Rise and Fall of the Ethnic Revival: Perspectives on Language and Ethnicity* (pp. 343–362). Berlin: Mouton de Gruyter.

Language and culture. In A. Kuper and J. Kuper (eds) *The Social Science Encyclopedia* (pp. 444). London: Routledge.

Language and ethnicity in the periodical publications of four American ethnic groups. In J.A. Fishman (ed.) *The Rise and Fall of the Ethnic Revival: Perspectives on Language and Ethnicity* (pp. 305–342). Berlin: Mouton de Gruyter (reprint of 1983).

Language maintenance and ethnicity. In J.A. Fishman (ed.) *The Rise and Fall of the Ethnic Revival: Perspectives on Language and Ethnicity* (pp. 57–76). Berlin: Mouton de Gruyter (reprint of 1981).

Language, ethnicity and racism. In J.A. Fishman (ed.) *The Rise and Fall of the Ethnic Revival: Perspectives on Language and Ethnicity* (pp. 3–14). Berlin: Mouton de Gruyter (reprint of 1977).

The lively life of a dead language or everyone knows that Yiddish died long ago. In N. Wolfson and J. Manes (eds) *Language of Inequality* (pp. 207–222). Berlin: Mouton (reprint, revision and expansion of 1982).

Macro-sociolinguistics/sociology of language in the early eighties. *Annual Review of Sociology* 11, 113–127.

Mother-tongue claiming in the United States since 1960. In J.A. Fishman (ed.) *The Rise and Fall of the Ethnic Revival: Perspectives on Language and Ethnicity* (pp. 107–194). Berlin: Mouton de Gruyter (reprint of 1983).

Nathan Birnbaum's first phase: From Zionism to Eastern European Jewry (in commemoration of his 120th birthday). *Shofar* 4 (1), 17–27.

Non-English language ethnic community schools in the USA: Instruments of more than literacy and less than literacy. *Working Papers on Migrant and Intercultural Studies* 1 (July).

'Nothing new under the sun' (Ecclesiastes 1:9): A case study at early stages of the 'language and ethnocultural identity' linkage. In J.A. Fishman (ed.) *The Rise and Fall of the Ethnic Revival: Perspectives on Language and Ethnicity* (pp. 77–104). Berlin: Mouton de Gruyter (reprint of 1983).

Positive bilingualism: Some overlooked rationales and forefathers. In J.A. Fishman (ed.) *The Rise and Fall of the Ethnic Revival: Perspectives on Language and Ethnicity* (pp. 445–456). Berlin: Mouton de Gruyter (reprint of 1978).

The rise and fall of the 'ethnic revival' in the USA. In J.A. Fishman (ed.) *The

Rise and Fall of the Ethnic Revival: Perspectives on Language and Ethnicity (pp. 489–526). Berlin: Mouton de Gruyter (reprint of 1983).

The significance of the ethnic community mother-tongue school. In J.A. Fishman (ed.) *The Rise and Fall of the Ethnic Revival: Perspectives on Language and Ethnicity* (pp. 363–372). Berlin: Mouton de Gruyter.

The societal basis of the inter-generational continuity of additional languages. In K.R. Jankowsky (ed.) *Scientific and Humanistic Dimensions of Language: Festschrift for Robert Lado* (pp. 551–558). Amsterdam: Benjamins.

The sociology of Jewish languages from the perspective of the general sociology of language: A preliminary formulation. In J.A. Fishman (ed.) *Readings in the Sociology of Jewish Languages* (pp. 3–21). Leiden: Brill (reprint of 1981).

Special issue on Yiddish (with G.S. Fishman). *Bilingual Family Newsletter*, Multilingual Matters (entire issue).

Spracherhalt. In D. Elschenbroich (ed.) *Einwanderung, Integration, Etnische Bindung* (pp. 155–178). Frankfurt: Stroemfeld/Roter Stern (translation into German of Language maintenance and ethnicity, 1980).

Toward multilingualism as an international desideratum in government, business and the professions. *Annual Review of Applied Linguistics* 6, 2–9.

Tsi iz nokh do a hofenung far yidish in amerike? *Melburner Bleter* November–December, 13–17 (reprint of 1981).

The Whorfian hypothesis: Varieties of valuation, confirmation and disconfirmation 1. In J.A. Fishman (ed.) *The Rise and Fall of the Ethnic Revival: Perspectives on Language and Ethnicity* (pp. 457–472). Berlin: Mouton de Gruyter (reprint of 1980).

Whorfianism of the third kind: Ethnolinguistic diversity as a worldwide societal asset (The Whorfian hypothesis: Varieties of validation, confirmation and disconfirmation 2). In J.A. Fishman (ed.) *The Rise and Fall of the Ethnic Revival: Perspectives on Language and Ethnicity* (pp. 473–485). Berlin: Mouton de Gruyter (reprint of 1982).

Why did Yiddish change? *Diachronica* 2 (1), 67–82.

Written Spanish in the United States: An analysis of the Spanish of the ethnic press (with O. García, M. Gertner and S. Burunat). *International Journal of the Sociology of Language* 56, 85–98.

1986 Baskn alekho shpanye! *Afn shvel* 264, 14–17.

Bilingualism and separatism. *Annals of the American Association of Political and Social Science* 487, 168–180.

Demographic and institutional indicators of German language maintenance in the United States, 1960–1980. In F. Trommler (ed.) *Amerika und die Deutschen: Bestandsaufnahme einer 300 jahrigen Geschichte* (pp. 263–278). Opladen: Westdeutscher Verlag (translation into German of 1985).

Der gezelshaftiker bazis funem tsvishn-doyresdikn hemshekh fun tsveyte shprakhn. *Afn shvel* 262, 3–5.

Ivrit v'yidish: Yitsug khizuti shel yakhasim sotsyolingvistim. *Hadoar* 66 (7), 12–16.

Nathan Birnbaum's third phase: The activization of Jewish sanctity. In J.A. Fishman (with A. Tabouret-Keller, M. Clyne, B. Krishnamurti and M. Abdulaziz, eds) *The Fergusonian Impact* (pp. 325–336). Berlin: Mouton de Gruyter.

Shprakh-planirung, oysleyg-planirung un yidish. *Afn shvel* 261, 6–10.

Yidish un yidishe sotsiolingvistik: Tsvishn yo un neyn. *Afn shvel* 263, 9–12.

1987   A naye farteydikung fun yidish in di khareydishe krayzn. *Afn shvel* 266, 3–6.

Continuity and change in Nathan Birnbaum's thought. In J.A. Fishman, *Ideology, Society and Language: The Odyssey of Nathan Birnbaum* (pp. 85–108). Ann Arbor, MI: Karoma.

Der noyekh hatsadik fun der yidisher shprakh. *Vegn mordkhe shekhter un zayn verk: tsu zayn 60stn geboyrntog* (pp. 20–22). New York: League for Yiddish.

English: Neutral tool or ideological protagonist? A 19th century East-Central European intellectual views English from afar. *English World Wide* 8, 1–10.

Ideology, society and language: The sociolinguist as biographer: Returning to initial questions and turning to new ones. In J.A. Fishman, *Ideology, Society and Language: The Odyssey of Nathan Birnbaum* (pp. 109–131). Ann Arbor, MI: Karoma.

Introduction (to *IJSL* issue on Progress in the sociology of Jewish languages). *International Journal of the Sociology of Language* 67, 5–6.

Language spread and language policy for endangered languages. In *Georgetown University Round Table on Language and Linguistics* (pp. 1–15). Washington, DC: Georgetown University Press.

Nathan Birnbaum's first phase: From Zionism to Eastern European Jewry (in commemoration of his 120th birthday). In J.A. Fishman, *Ideology, Society and Language: The Odyssey of Nathan Birnbaum* (pp. 11–25). Ann Arbor, MI: Karoma (reprint of 1985).

Nathan Birnbaum's second phase: The champion of Yiddish and Jewish cultural autonomy. In B. Narr and H. Wittje (eds) *Spracherwerb und Mehrsprachigkeit; Festschrift fur Els Oksaar zum 60 Geburtstag* (pp. 173–180). Tubingen: Gunter Narr.

Nathan Birnbaum's second phase: The champion of Yiddish and Jewish cultural autonomy. In J.A. Fishman, *Ideology, Society and Language: The Odyssey of Nathan Birnbaum* (pp. 26–37). Ann Arbor, MI: Karoma (reprint of 1987).

Nathan Birnbaum's third phase: The activization of Jewish sanctity. In J.A. Fishman, *Ideology, Society and Language: The Odyssey of Nathan Birnbaum* (pp. 72–84). Ann Arbor, MI: Karoma (reprint of 1986).

Nathan Birnbaum's view of American Jewry. *Judaica Book News* Fall/Winter 18 (1), 10–14 and 68–70.

Post-exilic Jewish languages and pidgins/creoles: Two mutually clarifying perspectives. *Multilingua* 6 (1), 7–24.

Reflections on the current state of language planning. In L. LaForge (ed.) *Proceedings of the International Colloquium on Language Planning* (pp. 406–428). Quebec: University of Laval Press.

The role of the Tshernovits language conference in 'The rise of Yiddish'. In J.A. Fishman, *Ideology, Society and Language: The Odyssey of Nathan Birnbaum* (pp. 38–71). Ann Arbor, MI: Karoma.

The sociolinguist as biographer: Questions. In J.A. Fishman, *Ideology, Society and Language: The Odyssey of Nathan Birnbaum* (pp. 1–10). Ann Arbor, MI: Karoma.

The sociolinguist as biographer: Reflections on taking leave. In J.A. Fishman, *Ideology, Society and Language: The Odyssey of Nathan Birnbaum* (pp. 132–141). Ann Arbor, MI: Karoma.

Translation into English of 15 selected German or Yiddish articles written by Nathan Birnbaum (with W. Kramer and M. Gertner). In J.A. Fishman,

Ideology, Society and Language: The Odyssey of Nathan Birnbaum (pp. 145–246). Ann Arbor, MI: Karoma.

What is happening to Spanish on the US mainland? *Ethnic Affairs* 1, 12–23.

1988 Der hebreyisher opruf af der tshernovitser konferents. *Afn shvel* 271, 8–13.

English only: Its ghosts, myths and dangers. *International Journal of the Sociology of Language* 74, 125–140.

The development and reform of writing systems. In U. Ammon, N. Dittmar and K.J. Mattheier (eds) *Sociolinguistics/Soziolinguistik 2* (pp. 1643–1650). Berlin: Mouton de Gruyter.

Ethnocultural issues in the creation, substitution and revision of writing systems. In B.A. Rafoth and D.L. Rubin (eds) *The Social Construction of Written Communication* (pp. 273–286). Norwood, NJ: Ablex.

Language spread and language policy for endangered languages. *Jakin* 48, 5–21 (translation into Basque of 1987).

Nosn birnboyms dray tshernovitser konferentsn. *Tsukunft* 95 (1), 85–90.

Research on national languages. In U. Ammon, N. Dittmar and K.J. Mattheier (eds) *Sociolinguistics/Soziolinguistik 1* (pp. 638–646). Berlin: Mouton de Gruyter.

1989 Attracting a following to high-culture functions for a language of everyday life: The role of the Tshernovits language conference in 'The rise of Yiddish'. In J.A. Fishman, *Language and Ethnicity in Minority Sociolinguistic Perspective* (pp. 498–529). Clevedon: Multilingual Matters (reprint of 1980).

Bilingualism and biculturalism as individual and as societal phenomena. In J.A. Fishman, *Language and Ethnicity in Minority Sociolinguistic Perspective* (pp. 181–201). Clevedon: Multilingual Matters (reprint of 1980).

Cross-polity linguistic homogeneity/heterogeneity and per-capita gross national product: An empirical exploration. *Language Problems and Language Planning* 13, 103–118.

Cross-polity perspective on the importance of linguistic heterogeneity as a 'contributory factor' in civil strife. In J.A. Fishman, *Language and Ethnicity in Minority Sociolinguistic Perspective* (pp. 605–626). Clevedon: Multilingual Matters.

Elites and rank-and-file: Contrasts and contexts in ethnolinguistic behavior and attitudes. In J.A. Fishman, *Language and Ethnicity in Minority Sociolinguistic Perspective* (pp. 481–484). Clevedon: Multilingual Matters.

English only: Its ghosts, myths and dangers. In J.A. Fishman, *Language and Ethnicity in Minority Sociolinguistic Perspective* (pp. 638–654). Clevedon: Multilingual Matters (reprint of 1988).

Ethnic activists view the ethnic revival and its language consequences: An interview study of three American ethnolinguistic minorities. In J.A. Fishman, *Language and Ethnicity in Minority Sociolinguistic Perspective* (pp. 530–549). Clevedon: Multilingual Matters (reprint of 1983).

Ethnic community mother tongue schools in the USA: Dynamics and distributions. In J.A. Fishman, *Language and Ethnicity in Minority Sociolinguistic Perspective* (pp. 452–464). Clevedon: Multilingual Matters (reprint of 1980).

The ethnic dimension in language planning. In J.A. Fishman, *Language and Ethnicity in Minority Sociolinguistic Perspective* (pp. 265–268). Clevedon: Multilingual Matters.

Ethnolinguistic homogeneity and heterogeneity: Worldwide causes, consequences and aspirations. In J.A. Fishman, *Language and Ethnicity in Minority Sociolinguistic Perspective* (pp. 561–563). Clevedon: Multilingual Matters.

Far vos zol undz ongeyn der matsev fun irlendish? *Afn shvel* 274, 3–7.

Institutional language maintenance resources of American Indians in the early 1980s. In M.R. Key and H.M. Hoenigswald (eds) *General and Amerindian Ethnolinguistics: In Remembrance of Stanley Newman* (pp. 107–122). Berlin: Mouton de Gruyter.

Language and ethnicity in education: The bilingual minority focus. In J.A. Fishman, *Language and Ethnicity in Minority Sociolinguistic Perspective* (pp. 419–424). Clevedon: Multilingual Matters.

Language and ethnicity. In J.A. Fishman, *Language and Ethnicity in Minority Sociolinguistic Perspective* (pp. 23–65). Clevedon: Multilingual Matters (reprint of 1977).

Language maintenance and ethnicity. In J.A. Fishman, *Language and Ethnicity in Minority Sociolinguistic Perspective* (pp. 202–223). Clevedon: Multilingual Matters (reprint of 1980).

Language maintenance and language shift in ethnocultural perspective. In J.A. Fishman, *Language and Ethnicity in Minority Sociolinguistic Perspective* (pp. 177–180). Clevedon: Multilingual Matters.

Language policy: Past, present and future. In J.A. Fishman, *Language and Ethnicity in Minority Sociolinguistic Perspective* (pp. 403–418). Clevedon: Multilingual Matters (reprint of 1981).

Language spread and language policy for endangered languages. In J.A. Fishman, *Language and Ethnicity in Minority Sociolinguistic Perspective* (pp. 389–402). Clevedon: Multilingual Matters (reprint of 1987).

Language, ethnicity and racism. In J.A. Fishman, *Language and Ethnicity in Minority Sociolinguistic Perspective* (pp. 9–22). Clevedon: Multilingual Matters (reprint of 1977).

Mit vos iz yidish andersh? *Afn shvel* 273, 7–11.

Modeling rationales in corpus planning: Modernity and traditions in images of the good corpus. In J.A. Fishman, *Language and Ethnicity in Minority Sociolinguistic Perspective* (pp. 367–388). Clevedon: Multilingual Matters (reprint of 1983).

Nathan Birnbaum's view of American Jewry. In J.A. Fishman, *Language and Ethnicity in Minority Sociolinguistic Perspective* (pp. 550–560). Clevedon: Multilingual Matters (reprint of 1987).

Non-English language ethnic community schools in the USA: Instruments of more than literacy and less than literacy. In E.Z. Sonino (ed.) *Literacy in School and Society* (pp. 25–31). New York: Plenum (reprint of 1985).

'Nothing new under the sun' (Ecclesiastes 1:9): A case study at early stages of the language and ethnocultural identity linkage. In J.A. Fishman, *Language and Ethnicity in Minority Sociolinguistic Perspective* (pp. 66–96). Clevedon: Multilingual Matters (reprint of 1983).

On the peculiar problems of smaller national languages. In J.A. Fishman, *Language and Ethnicity in Minority Sociolinguistic Perspective* (pp. 368–375). Clevedon: Multilingual Matters (reprint of 1983).

Philosophies of bilingual education in societal perspective. In J.A. Fishman, *Language and Ethnicity in Minority Sociolinguistic Perspective* (pp. 439–451). Clevedon: Multilingual Matters (reprint of 1979).

Puerto Rican intellectuals in New York: Some intragroup and intergroup contrasts. In J.A. Fishman, *Language and Ethnicity in Minority Sociolinguistic Perspective* (pp. 485–497). Clevedon: Multilingual Matters (reprint of 1969).

The rise and fall of the 'ethnic revival' in the USA. In J.A. Fishman, *Language and Ethnicity in Minority Sociolinguistic Perspective* (pp. 655–698). Clevedon: Multilingual Matters (reprint of 1983).

The societal basis of the inter-generational continuity of additional languages. In J.A. Fishman, *Language and Ethnicity in Minority Sociolinguistic Perspective* (pp. 224–233). Clevedon: Multilingual Matters (reprint of 1985).

The sociology of bilingual education. In J.A. Fishman, *Language and Ethnicity in Minority Sociolinguistic Perspective* (pp. 425–438). Clevedon: Multilingual Matters (reprint of 1974).

The spread of English as a new perspective for the study of language maintenance and language shift. In J.A. Fishman, *Language and Ethnicity in Minority Sociolinguistic Perspective* (pp. 233–263). Clevedon: Multilingual Matters (reprint of 1976).

Status planning for endangered languages. In I. Fodor and C. Hagege (eds) *Language Reform: History and Future* (pp. 1–11). Hamburg: Buske 4 (revision of Language spread and language policy for endangered languages, 1957; retitled).

Toward multilingualism as an international desideratum in government, business and the professions. In J.A. Fishman, *Language and Ethnicity in Minority Sociolinguistic Perspective* (pp. 627–637). Clevedon: Multilingual Matters (reprint of 1985).

The use of minority mother tongues in the education of children. In J.A. Fishman, *Language and Ethnicity in Minority Sociolinguistic Perspective* (pp. 465–480). Clevedon: Multilingual Matters (reprint of 1983).

Utilizing societal variables to predict whether countries are linguistically homogeneous or heterogeneous. In J.A. Fishman, *Language and Ethnicity in Minority Sociolinguistic Perspective* (pp. 580–604). Clevedon: Multilingual Matters.

Utilizing societal variables to predict whether countries are linguistically homogeneous or heterogeneous. *Cultural Dynamics* 1, 414–437 (reprint of 1988).

Utilizing societal variables to predict whether countries are linguistically homogeneous or heterogeneous. *Basque World Congress, Conference on the Basque Language*. 2: *Hizkuntza eta Gizzartes/Lengua y sociedad* (pp. 185–202). Vitoria-Gasteiz: Gobierno Vasco (reprint and revision of 1988).

What is ethnicity and how is it linked to language? Phenomenological and socio–historical considerations. In J.A. Fishman, *Language and Ethnicity in Minority Sociolinguistic Perspective* (pp. 5–8). Clevedon: Multilingual Matters.

Whorfianism of the third kind: Ethnolinguistic diversity as a worldwide societal asset. In J.A. Fishman, *Language and Ethnicity in Minority Sociolinguistic Perspective* (pp. 564–579). Clevedon: Multilingual Matters (reprint of 1982).

Yiddish dictionaries through the centuries. *Worterbicher* 3 (pp. 2246–2254). Berlin: Mouton.

Yidish bay di khareydim; frishe koykhes un naye tsores. *Afn shvel* 276, 1–5.

1990 Cross-polity perspective on the importance of linguistic heterogeneity as a contributory factor in civil strife. *Canadian Review of Studies in Nationalism* 17, 131–146 (reprint and revision of 1988).

Di farlegnheytn funem hayntikn yidishizm. *Afn shvel* 278, 1–5.

Empirical explorations of two popular assumptions: Interpolity perspective on the relationships between linguistic heterogeneity, civil strife and per capita gross national product. In F. Imhof (ed.) *Learning in Two Languages: From Conflict to Consensus in the Reorganization of Schools* (pp. 209–225). New Brunswick, NJ: Transaction Publishers.

English as a world language revisited. In L. Laforge and G.D. McConnell (eds) *Language Spread and Social Change: Dynamics and Measurement* (pp. 97–102). Sainte-Foy: Presses de l'Université Laval.

100 (hundert) yor ivrit-miduberet: Uftu un dayges. *Afn shvel* 279, 4–7.

The lexicography of Yiddish. *Worterbucher, Dictionaries, Dictionnaires* 2, 2246–2254.

Limitaciones de la eficacia escolar para invertir el desplazamiento lingüístico (IDL). *Ponencias Internacionales: Primer Congreso de la Escuela Pública Vasca* (pp. 127–141). Vitoria-Gasteiz: Gobierno Vasco.

Limitaciones de la eficacia escolar para invertir el desplazamiento lingüístico (IDL). *Ponencias y Comunicaciones, Tomo/Primer Congreso de la Escuela Pública Vasca* (pp. 191–196). Vitoria-Gasteiz: Gobierno Vasco (reprint of 1990 original).

Linguistic heterogeneity and civil strife. *Canadian Review of Studies in Nationalism* 17, 1–2.

My life through my work: My work through my life (autobiography). In K. Koerner (ed.) *First Person Singular II: Autobiographies by North American Scholars in the Language Sciences* (pp. 105–124). Amsterdam: John Benjamins.

Reflections on the current state of language planning. In U.N. Singh and R.N. Srivastava (eds) *Perspectives in Language Planning* (pp. 27–59). Calcutta: Mithila Darshan (reprint of 1987).

Towards a theory of reversing language shift. *Journal of Multilingual and Multicultural Development* 11, 5–36.

Tsu maks vaynraykhs 21stn yortsayt. *Afn shvel* 277, 10–14.

Vos iz der shaykhes tsvishn shprakh un kultur? *Afn shvel* 280, 11–16.

1991 Cartoons about language: A case study of the visual representation of sociolinguistic attitudes. In V. Ivir and D. Kalogjera (eds) *Languages in Contact and Contrast: Essays in Contact Linguistics* (pp. 179–193). Berlin: Mouton de Gruyter.

The centrality of language in the thinking of language ideologists. In B. Lakshmi Bai and B. Ramakrishna Reddy (eds) *Studies in Dravidian and General Linguistics: A Festschrift for Bh. Krishnamurti* (pp. 390–399). Hyderabad: Centre of Advanced Study in Linguistics, Osmania University.

Der onheyb fun visikn ahaves-yidish un sines-yidish in mizrekh-eyrope. *Afn shvel* 285 (Part I).

Dzudezme un yidish in 1492. New York: *Afn shvel* 287/288, 6–10.

The Hebraist response to the Tshernovits Conference. *Semitic Studies* 1, 437–449.

Hebrew and Yiddish: The Visual representation of sociolinguistic relationships. In V. Ivir and D. Kalogjera (eds) *Languages in Contact and Contrast: Essays in Contact Linguistics* (pp. 179–193). Berlin: Mouton de Gruyter (translation and revision of Ivrit v'yidish, 1986).

Inter-polity perspective on the relationship between linguistic heterogeneity, civil strife and gross national product. *International Journal of Applied Linguistics* 1, 5–18.

It Baskysk and it Frysk. *It Beaken* 53 (3/4), 119–149.

A methodological check on three cross-polity studies of linguistic homogeneity/heterogeneity (with G.D. McConnell and F.R. Solano). In M.E. McGroarty and C. Faltis (eds) *Languages in School and Society: Policy and Pedagogy* (pp. 21–30). Berlin: Mouton de Gruyter.

Nosn birnboyms: Di uvdes fun mizrekh–eyropeyishe yidn. *Yivo Bleter*, Yivo Institute for Jewish Research I, 109–128 (new series).

Putting the 'socio' back into the sociolinguistic enterprise. *The International Journal of the Sociology of Language* 92, 127–138.

Three dilemmas of organized efforts to reverse language shift. In U. Ammon and M. Hellinger (eds) *Status Change of Languages* (pp. 285–293). Berlin: Mouton de Gruyter.

Tsi ken eyn shprakh farmogn tsvey normes? Der norvegisher fal. *Afn shvel* 281, 7–11.

1992 Ahaves-yidish un sines-yidish. *Afn shvel* 284/285, 22–23.

Cross-polity analysis of factors affecting English language spread: Predicting three criteria of spread from a large pool of independent variables (with A. Rubal-López). *World English* I (2/3), 309–329.

Der onheyb fun visikn ahaves-yidish un sines-yidish in mizrekh-eyrope. *Afn shvel* 286, 10–16 (Part II).

Dzudezme un yidish in 1492. *Afn shvel* 287/288, 6–10.

The lexicography of Yiddish. In L. Zgusta (ed.) *History, Languages and Lexicographers* (pp. 2246–2254). Tübingen: M. Niemeyer.

Prospects for reversing language shift (RLS) in Australia: Evidence from its aboriginal and immigrant languages. *Vox: The Journal of the Australian Advisory Council of Languages and Multicultural Education* 6, 48–62.

The sociology of English as an additional language. In B.B. Kachru (ed.) *The Other Tongue: English Across Cultures* (pp. 20–25). Urbana, IL: University of Illinois Press.

Yiddish: Thesaurus of linguistic indexing terms. In *Handbook of Linguistics* (p. 96). Berlin: Mouton de Gruyter.

1993 A makhloykes leshem-shomayem vegn ... oysleyg. *Afn shvel* 289/290, 13–16 (simultaneous publication of 1993 below).

A makhloykes leshem-shomayem vegn ... oysleyg. *Forverts* April 30, 15 and 18 (simultaneous publication of 1993 above).

The content of positive ethnolinguistic consciousness. *Geolinguistics* 19, 16–25.

Eskolaren mugak hizkunta biziberritzeko saioan. *BAT: Soziolinguistika Aldizkaria* 10, 37–47 (translation into Basque of Limitaciones de la eficacia escolar para invertir el displazamiento lingulstico, 1990).

Ethnolinguistic democracy: Varieties, degrees and limits. *Language International* 5, 11–17.

The 'First Congress' phenomenon: Arriving at some general conclusions. In J.A. Fishman (ed.) *The Earliest Stages of Language Planning: The First Congress Phenomenon* (pp. 332–348). Berlin: Mouton de Gruyter.

Good conferences in a wicked world: On some worrisome problems in the study of language maintenance and language ahift. In W. Fase, K. Jaspaert and S. Kroon (eds) *The State of Minority Languages* (pp. 311–317). Lisse: Swets & Zeitlinger.

In praise of my beloved language. *Working Papers in Educational Linguistics* 9 (2/Fall), 1–11.

Introduction and Postscript to Magocsi's scholarly seminar on the codification of the Rusyn language. *The International Journal of the Sociology of Language* 100/101, 104, 119 and 123–125.

Introduction: Exploring an overlooked sociolinguistic phenomenon: The first congress for language. In J.A. Fishman (ed.) *The Earliest Stages of Language Planning: The First Congress Phenomenon* (pp. 1–10). Berlin: Mouton de Gruyter.

Language conflict and language planning. In F. Coulmas (ed.) *Trends in Linguistics, Studies and Monographs* (pp. 69–81). Berlin: Mouton de Gruyter.

Le Yiddich, de la tradition à la modernisation. In S. Trigano (ed.) *La Société Juive à Travers l'Histoire* (pp. 511–521). Paris: Fayard (translation into French of Ahaves-yidish un sines-yidish, 1992).

Linguistic heterogeneity, civil strife and per capita gross national product in inter-polity perspective. In A. Roca and J.M. Lipski (eds) *Spanish in the United States: Linguistic Contact and Diversity* (pp. 9–19). Berlin: Mouton de Gruyter.

One hundred issues of *IJSL. International Journal of the Sociology of Language* 100/101, 5–8.

Reversing language shift: Successes, failures, doubts and dilemmas. In E. Håkon Jahr (ed.) *Language Conflict and Language Planning* (pp. 69–81). Berlin: Mouton de Gruyter.

The Tshernovits Conference revisited: The first World Conference for Yiddish, 85 years later. In J.A. Fishman (ed.) *The Earliest Stages of Language Planning: The First Congress Phenomenon* (pp. 321–332). Berlin: Mouton de Gruyter.

Three successful cases (more or less): Modern Hebrew, French in Quebec and Catalan in Spain. *Treballs de Sociolinguistica Catalana* 19, 4.

Yidish un shtimrekht in nyu-york. *Afn shvel* 291, 11–14, Part I.

Yidish un shtimrekht in nyu york. *Afn shvel* 292, 12–14, Part II.

1994 Critiques of language planning: A minority languages perspective. *Journal of Multilingual and Multicultural Development* 15 (2/3), 91–99.

Di tshernovitser konferents. *Afn shvel* 292, 1–5.

Di 'moderne ortodoksye' un yidish. *Afn shvel* 294, 2–5.

Di sotsiologye fun yidish mitn ponem tsum 21stn yorhundert. *Afn shvel* 295, 1–5.

Dictionaries as culturally constructed and as culture-enacting artifacts: The reciprocity view as seen from Yiddish sources. In B.B. Kachru and H. Kahana (eds) *Cultures, Ideologies and the Dictionary* (pp. 29–34). Tubingen: Max Neimayer Verlag.

'English only'. *Sociolinguistica* 8, 65–72.

The limits of ethnolinguistic democracy. T. Skutnabb-Kangas and R. Phillipson (eds) *Contributions to the Sociology of Language: Linguistic Human Rights* (pp. 49–61). Berlin: Mouton de Gruyter.

The neo-Marxist and post-structural critiques of 'classical language planning.' *Mosaica Digest* 3, 65–67 (reprint of 1994 original).

Neo-Marxist and post-structural critiques of 'classical language planning.' In I. Fodor and Claude Hagège (eds) *Language Reform: History and Future* (pp. 1–8). Hamburg: Helmut Buske Verlag.

In praise of my language or what do minorities want? In A. Strijbosch (ed.) *Grensverkenningen: Over groepsvorming, minderheden en tolerantie* (pp. 141–150) (Series: *Reeks Recht & Samenleving* nr. 9). Nijmegen: Katolieke Universiteit.

Sociologie du Yiddish. In J. Baumgarten (ed.) *Mil ans de Cultures Ashkenazes* (pp. 427–436). Paris: Editions du Cerf (reprint of Di sotsiologye fun yidish mitn ponem tsum 21stn yorhundert, 1994).

The truth about language and culture (and a note about the relevance of the Jewish case). *International Journal of the Sociology of Language* 109, 83–96.

Vos far a min konferents iz geven di tshernovitser konferents fun 1908. *Afn shvel* 293, 1–5.

Yiddish and voting rights in New York: 1915 and 1921. *Language Problems and Language Planning* 181, 1–17.

1995 Der gebitener tsugang tsu shprakh un kultur. *Afn shvel* 298, 12–16.

Einar Haugen. *Language* 71, 558–564.

Einar Haugen. *BAT: Soziolinguistika Aldizkaria* 2, 57–64 (translation and reprint of 1995).

Einar Haugen. *Journal of the Linguistic Society of America* 71 (3), 558–564 (reprint of 1995).

In appreciation of Einar Haugen. *The International Journal of the Sociology of Language* 116, 165–173.

Maks vaynraykh in amerike: A talmids zikhroynes. *Goldene keyt* 140, 5–12.

Yiddish scholarship today. In D.W. Halwachs, G. Penzinger and G. Ambrosch (eds) *Linguistics With a Human Face: Festschrift fur Norman Denison zum 70 Geburstag* 10 (pp. 73–80). Graz: Institut fur Sprachenwissenschaft der Universitat.

Yiddish scholarship today. *Oerprintsel u twat oars ah mei in echte taal.* [City: publisher missing] (translation into Frisian of 1995).

1996 Di 'moderne ortodoksiye' un der frumer politisher ekstremizm. *Afn shvel* 302, 3–7.

Language and nationalism. In S. Woolf (ed.) *Nationalism in Europe: 1815 to the Present: A Reader* (pp. 55–170). London: Routledge (reprint of excerpts from *Language and Nationalism*, 1972).

Language revitalization. In H. Goebel, P.H. Nelde, Z. Stary and W. Wolsk (eds) *Kontaktlinguistik/Contact Linguistics/Linguistiquede Contact: An International Handbook of Contemporary Research* (pp. 902–906). Berlin: Mouton de Gruyter.

Perfecting the perfect: Improving the beloved language. *Text and Nation* 3–16.

What do you lose when you lose your language? ERIC document (Education Resources Information Center, US Microfiche) ED395732.

Yiddish revival confounds experts. *Mosaica Digest 3*, 65–67 (reprint of 1996 original).

Yiddish revival confounds experts. *Yeshiva University Review* (winter), 14–16.

1997 Bloomington, summer of 1964: The birth of American sociolinguistics. In C.B. Paulston and G.R. Tucker (eds) *The Early Days of Sociolinguistics: Memories and Reflections* (pp. 87–95). Dallas, TX: Summer Institute of Linguistics Publications.

Do ethnics have culture? And what's so special about New York anyway? In O. García and J.A. Fishman *The Multilingual Apple: Languages in New York City* (pp. 341–351). Berlin: Mouton de Gruyter.

The First Congress phenomenon. *Rusinski Zhivot* 4 (April 14), 1–3 (translation into Rusyn of 1993, abbreviated).

Kedushe shebeyidish. *Afn shvel* 307, 3–8.

Language and ethnicity: The view from within. In F. Coulmas (ed.) *The Handbook of Sociolinguistics* (pp. 327–343). Oxford: Blackwell Publishers.

Language maintenance and language shift as a field of inquiry. *Estudios sobre comunicación interlingüística e intercultural* 7, 3–53 (translation and reprint of 1964).

Predictors and criteria in multisite census survey research: From Einar Haugen to today. In S. Eliasson and E. Håkon Jahr (eds) *Language and its Ecology: Essays in Memory of Einar Haugen* (pp. 3–21). Berlin: Mouton de Gruyter.

Reflections about (or prompted by) *International Journal of the Sociology of Language (IJSL)*. In C.B. Paulston and G.R. Tucker (eds) *The Early Days of Sociolinguistics: Memories and Reflections* (pp. 237–241). Dallas, TX: Summer Institute of Linguistics Publications.

Uriel Weinreich (1926–1967): A sociolinguistic appreciation. In C.B. Paulston and G.R. Tucker (eds) *The Early Days of Sociolinguistics: Memories and Reflections* (pp. 307–313). Dallas, TX: Summer Institute of Linguistics Publications.

Yiddish in the universities: Possibilities and problems. *Jewish Currents* 51, 30–32.

Zikhroynes vegn maks vaynraykh. *Yivo bleter* III, 349–353 (new series).

1998 Maintaining languages: What works? What doesn't? In G. Cantoni (ed.) *Stabilizing Indigenous Languages* (pp. 186–198). Flagstaff, AZ: Northern Arizona University Press.

Nyelvi modernizacio es nyelvi tervesez a nemzeti modernizacio es tervezes mas tipusaival osszehasonlitva. In *Nyelvi Tervezes* (pp. 11–30). Budapest: Universitas Kiado (translation into Hungarian of Language modernization and planning in comparison with other types of national modernization and planning, 1973).

On the importance of new sociolinguistic journals. *Japanese Journal of Language in Society* 1, 5–7.

Sociolinguistic impressions/Impressions sociolinguistiques. *Treballs se Sociolinguistica Catalana* 14/15, 229–230.

The third century of non-English language maintenance and non-Anglo ethnic maintenance in the United States. In *Nyelvi Tervezes* (pp. 31–50). Budapest: Universitas Kiado (translation into Hungarian of 1973).

Vi vet oyszen der yidishizm inem 21stn yorhundert? *Afn shvel* 309, 3–5.

What do you lose when you lose your language? In G. Cantoni (ed.) *Stabilizing Indigenous Languages* (pp. 80–91). Flagstaff, AZ: Northern Arizona University Press (originally ERIC document ED395732, 1996).

Zhitlovski un tshernovits. *Afn shvel* 311, 1–4.

1999 The City as the root of all evil. *Educators for Urban Minorities* 1, 45–50.

Comments and reflections. *Anthropology and Education Quarterly* 30, 116–124.

Concluding comments. In J.A. Fishman (ed.) *Handbook of Language and Ethnic Identity* (pp. 444–454). New York: Oxford University Press.

Honoring an honorable, serious and most knowledgeable friend: Koen Zondag. In D. Gorter *Liber Amicorum Koen Zondag* (pp. 23–25). Ljouwert, Friesland.

Maks vaynraykh: shtrikhn un meynungen. *Afn shvel* 313, 2–5.

The new linguistic order. *Foreign Policy* 113, 26–40.

The new linguistic order. In P. O'Meara, H.D. Mehlinger and M. Krain (eds) *Globalization and the Challenges of a New Century* (pp. 435–442). Bloomington, IN: Indiana University Press (reprint of 1999).

Sociolinguistics. In J.A. Fishman (ed.) *Handbook of Language and Ethnic Identity* (pp. 152–163). New York: Oxford University Press.

2000 Business as usual for threatened languages. *He Pukenga Korero, A Journal of Māori Studies* 5 (2), 16–20.

La linguistica de Pompeu Fabra. In J. Ginebra, R-D. Martínez Gili and M.A. Pradilla (eds) *La lingüística de Pompeu Fabra* (pp. 41–55). Alacant: Institut Interuniversitari de Filologia Valenciana and Barcelona: Universitat Rovira i Virgili.

Language planning for 'the other Jewish languages' in Israel: An agenda for the beginning of the 21st century. *Language Problems and Language Planning* 24 (3), 215–231.

Lezikorn shloyme birnboymen. *Afn shvel* 320, 3–5.

Obituary: Charles A. Ferguson. *Journal of Sociolinguistics* 4, 120–128.

Rethinking language defense. In R. Phillipson (ed.) *Rights to Language, Equity, Power and Education: Celebrating the 60th Birthday of Tove Skutnabb-Kangas* (pp. 23–27). Mahwah, NJ: Lawrence Erlbaum Associates.

Reversing language shift: RLS theory and practice revisited. In G. Kindell and M.P. Lewis (eds) *Assessing Ethnolinguistic Vitality: Theory and Practice: Selected Papers from the Third International Language Assessment Conference* (pp. 1–25). Dallas, TX: SIL International.

The status agenda in corpus planning. In R.D. Lambert and E. Shohamy (eds) *Language Policy and Pedagogy: Essays in Honor of A. Ronald Walton* (pp. 43–51). Amsterdam: John Benjamins.

2001 L'agenda de l'estatus en la planificació del corpus. In J.A. Fishman *Llengua i identitat* (pp. 265–278). Alzira: Bromera (translation into Catalan of The status agenda in corpus planning, 2000).

A decade in the life of a two-in-one language: Yiddish in New York City (secular and ultra-orthodox). In J.A. Fishman (ed.) *Can Threatened Languages Be Saved?* (pp. 74–100). Clevedon: Multilingual Matters.

Di eybike shtotishkeyt funem eybikn folk. *Afn shvel* 324, 3–6.

Digraphia maintenance and loss among Eastern European Jews (Intertextual and interlingual print-conventions since 1800). *International Journal of the Sociology of Language* 150, 27–41.

From theory to practice and vice versa. In J.A. Fishman (ed.) *Can Threatened Languages Be Saved?* (pp. 451–483). Clevedon: Multilingual Matters.

Greetings from a viewer from afar: The objectives of Israel's sociology of language. In H. Herzog and E. Ben-Rafael (eds) *Language and Communication in Israel* (pp. 625–632). New Brunswick: Transaction Publishers.

If threatened languages can be saved, then can dead languages be revived? *Current Issues in Language Planning* 2 (2–3), 222–230.

Interwar Eastern European Jewish parties and the language issue. *International Journal of the Sociology of Language* 151, 175-189.

Introducing Khayem Zhitlovski. In R. Cooper, E. Shoshamy and J. Walters (eds) *New Perspectives and Issues in Educational Language Policy* (pp. 145-154). Amsterdam: John Benjamins.

Language policy: Linguistic perspectives. In N.J. Smelser and P.B. Baltes (eds) *International Encyclopedia of the Social and Behavioral Sciences* (Vol. 12; pp. 8361-8365). Oxford: Elsevier.

Llengua i etnicitat: La visió des de dins. In J.A. Fishman, *Llengua i identitat* (pp. 191–220). Alzira: Bromera (translation into Catalan of Language and ethnicity: The view from within, 1997).

Manteniment lingüístic i etnicitat. In J.A. Fishman, *Llengua i identitat* (pp. 21–56). Alzira: Bromera (translation into Catalan of Language maintenance and ethnicity, 1980).

Observacions finals (sobre llengua i identitat ètnica). In J.A. Fishman, *Llengua i identitat* (pp. 243–264). Alzira: Bromera (translation into Catalan of Concluding comments, 1999).

Recapitulació teòrica: Què és la inversió de la substitució lingüística (ISL) i com pot tenir èxit? In J.A. Fishman, *Llengua i identitat* (pp. 107–174). Alzira: Bromera (translation into Catalan of *Reversing Language Shift: Theoretical and Practice of Assistance to Threatened Languages*, 1991: pp. 381–419).

Reversing language shift. In R. Mesthrie (ed.) *Concise Encyclopedia of Sociolinguistics* (pp. 673–679). Amsterdam: Elsevier.

Shprakh-planirung far 'di andere yidishe leshoynes' in yisroel. *Afn shvel* 323, 2–5 (Part II).

Shprakh-planirung far 'di andere yidishe leshoynes' in yisroel. *Afn shvel* 321, 8–11 (Part I).

Sociolingüística (I identitat ètnica). In J.A. Fishman, *Llengua i identitat* (pp. 221–242). Alzira: Bromera (translation into Catalan of Sociolinguistics, 1999).

Three hundred plus years of heritage language education in the United States. In J.K. Peyton, D.A. Ranard and S.McGinnis (eds) *Heritage Languages in America: Preserving a National Resource* (pp. 81–98). McHenry, IL: Center for Applied Linguistics.

Tornant a la llengua i l'etnicitat. In J.A. Fishman, *Llengua i identitat* (pp. 175–190). Alzira: Bromera (translation into Catalan of Revisiting language and ethnicity, 1997).

Una perspectiva interestatal de les relacions entre l'heterogeneïtat lingüística, el conflicte civil i el producte nacional brut per capita. In J.A. Fishman, *Llengua i identitat* (pp. 83–106). Alzira, Valencia: Bromera (translation into Catalan of Inter-polity perspective on the relationship between linguistic heterogeneity, civil strife and gross national product, 1991).

Uriel vaynraykh: A sotsiolingvistisher opshats. *Afn shvel* 322, 1–4.

El whorfianisme del tercer tipus: La diversitat etnolingüística com a avantatge social universal. In J.A. Fishman, *Llengua i identitat* (pp. 57–82). Alzira: Bromera (translation into Catalan of Whorfianism of the third kind, 1982).

Whorfianismo del tercer tipo. In Y. Lastra (ed.) *Estudios de Sociolingüística* [page numbers missing]. Mexico, DF: Universidad Nacional Autónoma (translation into Spanish of Whorfianism of the third kind, 1982).

Why is it so hard to save a threatened language? In J.A. Fishman (ed.) *Can Threatened Languages Be Saved?* (pp. 1–22). Clevedon: Multilingual Matters.

2002 Diglossia and societal multilingualism: Dimensions and differences. *International Journal of the Sociology of Language* 157, 98–100.

Do ethnics have culture? And what's so special about New York anyway? In O. García and J.A. Fishman, *The Multilingual Apple: Languages in New York City* (2nd edn; pp. 341–354) Berlin: Mouton de Gruyter (reprint of 1997).

Endangered minority languages: Prospects for sociolinguistic research. *International Journal on Multicultural Societies* 4 (2), 270–275.

The holiness of Yiddish: Who says Yiddish is holy and why? *Language Policy* 1, 123–141.

'Holy languages' in the context of societal bilingualism. In L. Wei, J-M. Dewaele and A. Houston (eds) *Opportunities and Challenges of Bilingualism* (pp. 15–24). Berlin: Mouton de Gruyter.

Introduction. *MOST Journal on Multicultural Societies* 4 (2), i–x.

La perception du 'fait français' québécois aux États-Unis. In P. Bouchard and R.Y. Bourhis (eds) *L'Aménagement Linguistique au Québec: 25 ans d'application de la langue française, Revue d'aménagement linguistique* hors série (pp. 197–200). Québec: Office Québécois de la Langue Française.

What a difference 40 years make! *Journal of Linguistic Anthropology* 12, 144–149.

2003 An empirical test of two popular assumptions: Interpolity perspective on the relationships between linguistic heterogeneity, civil strife and per capita gross national product. In C. Bratt Paulston and G.R. Tucker (eds) *Sociolinguistics: The Essential Readings* (pp. 382–393). Oxford: Blackwell (reprint of 1990).

Bilingualism with and without diglossia: Diglossia with and without bilingualism. In C. Bratt Paulston and G.R. Tucker (eds) *Sociolinguistics: The Essential Readings* (pp. 359–366). Oxford: Blackwell (reprint of 1967).

Interwar Eastern European Jewish parties and the language issue. In S.M. Lyman (ed.) *Essential Readings on Jewish Identities, Lifestyles & Beliefs: Analyses of the Personal and Social Diversity of Jews by Modern Scholars* (pp. 80–94). New York: Richard Altschuler & Associates (reprint of 2001).

Languages late to literacy (A place in the sun on a crowded beach). In B.D. Joseph, J. Destefano, N.G. Jacobs and I. Lehiste (eds) *When Languages Collide: Perspectives on Language Conflict, Language Competition and Language Coexistence* (pp. 97–108). Columbus, OH: Ohio State University Press.

The primordialist/constructivist debate today: The language and ethnicity link in academic and in everyday-life perspective. In D. Conversi (ed.) *Ethnonationalism in the Contemporary World: Walker Connor and the Study of Nationalism* (pp. 83–91). London: Routledge.

2004 Ethnicity and supra-ethnicity in corpus planning: The hidden status agenda in corpus planning. *Nations and Nationalism* 10 (1/2), 79–94.

The hidden status agenda in corpus planning. In M. Guibernau and J. Hutchinson (eds) *History and National Destiny: Ethnosymbolism and its Critics* (pp. 79–94). Oxford: Blackwell (reprint of 2000).

Language maintenance, language shift and reversing language shift. In T.K. Bhatia and W.C. Ritchie (eds) *The Handbook of Bilingualism* (pp. 406–436). Oxford: Blackwell.

Multilingualism and non-English mother tongues. In E. Finegan and J. Rickford (eds) *Language in the USA: Perspectives for the 21st Century* (pp. 115–132). New York: Cambridge University Press.

Who speaks what language to whom and when? In J. Stefanik (ed.) *Antologia*

Bilingvizmu (pp. 114–128). Bratislava: Academic Electronic Press (translation into Slovak of 1965).

Why is it so hard to save a threatened language? *Kotoba to Syakai 7-go 7*, 6–36 (translation into Japanese of 2001).

Yiddish and German: An on-again, off-again relationship and some of the more important factors determining the future of Yiddish. In A. Gardt and B. Huppauf (eds) *Globalization and the Future of German* (pp. 213–227). Berlin: Mouton de Gruyter.

2005 Language policy and language shift. In T. Ricento (ed.) *An Introduction to Language Policy: Theory and Method* (pp. 311–328). Malden, MA: Blackwell.

Una doble minoría. Las contribuciones de una comunidad a la innovación educativa. In L. Meyer and B. Maldonado (eds) *Entre la Normatividad y la Comunalidad: Experiencias Educativas Innovadoras del Oaxaca Indígena Actual* (pp. 601–611). Oaxaca: Instituto Estatal.

Works in progress and accepted for publication (as of 2005)

Are secular Jews only secular or are they also secular? In B. Zumoff (ed.) *Secular Jewishness for Our Time: A Three-Part Symposium by Three Generations of Writers, Educators and Cultural Activists in 1938–40, 1968–69, 1998–2000.* [City: publisher missing].

Diasporas and diasporas and diasporas: Dimensions of Jewishness. In B. Zumoff (ed.) *Secular Jewishness for Our Time: A Three-Part Symposium by Three Generations of Writers, Educators and Cultural Activists in 1938–40, 1968–69, 1998–2000.* [City: publisher missing].

Imagining linguistic pluralism in the USA. *Developing Minority Language Resources: Spanish for Native Speakers in California* (with G. Valdés). Clevedon: Multilingual Matters.

Language and culture. *Social Science Encyclopedia* (revised edition).

Leadership trajectories in the language planning process.

Research methods in the sociology of language and education. In K.A. King and N. Hornberger (eds) *Research Methods in Language and Education: Encyclopedia of Language and Education*, 10.

Sociolinguistics: More powers to you (on the explicit study of power in sociolinguistic research*).* In M. Pütz and J.A. Fishman (eds) *'Along the Routes to Power': Explorations of Empowerment Through Language.* Berlin: Mouton de Gruyter.

A sociology of bilingualism: From home to school and back again (proceedings of the Vigo Conference).

Speaking, reading, writing and attituding Spanish among Californian Hispanic professionals. In G. Valdés *Developing Minority Language Resources: Spanish for Native Speakers in California.* Clevedon: Multilingual Matters.

The Tshernovits conference, 1908. *YIVO Encyclopedia of Jews in Eastern Europe.*

Yiddish language planning and standardization. *YIVO Encyclopedia of Jews in Eastern Europe.*

Yiddishism, secularism, Jewishness: 1938, 1968, 1998, A personal odyssey. In B. Zumoff (ed.) *Secular Jewishness for Our Time: A Three-Part Symposium by Three Generations of Writers, Educators and Cultural Activists in 1938–40, 1968–69, 1998–2000*

Reviews, Prefaces, Comments and Notes

1949 Review (in Yiddish) of N. Ausubel (ed.) *A Treasury of Jewish Folklore: Stories, Traditions, Legends, Humor, Wisdom and Folk Songs of the Jewish People. Yivo-bleter* 33, 195–206.

1951 Review (in Yiddish) of M. Leach (ed.) *Standard Dictionary of Folklore, Mythology and Legend. Yivo-bleter* 35, 264–272.

1953 Review of R.H. Becketal (ed.) *Curriculum in the Modern Elementary School. Jewish Education Bulletin* 1953–1954, [page number/s missing].
Review of N. Cantor *The Teaching–Learning Process. Jewish Education Bulletin* 1953–1954, [page number/s missing].
Review of M.F. Clough (ed.) *Psychology in the Services of the School. Jewish Education Bulletin* 1953–1954, [page number/s missing].
Review of W.E. Martin and C.B. Stendler (eds) *Child Development: The Process of Growing Up in Society. Jewish Education Bulletin* 1953–1954, [page number/s missing].
Review of A.A. Roback *History of American Psychology. Jewish Education Bulletin* 1953–1954, [page number/s missing].
Review of M. Thomson (ed.) *Talk It Out With Your Child. Jewish Education Bulletin* 1953–1954, [page number/s missing].

1954 Addition to *Guides to Psychological Literature. American Psychologist* 9, 159.
Abstract: *The Role of the Culture-Group Affiliation of the Judge in Thurstone Attitude-Scale Construction* (with I. Lorge). *American Psychologist* 9, 368–369.

1955 Comments on D. Hildebrand, Editorial: The social responsibility of scientists. *American Scientist* 43, 90–92.
Review of N. Berdyaev, *The Roots of Hatred: Christianity and Anti-Semitism. The Humanist* 15, 284.
Review of J.B. Carroll *The Study of Language, A Critical Review. Journal of Social Psychology* 41, 169–179.
Suggestions on the reading of papers. *American Psychologist* 10, 174.
What's happening to the Society for the Psychological Study of Social Issues today. *SPSSI Newsletter* April 2 and 4, [page number/s missing].

1956 Review of S.I. Hayakawa (ed.) *Language, Meaning and Maturity (A Loyal Opposition View). A Review of General Semantics* 13, 225–232.

1957 College Board research notes. *College Board Review* 31, 3–4; *College Board Review* 32, 3; *College Board Review* 33, 2–3.

1958 College Board research notes. *College Board Review* 34, 2; *College Board Review* 35, 2–3.
Review of B. English and A.C. English *A Comprehensive Dictionary of Psychological and Psychoanalytical Terms* [journal, vol/issue and page numbers missing].
Review of M.G. Field *Doctor and Patient in Soviet Russia. American Scientist* 46, 152A–154A.

1959 Review of O. Buros (ed.) *SRA Tests of Educational Ability. Fifth Mental Measurements Yearbook* (pp. 510–511). Highland Park, NJ: Gyphon Press.
Review of O. Buros (ed.) *Thurstone Test of Mental Alertness. Fifth Mental Measurement Yearbook* (pp. 529–530). Highland Park, NJ: Gyphon Press.

Review of A.A. Roback *Destiny and Motivation in Language. A Review of General Semantics* 16, 250–251.

1961 Review of D.K. Berlo (ed.) *The Process of Communication: An Introduction to Theory and Practice (from Language to Communication). Contemporary Psychology* 6, 7.

1962 Review of M. Carpenter. *The Larger Learning. Personnel and Guidance* 40, 746–747.
Review of J.L. Moreno with H.H. Jennings (and others). *The Sociometry Reader. Psychometrika* 27, 216–218.
Review of H. Toch *Legal and Criminal Psychology (Cops, Robbers and Psychology). Contemporary Psychology* 7, 292.

1963 Review of J. Gottmann *Megalopolus: The Urbanized Northeastern Seaboard of the United States. The Journal of Higher Education* 34 (3), 176–178.

1966 Preface to W. Ravid *Doctoral Dissertations and Masters Theses* 1 (pp. 3–4 and back). New York: YIVO Institute for Jewish Research.
Review of J.J. Gumperz and D. Hymes (eds) *The Ethnography of Communication. International Journal of American Linguistics* 32 (2), 193–195.

1967 Review of J.O. Hertzler *A Sociology of Language. Language* 43, 586–604.
Review of J. Macnamara *Bilingualism and Primary Education. The Irish Journal of Education* 1, 79–83.

1968 Preface to P. Disenhouse *Doctoral Dissertations and Masters Theses* 2 (p. 3 and back). New York: YIVO Institute for Jewish Research.
Preface to A. Verdoodt *Zweisprachige Nachbarn* (pp. v–vii). Vienna: Braumuller.
Remarks (on establishing the Graduate School of Humanities and Social Sciences at Yeshiva University) in J.A. Fishman (ed.) *Expanding Horizons of Knowledge About Man* (pp. 22–24). New York: Yeshiva University.
Review of W. Bright (ed.) *Sociolinguistics: Proceedings of the UCLA Sociolinguistics Conference 1964. Lingua* 19 (4), 428–432.

1969 Review of A. Ansel *Judaism and Psychology. Journal of Jewish Communal Service* 46, 197–198.
Review of J.C. Baratz and R.W. Shuy *Teaching Black Children to Read. Science* 165, 1108–1109.
Review of D.L.Sills *International Encyclopedia of the Social Sciences* (with J. Findling). *Language* 45 (2), 458–463.
Review of P.E. Vernon *Intelligence and Cultural Environment; and Literacy and the Language Barrier. Science* 165, 1108–1109.

1970 Preface to P. Disenhouse, *Doctoral Dissertations and Masters Theses* 3 (p. 3 and back). New York: YIVO Institute for Jewish Research.

1971 Preface to P. Disenhouse *Doctoral Dissertations and Masters Theses* 4 (p. 3 and back). New York: YIVO Institute for Jewish Research.
Preface to *The Impact of Migration on Language Maintenance and Language Shift. International Migration Review* 5 (2), 121–124.

1972 Preface to P. Disenhouse *Doctoral Dissertations and Masters Theses* 5 (p. 3 and back). New York: YIVO Institute for Jewish Research.
Preface to R. Kjolseth and F. Sack *Zur Sociologie der Sprache* [page number/s missing]. Opladen: Westdeutscher Verlag.

Preface to G. Lewis *Multilingualism in the Soviet Union* (pp. vii–ix). The Hague: Mouton.

Preface to W.F. Mackey *Bilingual Education in a Binational School* (pp. xviii). Rowley, MA: Newbury.

Review of J.R. Rayfield *The Languages of a Bilingual Community*. *Language* 48 (4), 969–976.

1973 Review of E. Haugen *The Ecology of Language*. *American Anthropologist* 75, 1078.

Review of H.C. Triandis in association with V. Vassiliou and others and with the assistance of E.E. Davis and others *The Analysis of Subjective Culture*. *Contemporary Psychology* 18, 557–558.

1974 Discussant: Contemporary Jewish Studies at the College–University Level. *American Jewish Historical Quarterly* 63, 369–378.

Preface to P. Disenhouse *Doctoral Dissertations and Masters Theses* 6 (p. 3 and back). New York: YIVO Institute for Jewish Research.

Review of P. Ladefoged, R. Glick and C. Griper *Language in Uganda*. *American Anthropologist* 76, 646.

1975 Preface to P. Disenhouse *Doctoral Dissertations and Masters Theses* 7 (p. 3 and back). New York: YIVO Institute for Jewish Research.

Review of D. Hymes *Foundations in Sociolinguistics: An Ethnographic Approach*. *General Linguistics* 15, 257–260.

Review of A.D. Svejcer *Voprosy sociologii jazyka v sovrennoj amerikansko lingvistike*. *Linguistics* 143, 88–97.

Review of W.Wolfram *Sociolinguistic Aspects of Assimilation: Puerto Rican English in New York City*. *Language* 51, 776–779.

1977 Preface to *Language Maintenance (A Demonstration of Language Retrieval via Computer Annotated Bibliography)* [page number/s missing]. Washington, DC: Educational Resource Division, National Institute of Education.

Review of M. Fox and B. Skolnick *Language in Education: Problems and Prospects in Research and Training*. *Language in Society* 6, 82–84.

1978 Foreword to L. Jessel *The Ethnic Process* (pp. 9–10). The Hague: Mouton.

1979 Postscript to *Dialect and Standard in Highly Industrialized Societies, The International Journal of the Sociology of Language* 21, 153–155.

Review of D.D. Laitin *Politics, Language and Thought*. *Language* 55, 471–473.

Review of J.A. Matisoff *Blessings, Curses, Hopes and Fears: Psycho-Extensive Expressions in Yiddish*. *Library Journal* 104, 1339.

Review of B. Spolsky and R.L. Cooper (eds) *Case Studies in Bilingual Education*. *International Migration Review* 13, 353–354.

1980 Review of S.A. Birnbaum (ed.) *Yiddish, A Survey and a Grammar*. *Language Problems and Language Planning* 4, 157–159.

Review of G. Gilbert and J. Ornstein (eds) *Problems in Applied Educational Sociolinguistics: Readings on Language and Culture Problems of United States Ethnic Groups*. *International Migration Review* 14, 428–429.

Review of T. Hauptfleisch (ed.) *Language Loyalty in South Africa* (Vol. 1); *Opinions of White Adults in Urban Areas* (Vol. 2); *Using and Improving Usage in the Second Language, Some Opinions of White Adults in Urban Areas* (Vol. 3); *Motivations to Language Use: Opinions and Attitudes of White Adults in Urban Areas*. *English World Wide* 1, 143–144.

Review of E.M. Pascasio (ed.) *The Filipino Bilingual: Studies on Philippine Bilingualism and Bilingual Education. Language Problems and Language Planning* 4, 89–91.

1981 Comment: Yeshiva University and Yiddish. *Jewish Daily Forward* (Sunday English supplement) January 11, 3.

Review of E. Allardt *Implications of the Ethnic Revival in Modern Industrial Society. Language in Society* 10, 288–289.

Review of H. Giles and R. St Clair (eds) *Language and Social Psychology. Language* 57, 220–222.

Review of E.G. Lewis *Bilingualism and Bilingual Education: A Comparative Study. Harvard Educational Review* 51, 608–610.

Review of R.V. Padilla (ed.) *Bilingual Education and Public Policy in the United States. International Migration Review* 15, 779–780.

Review of W.R. Schmalstieg and T.F. Magner (eds) *Sociolinguistic Problems in Czechoslovakia, Hungary, Romania and Yugoslavia. General Linguistics* 21, 147–148.

1982 Reply to T. Feitsma, Comments in *Fryx* 3 (7), 102–103. Replyk oangeande twataligens.

Reply to T. Feitsma, Comments in *Fryx* 3 (8), 117 and 120. Replyk oangeande twataligens.

Review of P. Schach (ed.) *Languages in Conflict: Linguistic Acculturation on the Great Plains. Journal of American Ethnic History* 1, 114–115.

1983 Preface to I. Fodor and C. Hagege (eds) *Language Reform: History and Future* (pp. i–iii). Hamburg: Buske Verlag.

Review of N. Conklin and M. Louries (eds) *A Host of Tongues: Language Communities in the United States. American Journal of Education* [vol/issue number missing], 295–297.

Review of M. Ridge (ed.) *The New Bilingualism. Language* 59, 676–677.

Review of G. Sankoff *The Social Life of Language. Modern Language Journal* 66, 74.

1984 Review of P. Brang and M. Zullig, (with the assistance of K. Brong) *Kommentierte Bibliographic zur Slavischen Soziolinguistik. Slavica Helvetica* 17. *International Journal of the Sociology of Language* 46, 147–148.

1985 Preface to I. Kreindler *Sociolinguistic Perspective on Soviet National Languages* (pp. vii–viii). Berlin: Mouton de Gruyter.

1986 Foreword to A.D. Evans and W.W. Falk *Learning to be Deaf* (pp. v–vi.). Berlin: Mouton de Gruyter.

Review of J. Edwards (ed.) *Linguistic Minorities: Policies and Pluralism. Modern Language Review* 70, 57–58.

Review of R. Fasold *The Sociolinguistics of Society. Language* 62 (1), 188.

Review of K. Hakuta *Mirror of Language: The Debate on Bilingualism. Los Angeles Times* March 23, p. 13.

1987 Foreword to N.H. Hornberger *Bilingual Education and Language Maintenance: A Southern Peruvian Quechua Case* (pp. vii–viii). Dordrecht: Foris.

Preface to Annenberg, L. *Raising Children Bilingually: The Pre-School Years* (pp. xi–xiii). Clevedon: Multilingual Matters.

Preface to J. Maurais *Politique et Aménagement Linguistiques* (pp. 3–4). Quebec: Conseil de la langue française.

Review of S. Churchill (ed.) *The Education of Linguistic and Cultural Minorities in the OECD Countries. The Modern Language Journal* 72 (2), 227–228.
Review of J. Edwards *Language, Society and Identity. International Migration Review* 21, 168–169.
Review of F. Hershteyn *A pekl ksovem fun a lerer a khoyvev-yidish un yidishkeyt. Afn shvel* 267, 5–8.
Review of B.B. Kachru *The Alchemy of English: The Spread, Functions and Models of Non-Native Englishes (The Spread of English). World Englishes* 6 (2) 169–175.
Review of Y. Mark (ed.) *Groyser verterbukh fun der yidisher shprakh, band iv. International Journal of the Sociology of Language* 67, 201–203.

1988 [Title missing]. Three brief talks presented on May 26, June 2 and June 6 (in connection with becoming Distinguished University Research Professor of Social Science, Emeritus). Unpublished manuscript, Ferkauf Graduate School of Psychology, Albert Einstein College of Medicine Campus, Yeshiva University.

1989 Comments on R.M. Keesing, Exotic readings of cultural texts. *Current Anthropology* 30 (4), 471–472.
Review of J.A. Laponce *Languages and Their Territories. Canadian Review of Studies in Nationalism* 16, 283–285.
Review of F.J. Neumeyer (ed.) *Language: The Sociocultural Context (Linguistics: The Cambridge Survey*, Vol. 4). *Contemporary Sociology* 18, 260–261.
Review of T. Skutnabb-Kangas and J. Cummins (eds) *Minority Education from Shame to Struggle: Language, Culture and Curriculum. Multilingual Matters* 2, 71–72.

1990 Review of J. Crawford *Bilingual Education: History, Politics, Theory and Practice. International Journal of the Sociology of Language* 86, 151–152.

1991 Review of B. Harshav *The Meaning of Yiddish. Transactions* (Rutgers University Press) [vol/issue and page numbers missing].
Review of W.E. Lambert and D.M. Taylor *Coping with Cultural and Racial Diversity in Urban America. Contemporary Sociology* 20 (2), 198.

1992 Foreword to G. Williams *Sociolinguistics: A Sociological Critique* (pp. vii–ix). London: Routledge.

1993 Review of C. Myers-Scotton (ed.) *Social Motivations for Codeswitching: Evidence from Africa. Oxford Studies in Language Contact* 177, 99–100.
Review of R. Phillipson (ed.) *Linguistic Imperialism. Modern Language Journal* 77, 399–400.
Review of C.H. Williams (ed.) *Called unto Liberty: On Language and Nationalism. Journal of Sociolinguistics* 1 (1), 145–149.

1994 Review of D. Bering (ed.) *Stigma of Names. Journal of Pragmatics* 22, 562–565.
Review of B. Harshav *Language in Time of Revolution. Society Review* 31 (5), 80–81.
Foreword to F. Sadiqi and M. Ennaji *Applications of Modern Linguistics* (pp. 9–10). Casablanca: Afrique Orient.

1995 Foreword to S.I. Hasnain *Standardization and Modernization: Dynamics of Language Planning* (pp. xii–xiv). New Delhi: Bahri Publications.
Review of V. Altaio (ed.) *Europe: Els intellectuals i la question europea. International Journal of the Sociology of Language* 3, 106–107.

1996 Preface to *International Journal of the Sociology of Language, Index to Issues 1–116* (1974–1995) (pp. v–vi). Berlin: Mouton de Gruyter.

Preface to *Italian-Esperanto, Esperanto-Italian Dictionary* (1st and 2nd edn; pp. x). Mantua: Editorial cooperativo.

1997 Foreword to S. Khanis, *Yidishe vertlekh fartaytsht* (pp. 1–3). New York: J.A. Fishman (in Yiddish).

Preface to M.C. Colombi and F.X. Alarcon (eds) *La enseñanza del español a hispanohablantes: Praxis y teoría* (pp. 12–14). Boston and New York: Houghton Mifflin Company.

Review of T. Skutnabb-Kangas (ed.) *Multilingualism for All. Language in Society* 27 (3), 413–415.

Review of C.H. Williams *Called Unto Liberty: On Language and Nationalism. Journal of Sociolinguistics* 1 (1), 145–149.

1998 Definitions of the 20 most common 'Yinglish' words. *Encarta World English Dictionary* [page number/s missing]. New York: Martins Press.

Foreword to M. Schaechter *The Standardized Yiddish Orthography* (pp. 1–3). New York: YIVO Institute for Jewish Research and Yiddish Language Resource Center of the League for Yiddish.

Foreword (in Yiddish) to M. Schaechter *The Standardized Yiddish Orthography. Afn shvel* 318, 1–3 (reprint).

Foreword to B. Sibayan *The Intellectualization of Filipino and other Sociolinguistic and Educational Essays* (pp. i–iii). Manila: The Linguistic Society of the Philippines.

Review of C. Baker and S. Prys Jones (eds) *Encyclopedia of Bilingualism and Bilingual Education. Bilingual Research Journal* 22, 317–319.

Review of D. Kerler *The Origins of Modern Literary Yiddish. Journal of Multilingual and Multicultural Development* 24 (4), 353–354.

Review of H.F. Schiffman *Linguistic Culture and Language Policy. International Journal of the Sociology of Language* 134, 31–35.

2001 Review of S.B. Ajulo and the Festschrift Committee (eds) *Language in Education and Society: Festschrift in Honor of Conrad Max Benedict Brann. International Journal of the Sociology of Language* 151, 191–194.

2002 Foreword to T.L. McCarty *A Place to be Navaho* (pp. xi–xiii). Mahwah, NJ: Lawrence Erlbaum Associates.

2003 A few reflections prompted by the articles in this issue. *MOST Journal on Multilingual Societies* (UNESCO) 5, 1.

Preface to R. Breton *Un atlas des langues du monde, miracle des temps modernes* (pp. 6–7). Paris: Utremont.

2005 Foreword to D. Ó Néill (ed.) *Rebuilding the Celtic Languages: Reversing Language Shift in the Celtic Countries* (pp. 9–12). First printing, Toronto: J.A. Fishman; second printing, Talybont: Y Lolfa.

Works in progress and accepted for publication (as of 2005)

Footnote to G.R. Tucker and C.B. Paulson (eds) *The Early Days of Sociolinguistics* on Heinz Kloss's recently revealed Nazi-party affiliations. Dallas, TX: Summer Institute of Linguistics (revised second printing).

Review of D. Lefkowitz *Words and Stones: The Politics of Language and Identity in Israel. The Journal of the Royal Anthropological Institute.*

Popular Articles

1948 Di shulyugnt: Ire shtrikhn un hofenungen. *Shul-pinkes-shikago* [Sholem Aleichem Folk Institut, Chicago], pp. 503–515.

1949 Nokh der mitlshul: Vos vayter? Yugntruf November 1948 to February 1949, 26–27.

1950 Etlekhe verter tsum graduir-klas. *Sholem aleykhem folkshul 21 Annual School Journal* June, [page number/s missing].

1964 Mayn tatns shir hashirim. *Afn shvel* January–February, 5–7.

1967 Briv in der redaktsye/Letter to the editor. *Kultur un dertsiyung* [vol/issue and page numbers missing].

Briv in der redaktsiye/Letter to the editor. *Morgn-zhurnal* [vol/issue and page numbers missing].

Dimensiyes fun yidishkeyt. *Kultur un dertsiyung* 3, 5–6.

Jewish students and Yiddishkeit. *The Call* (Workmens Circle) 36 (5), 13–15.

Serbish un kroatish. *Afn shvel* 178, 6–8.

Ufklerung fun yeshive-koledzsh. *Der tog* February 9, [page number/s missing)]

Ume veloshn. *Afn shvel* 179, 4.

Vos vet zayn mit dzshudzmo un mugrabish? *Yidishe tsaytung* March 29, [page numbers missing].

1968 A bagrisung un a bisl muser. *Yugntruf* 12, 4–6.

Dimensyes fun yidishkeyt, in simpozium: Veltlekhkeyt, traditsiye, undzer yidishkeyt (a frayer oystoysh fun meynungen). *Kultur un dertsiyung* [vol/issue number missing], 41–45.

Oriyentirtkeyt un organizirtkeyt: Dos naye gezets letoyves tsvey-shprakhiker bildung. *Afn shvel* 183, 3–5.

Planirter shprakh-iberruk. *Afn shvel* 182, 6–7.

Shprakh-planirung bay di umes-haoylem. *Afn shvel* 185, 11–12.

1970 Derhayntikn, faryidishn, fareynikn. *Yugntruf* 19, 14–18.

1972 Pluralizm in der efntlekher yisroeldiker yidishkeyt. *Yidishe tsaytung* September 25, [page number/s missing].

Traditsyonele gezelshaftlekhe rol fun yidish. *Yidishe tsaytung* [vol/issue and page numbers missing].

Vos vet zayn mit dzshudzmo un mugrabish? *Yidishe tsaytung* March 29, [page number/s missing].

1973 An amerikaner in yisroel; Ayndrukn un notitsn. *Tsukunft* 80, 260–262.

Lib hobn un tsuzogn. *Letste nayes* August 8, 10–11.

Shprakhiker monizm. *Yidishe tsaytung* [vol/issue and page numbers missing].

1974 Briv in redaktsiye. *Yidishe tsaytung* August 8, 4.

Ken di yidishe medine hobn gelt far alts? *Yidishe tsaytung* April 5, [page number/s missing].

Mit aza korn vet men keyn broyt nit bakn. *Yidishe tsaytung* March 22 and 29 (Part I).

Mit aza korn vet men keyn broyt nit bakn. *Yidishe tsaytung* April 5, 12 and 19 (Part II).

1978 'Di arbeter-ring heym': Nokh a sheferishe pozitsye. *Undzer heym/Our Home* (Workmens Circle) 6, 8.
Letter to the editors. *Commentator and Hamevaser* (Yeshiva University) January 15, [page number/s missing].
Mayn mame, di kishef–makherin. *Afn shvel* 234, 6–7.

1981 Briv in der redaktsiye/Letter to the editor (in response to 'Vifl darf men ongebn dem kval un bay vos'). *Forverts* December 17, [page number/s missing].
Dokter fishman entfert af a briv in der redaktsiye: An entfer af a briv mit a tayne tsu im. *Forverts* December 29, [page number/s missing].

1982 Briv in der redaktsiye [Letter to the editor]. *Kanader odler* June 25, 7.
Der tkhiyes-hameysim fun di frizn. *Afn shvel* 249, 8–9.
Yidish in yeshive-universitet un a simkhe fun hashoves-aveyde. *Algemeyner zhurnal* [vol/issue and page numbers missing].

1983 Umzister agmes-nefesh? *Afn shvel* 253/254, 8.
Vos vet vayter zayn? Vos vet undz nokh blaybn? *Afn shvel* 251, 2–4.

1984 Afile on gefilte fish. Tsu di shloyshim fun mayn shvester rukhl, oleho hasholem. *Afn shvel* [issue number missing], 9–11.
Afilu b'li gefilte fish. *Hashavua* x/8, 3–5 (expanded, revised and translated into Hebrew).
Gute nayes vegn yidish. *Afn shvel* 253/254, 5–8.
Max un moritz un motl un kopl. *Afn shvel* 252, 16.

1985 Laytish mame-loshn. *Afn shvel* 259, 1–2.
Tsulib vos darfn mir nokh yidish? *Tsukunft* 91 (1), 1–4.
Yidn, yidishkeyt un yidish in melburn, ostralye. *Afn shvel* 260, 11–14.

1986 Der tsushtayer fun veltlekhkeyt tsum yidishn lebn. *Tsukunft* 92 (11–12), 201–208.
'Yiddish watching': Nit ayndrimlen. *Sh'ma* 16 (309), 67–68.

1987 A pekl ksovim fun a lerer a khovevey-yidish un yidishkeyt. *Afn shvel* 267, 5–8.
Bamerkung tsu M. Tsanins briv in der redaktsye. *Afn shvel* [issue number missing], 8–9.
Himl un erd un rus vays. *Afn shvel* 265, 2–4 and 16.
Nosn birnboyms tsugang tsum amerikaner yidntum onheyb 20stn yorhundert. *Yediyes fun yivo* 171, 6–7.
Shpaltung, shrek un hofnung. *Afn shvel* 268, 3–4.

1988 Di veyniker banutste shprakhn. *Afn shvel* 270, 4–8.
Shoel gutmans profil. *Afn shvel* 272, 3–6.
Tsi darf amerike an ofitsyele shprakh? *Afn shvel* 269, 10–14.

1989 Editor's note: Error in Dov Noy's article. *Folklife Center News* 12 (2), 3.
Vos hot di yidishe literature geton far der yidisher shprakh? *Der pakn-treger/The Book Peddler* 10–11, 55–54.

1990 Ester. *Afn shvel* 275, 10–13.
Zikhroynes vegn ester. *The Esther Codor Cohen Memorial Committee*: Gella Schweid Fishman, Joshua A. Fishman, Chana Schachner, Lyvia Schaefer. Autumn, 26–33 (bilingual).

1991 A benkenish nokh yidisher veltlekhkeyt. *Tsukunft* 8–11.

Mit 50 (fuftsik) yor tsurik in filadelfiye: A yugnt-zhurnal af yidish. *Forverts* (95th Jubilee issue), 22–23.

1992 Lekoved 'di tsukunft' tsum vern a ben-meye-shonem. *Tsukunft* May–June, 8–11.
Yidish: Mayn ershte heym. *Tsukunft* 97 (1), 7–9.

1993 A benkenish nokh yidisher veltlekhkeyt. *Di prese* January 27, [page number / s missing].

1994 S'iz geshtorbn a vikhtiker tuer far a kleyner shprakh. *Afn shvel* 296, 12–15.
Tikn-toes tsu dokter Fishmans artikl in forikn numer [Letter to the editor]. *Afn shvel* May–June, [page number / s missing].

1995 A bagrisung tsu tsvey khosheve yubilarn. *Kheshbn* 27, 90.
Der kishef bay undz in der heym. *Afn shvel* 297, 3–7.
Yiddish revival confounds experts. *Yeshiva University Review* [vol/issue number missing], 14–16.

1996 Ahaves-haloshn: Di libe tsu der eygener shprakh. *Forverts* October 18, 18.
A por verter baym ibergebn a premye. *Tsukunft* May–June, 37–38.
Di hashpoe fun universitetn afn shprakhbanuts: Di volozhiner yeshive un ire nokhgeyers. *Afn shvel* 304, 13–17.
Dovid un golyes: Yidish un english. *Forverts* December 13, 8 and 15.
Dovid un golyes. *Forverts* (Russian edn) January 10–16, [page number / s missing] (reprint, translated into Russian).
Gevald, mir vern dertrunken in a yam fun english. *Forverts* August 16, 15.
Mit libe, mit humor un mit aynfalerishkeyt. *Kind un keyt* 2, 14–15.
Ongekhapt dem emes bay der bord. *Afn shvel* 303, 1–6.
Pakhed-haleshoynes: di moyre far shprakhn. *Forverts* September 27, 15.
Tsi muz untergeyn di veltlekhe yidish-redndike svive? *Afn shvel* January–March, 2–4.
Tsu gast bay galitsyaner in shpanye. *Forverts* July 19, 15.

1997 A berishe toyve? Di virkung fun yidish af english. *Forverts* January 3, 9.
A kurstn entfer af leyon yaneses taynes *Afn shvel* [vol/issue and page number / s missing].
Alte sonim betn zikh iber. *Forverts* December 5, 6 and 27.
Bonim godalti veroymemosi. *Afn shvel* 305, 1–2.
Daytsh vi di lernshprakh in khayfer tekhnikum. *Forverts* August 18, 15.
Di 'magna carta' fun undzer shprakh-frayheyt. *Forverts* June 13, 10.
Di ershte nayes vegn 4tn yuli af yidish. *Forverts* June 27, 15.
Di yerusholayimer verter-fabrik. *Forverts* March 14, 15.
Dos khsidishe yidish: Gut tsi shlekht? *Forverts* August 29, 15.
Ebonik: A negerisher variant fun english? *Forverts* May 2, 14.
English bay (teyl) kh'sidim. *Forverts* October 3, 15 and 19.
Farvalters. *Forverts* October 26, 18–19.
Fremdshprakhike tsaytungen in amerike: 1897. *Forverts* May 16, 5.
Hebreyish bay fraye un bay frume. *Forverts* April 11, 15.
Tayne vetshuve. *Afn shvel* 306, 31.
Velkher iz der emeser dokter nosn birnboym? *Forverts* June 11, 10.
Vilne vu bistu? *Forverts* November 14, 6.
Yidish in di efntlekhe mitlshuln: Meglekh tsi ummeglekh? *Forverts* January 17, 14 and 18.
Yidish in di universitetn: Meglekhkeytn un problemen. *Forverts* February 14, 8.
Zey un mir. *Forverts* March 28, 19–20.

1998 A naye sakone fun ... kalifornye. *Forverts* April 24, 15.
A zhest letoyves yidish metsad ... holand. *Forverts* May 8, 8.
Der koyekh fun fundamentalizm. *Forverts* August 28, 11.
Der sod fun 'fundamentalizm': Kleyne entfers af groyse frages. *Forverts* September 18, 8 and 27.
Di ershte shprakh-konferentsn un der goyrl fun yidish. *Forverts* March 13, 6.
Fun shtetl iz gevorn di velt. *Forverts* October 30, 14 and 22.
Fundamentalizm, religye un veltlekhkeyt. *Forverts* (Russian edn), November, 13–19.
Indiyaner dertseyln. *Forverts* July 24, 11 and 22.
Khayem Zhitlovskis peule in yidishn lebn. *Yidishe kultur* 60, 19–20.
Mer vi stam 'gute literatur?' *Forverts* December 4, 10–11.
Naye leyenshprakhn un naye leyeners. *Forverts* April 10, 12.
Russian paraphrase of 'Di ershte konferentsn un der goyrl fun yidish.' *Forverts* (Russian edn) April 24, 30.
Shprakh-nisim. *Forverts* February 10, 15.
Tsivile gezelshaft. *Forverts* December 25, 16 and 17.
Tsvishn indiyaner. *Forverts* July 10, 9 and 22.
Vifl bikher farmogt der am-haseyfer? *Forverts* January 30, 15.
Yidish un yidish-shpanish: An eyropeyishe yerushe. *Forverts* June 12, 7 and 22.

1999 A briv in redaktsye. *Forverts* August 20, 19.
A vort vegn lerer shoel gutman, z'l (with G. Schweid Fishman). *Forverts* January 22, 20.
Baym bakumen di manger-premye. *Forverts* June 11, 17.
Bravo shvedn! *Forverts* July 9, 11.
Di dimensye fun yidisher naykeyt. *Forverts* April 16, 11.
Farvortsltkeyt un heylikeyt: Tsvey fun di dray dimensyes fun yidishkeyt. *Forverts* June 18, 11.
Frume shtimen. *Forverts* September 10, 14.
Katalaner, katalanish, katalunye. *Forverts* February 5, 11.
Y2K un der nayer yortoyznt. *Forverts* February 26, 15.
Yidishizm, veltlekhkeyt, yidishkeyt (1938, 1968, 1998) a perzenlekhe odeseye (Part I). *Forverts* January 15, 18.
Yidishizm, veltlekhkeyt, yidishkeyt (1938, 1968, 1998) a perzenlekhe odeseye (Part II). *Forverts* January 22, 18 and 22.

2000 A farshvundene velt. *Forverts* December 8, 11.
A vort friyer. *Afn shvel* 318, 1–3.
Der groyser tsushtayer fun di yidish-veltlekhe shuln. *Shulgrusn* 1, 6.
Di dekonstruktsye un rekonstruktsye fun der shite 'yidish-veltlekh.' *Forverts* December 29, 10.
Maoris: A kleyn folk mit groyse plener. *Forverts* October 6, 14.
Tsi veln mir inem nayem yorhundert blaybn bay di zelbe alte gedanken? *Afn shvel* 317, 6–9.
Veltlekh, harbstik. *Forverts* November 3, 11.
Vi azoy darf yidish vayter normirt vern inem 21stn yorhundert? *Afn shvel* 319, 3–4.
Yiddish: That's entertainment! A loshn tsi a gelekhter? *Forverts* September 22, 10.

2001 A limed on a balebos. *Forverts* May 4, 10.
Antdekt amerike! *Forverts* November 2, 11.
Der forsh-seminar. *Forverts* July 13, 11.

If not even higher. *Jewish Currents* 55 (4), 19–21.
Kloyster un melukhe. *Forverts* December 7, 11.
Kultur-tuers. *Forverts* June 22, 14.
Moderne ortodoktsye: An amerikaner fenomen. *Forverts* September 7, 9.
Perets, dubnov, zhitlovski un oyb nit nokh hekher. *Forverts* February 2, 6.
Tsi darfn mir oykh ton tshuve? *Forverts* October 12, 16.
Vi azoy ken nokh der yidish-veltlekher 'sektor' mamoshesdik mashpiye zayn
      dem osid fun yidish in amerike? *Forverts* April 6, 11.
Vos heyst bay yidn 'normalkeyt'? *Forverts* June 1, 11.
Yidishe lerers. *Forverts* August 10, 10.
Yidishe veltlekhkeyt un veltlekhe yidishkeyt. *Forverts* March 2, 11.

2002   A yidishe melukhe raboysay: Paradoksn. *Forverts* June 21, 11.
Der emes in ponim arayn [Letter to the editor]. *Forverts* February 8, 21.
Der yidisher oto bauer. *Forverts* August 2, 10.
Di frume prese af yidish in nyu-york. *Forverts* October 4, 11.
Di mapole fun english: Der netsokhn fun 'amerikanish.' *Forverts* July 12, 11.
Dos loshn funem taykh: Gegntn. *Forverts* May 17, 10 and 14.
Modernizirung: A shtekn mit tsvey ekn. *Forverts* February 8, 14 and 21.
Nosn birnbaums 'Das Volk.' *Forverts* December 6, 14 and 16–17.
Nosn birnboym un y.n. shteynberg. *Forverts* April 19, 27.
S'iz nit meglekh. *Afn shvel* 326, 1–2.
Tshuve bay veltlekhe yidn. *Forverts* September 6, 11.
Tsvey hundert yor 'rosetta-shteyn': A shlisl tsu der eybikeyt. *Forverts*
      November 1, 10 and 20.
Vos kenen mir zikh oplernen fun english? *Forverts* March 8, 10 and 19.
Yortsaytn un doyres. *Forverts* January 11, 11.

2003   A velt mit antoyshungen. *Forverts* March 7, 11.
Antisemitizm alekho, yankev! *Forverts* October 10, 11.
Birnboym in tshernovits. *Afn shvel* 329/330, 10–11 and 19.
Di 'konservative' shite bay yidishe fundamentalistn. *Forverts* August 1, 10.
Di geshikhte khazert zikh iber. *Forverts* July 8, 11.
Di tshernovitser konferents gufe. *Afn shvel* 329/330, 3–4.
Golusn un golusn. *Forverts* July 4, 11 and 22.
Katolikn, shvartse un mir. *Forverts* November 7, 11.
Peysekhdiks. *Forverts* April 11, 11.
Rosh-hashone, veltlekhkeyt un religye. *Forverts* September 26, 10.
'Tentse,' 'gezenge' un festivaln. *Forverts* May 2, 11.
Yidish inem 21stn yorhundert. *Forverts* December 5, 11.

2004   A naye peysekh kashe: Tsi iz tsurikforn ken daytshland punkt azoy oser vi
      tsurikgeyn ken mitsrayem? *Forverts* April 2, 11.
Basheves af baskish. *Forverts* August 6, 11.
Der 'revolutsyonerer' yidisher fundamentalizm. *Forverts* January 2, 11.
Der nayer dor daytshn (un 'rusn') in daytshland. *Forverts* June 4, 11.
Di tsores fun yidishe leshoynes. *Forverts* September 3, 11.
Gotenyu, shrek mikh nor shtrof mikh nit! *Forverts* October 1, 11.
Katalunye un di politik fun kleyne leshoynes. *Forverts* July 9, 11.
Kleyne leshoynes mit groyse tsores. *Forverts* October 5, 11.
Oykh tsu hebreyish tshepet men zikh. *Forverts* December 3, 14.
Purimdike tshikavesn. *Forverts* March 5, 11 and 22.
Tsigayner. *Forverts* May 7, 11.

Yidn in a kleyner shtot. *Forverts* February 6, 11.

2005 A yontev fun di yidish-veltlekhe shuln in tsofn-amerike. *Forverts* January 7, 14.
Az men lebt derlebt men. *Forverts* May 6, 11.
Di fir koyles fun shpanye. *Forverts* September 2, 11.
Farzikhdikeyt-tog. *Forverts* July 1, 7.
Leshoynes, tsenzusn un yidish. *Forverts* June, [page number/s missing].
Mizrekh-eyrope, yisroel, amerike un veltlekhkeyt. *Forverts* March 4, 11.
Purim freyd, purim tsiter. *Forverts* April 1, 11.
Tsi iz peysekh tsu lang? *Forverts* April 22, 5.
Vi got in odes: English in yisroel. *Forverts* November 4, 11.
Yidish in di amerikaner togshuln. *Forverts* August 5, 11.
Yidishe veltlekhkayt: Vu un vuhin. *Forverts* February 4, 11 and 14.
Yom-hatfutsot! *Forverts* October 7, 11.

Works in progress and accepted for publication (as of 2005)
Islamisher fundamentalizm. *Forverts*.

Interviews

1966 *Intervyu* mit D"r Shikl Fishman. *Yugntruf* 12–14 (in Yiddish).

1967 Un judío en Nueva York. J.A. Fishman. Interview conducted by P. Marcelino Pando. Diálogo, *Nueva York Hispano* May 1967 (21), 22–23.

1976 Interview with Dr J.A. Fishman on bilingual education. *Bilingual Review* 2 (2), 4–5 (Regional Cross-Cultural Training and Research Center, Board of Education, Office of Bilingual Education).
Success and failure in language education. *Melton Research Center Newsletter* 4, 1–4 and 6.

1981 Shikl un gele fishman dertseyln vi zey zenen gevorn religyez. *Algemeyner Zhurnal*, September 25, 24 (in Yiddish).

1982 J.A. Fishman. *De Pompebleden* 53 (11), 80 (in Frisian).

1983 In de serie taalwetenschap en moedertaalonderwijs, nu een gesprek met een Amerikaan. Moer, 31–39 (in Dutch).

1985 Yiddish alive in Melbourne. *Australian Jewish News* July 19, 12.

1986 Interview with Dr J.A. Fishman, conducted by J. Bergara, editor of *Zutabe*, summer (in Basque) (audiocassette).

1987 J.A. Fishman. *Zutabe* 15, 85–101 (in Basque).
Fraachpetwar mei J.A. Fishman. *Fryx*, 3, 8, 113–116 (in Frisian).

1989 J.A. Fishman: El estudio de las lenguas minoritarias desde el Bronx. *El País* (Madrid, Spain), May 13 (in Spanish).
Un judío con valija propia en Euskadi. *El correo español* (Bilbao, The Basque Country, Spain) May 18 (in Basque).

1990 Interview with Joshua Fishman: Schooling, bilingual education, sociology of language and Yiddish, O. García, Bronx, NY, 8/23/90 (audiocassette).

1991 Interview with Bertie Kaal on the *Sociology of Language. Language International* 3.5, November 17, 27–31.

1993 Holi Arbenigwr Iaith. *Golwg* 5 (44), 8–9 (in Welsh).
Interview with Dr J.A. Fishman. *BEOutreach* 5 (2), 26–29.
Navajo Language Week. *Navajo Radio Station*, Tuba City, New Mexico. September (audiocassette).

1994 Fishman, Joshua A. (1926–) Bibliographical information. *The Encyclopedia of Language and Linguistics*. Pergamon Press 3, pp. 1265–1266.

1996 Interview with Dr J.A. Fishman. T.L. McCarty, Tuscon, AZ, April 9 (audiocassette).
Interview with sociolinguist J.A. Fishman, conducted by Mark David. *The Yiddish Voice (WUNR, Boston: 1600 AM)*, November 6 (in Yiddish) (audiocassette).

1997 Socioloxia da linguaxe, bilinguismo e planificacion. Unha conversa con J.A. Fishman. Interview with Anxo M. Lorenzo Suarez and Xoan Paulo Rodriguez Yanez, *Grial* October/November/December (136), 583–599 (in Galician).

1998 An interview with J.A. Fishman, conducted by John Rawlings. *Stanford Oral History Project*, Stanford University Libraries, Stanford Historical Society, Stanford, CA.
An interview with Dr J.A. Fishman. University of Arizona, Tuscon, AZ, June 4 (videocassette).

1999 Interview with Professor J.A. Fishman, conducted by Xabier Erize (Vioria Gasteiz) New York University, August 5 (audiocassette).
Two languages will never be in a fully balanced situation in the same community. *Administration in Basque* 27, 10–11.

2000 Interview with Dr J.A. Fishman. (Elkarrizketa J.A. Fishman, Ekin Sociolinguistika ez da nik espero nuen moduan garatu). *BAT-Soziolinguistika aldizkaria elkarrizke* 32, 113–123 (in Basque).
Interview with J.A. Fishman, conducted by Eva Radich. Radio interview in Melbourne, June 30 (audiocassette).
Making good boundaries. Xabier Erize, *The Welsh Internationalist* April–May, 66–75.

2002 Interview with J.A. Fishman, conducted by A. Romariz. *Nos/Outras*, University of Vigo, Catalonia. October 23 (in Galiego).
Interview with Professor J.A. Fishman for a Documentary about Yiddish, conducted by Barbara Sostaric and Renato Porrini (audiocassette).

2004 Interview with J.A. Fishman for The Riverdale Press, NY (audiocassette).
Interview with J.A. Fishman, conducted by Berl Sandler, for the *Yiddish Forward Radio Program* NY, June 12 (in Yiddish) (audiocassette).
Interview with J.A. Fishman, Yiddish: The secret language, conducted by Barbara Sostaric. Anke Schaefer, http://www.rollingturtles.com (videocassette).
Joshua A. Fishman comments about himself, Yiddish, his reversing language shift theory and practice revisited. *Nasha Slova*, 12 (647), 31 (in Belorussian).

2005 Interview with J.A. Fishman (in preparation for his 80th birthday celebration), conducted by Nancy Hornberger and Martin Putz (Part I on two audiocassettes; Part II on CD – digital recording), May 17.

Index*

* Our gratitude to Cambria Russell and Zeena Zakharia for the preparation of this index and their generous reading of the manuscript.